ART LAW
IN A NUTSHELL®

FIFTH EDITION

LEONARD D. DuBOFF
Attorney at Law

CHRISTY A. KING
Attorney at Law

MICHAEL D. MURRAY
University of Kentucky College of Law

WEST ACADEMIC PUBLISHING

The publisher is not engaged in rendering legal or other professional advice, and this publication is not a substitute for the advice of an attorney. If you require legal or other expert advice, you should seek the services of a competent attorney or other professional.

Nutshell Series, In a Nutshell and the Nutshell Logo are trademarks registered in the U.S. Patent and Trademark Office.

COPYRIGHT © 1984, 1993 WEST PUBLISHING CO.
© West, a Thomson business, 2000
© 2006 Thomson/West
© 2017 LEG, Inc. d/b/a West Academic
    444 Cedar Street, Suite 700
    St. Paul, MN 55101
    1-877-888-1330

West, West Academic Publishing, and West Academic are trademarks of West Publishing Corporation, used under license.

Printed in the United States of America

ISBN: 978-1-63459-925-2

To Mary Ann Crawford DuBoff, my partner in law and in life, and to the memory of my mother and father, Millicent Barbara DuBoff and Reuben Robert DuBoff, for everything they did to inspire me.

Leonard D. DuBoff

To my husband, Bob, whose love and support make me strong, and to my son, Drew, whose big heart, passion and hard work make me proud.

Christy A. King

To Denise, Olivia, and Dennis, who fill my life with humor and fun, and to Leonard DuBoff and Christy King, whose collaboration over the last fourteen years has enriched my academic and scholarly life.

Michael D. Murray

INTRODUCTION TO THE FIFTH EDITION

The Fifth Edition of Art Law in a Nutshell continues to address a wide scope of national and international issues concerning law and the arts. Professor Michael D. Murray of the University of Kentucky College of Law has joined the author team of Leonard DuBoff and Christy King. The text continues to focus on the world of art law for artists, dealers, collectors, lawyers, and members of the public. Each chapter of the book has been updated, and material up to and including June 2016 is featured and discussed. We welcome you to the study of this fascinating area of the law.

LEONARD D. DUBOFF
CHRISTY A. KING
MICHAEL D. MURRAY

June 30, 2016

INTRODUCTION TO THE FOURTH EDITION

Art law is complex and obscure. Leonard DuBoff and his collaborator Christy King's well written *Art Law in a Nutshell* responds to this. It demystifies the world of art law for artists, dealers, collectors, lawyers, and members of the public. This easily understood book covers a broad range of legal topics and federal and state laws. They include, for example, copyrights, artists' moral rights, artists' resale royalties, trademarks, contracts, and taxation. Other issues, such as marketing, auctions, collecting, acquisitions, museums, insurance, authentication, and forgeries are covered. Today's international headlines concerning art are not ignored; indeed, analysis of the issues and the historical background are carefully laid out here. For example, DuBoff and King include discussions of high profile thefts of masterpieces, the destruction of cultural artifacts, and art as the spoils of war.

DuBoff cares deeply about his subject. He is an expert, having written important works in this area for more than 30 years. Here he and King take the reader through numerous complex issues. They discuss applicable laws and regulations, as well as actual cases. Their explanations are clear and understandable and at the same time legally and technically accurate. Additionally, this work is full of practical advice, insights, and perceptive observations. It is a book for those who want to be informed, and they will want it on their desks or in their workspaces.

For more than 40 years my life has focused on copyright law, a law that protects artists and their works. My focus, therefore, was narrow. This book has increased my appreciation of artists and others who work in the art world. It certainly enriched my understanding of the breadth of issues and the challenges that artists, institutions, dealers, and even governments face. It also made me aware of important issues that remain unresolved and that need to be addressed.

MARYBETH PETERS
Register of Copyrights
U.S. Copyright Office
Library of Congress

INTRODUCTION

Art Law in a Nutshell by Professor Leonard D. DuBoff is admirable for a number of significant reasons. It is written in clear, precise prose, readily understandable to the layman (i.e., one not attuned to the full complexities of legal phraseology). At the same time, it contains an excellent and wide range of legal references, cases in summary and citations to satisfy the true professional in law, and a thorough authoritative background for further study and action. It is a provocative book. It is full of insights, both fascinating and informative. It provides the basis for recommendations on improvements in the law; the simplification of legal labyrinths which have evolved over the years. And, of immense importance, it is a treasury of practical advice to the purchaser of art, to the collector of art and above all, to the individual artist.

As one who has worked in the arts for many years as a novelist, and many more as developer of legislation to create a National Endowment for the Arts (NEA) in the early 1960's, and subsequently as its Chairman, I find Professor DuBoff's work uniquely absorbing.

Since the Endowment's establishment less than twenty years ago, we have witnessed an extraordinary growth in the wide variety of all the arts, and in the importance we as a nation place on them as such technicalities of estate planning for all involved in the arts. We learn the legal protections for artists and works of art.

Throughout the text, in its details and examples of individuals caught in moments of travail and triumph, runs a unifying threat of wisdom from an author who deeply cares about his subject matter and wants to clarify it for now and also for a future time.

I feel inherent in this book that constant eye toward a better and wiser future, and a call for action wherever needed. In addition to providing an illuminating analysis of present-day conditions, *Art Law in a Nutshell* contains a wide assortment of areas for improvement, a rich vein to be mined, to form a base for enlightened discussion and action.

It was once said about my own work in designing the legislation for the National Endowment that a novelist's experience with broad concepts was not out of place. I wish I had enjoyed the pleasure of Professor DuBoff's collaboration then. I know his intelligent views and articulate voice will continue to be welcomed by the arts community and those who share in its myriad of benefits and potentials.

> LIVINGSTON BIDDLE
> Washington, D.C.
> (Chairman, National
> Endowment for the
> Arts, 1977–1981)

ACKNOWLEDGMENTS

When, more than four and a half decades ago, I combined my art background with my professional training as a lawyer, I had no idea how dynamic the field would become. As the melding of art and law continued and more professionals became involved with the arts, it became clear to the academic community, as well as to the legal profession, that Art Law had arrived. Today, there is an Art Law section of the Association of American Law Schools, a committee within the American Bar Association, which, among other things, is involved with Art Law, approximately 28 states have Volunteer Lawyers for the Arts programs, and there are several law reviews that are devoted entirely to this field.

Not too long ago, Art Law conferences were rare. Today, conferences and symposia devoted to this field have become quite common. Publications have also proliferated, and most law libraries contain a respectable collection of Art Law material. Indeed, there have been several bibliographies published for the field.

Law schools, too, have become involved with Art Law. Not long ago, it was unusual to find a school that offered a class on Art Law. Today, there are over fifty schools which offer the course on a regular basis, and others are coming online at a rapid pace. In fact, a law school casebook, *Art Law: Cases and Materials*, which is published by Aspen/Wolters Kluwer, is now used in numerous schools and is in the process of being revised again. Students interested in the field can find classes offered at law schools throughout the United States.

The growth of Art Law is by no means limited to the United States. As the reader will observe throughout this book, there is a significant international dimension to the field. In fact, the second and fourth editions of this volume have been translated into Mandarin Chinese and distributed throughout the People's Republic of China. The field is, indeed, global. One need only surf the Web in order to verify this fact.

West Academic has been an active participant in the field of Art Law. Beginning with its *Art and the Law* exhibition, West has been sensitive to the blending of these two disciplines. The publication of *Art Law in a Nutshell* is also indicative of West Academic's dedication to the field. This fifth edition continues the publisher's support and underscores its desire to have the most current material available to its readers.

In order to assemble the vast quantity of statutes, cases, articles, and books that have become available since the fourth edition was published, it was necessary to enlist the aid of numerous friends and colleagues. Their help is greatly appreciated, and some deserve special recognition. I would, therefore, like to express my sincere thanks to my collaborator Christy A. King, Esq., for her extraordinary help with this revision. She has sacrificed many evenings and weekends to bring this project to fruition. I would also like to thank my other collaborator, Professor Michael D. Murray, for his dedication and hard work on this book and others over the last fourteen years.

Christy and I would like to thank Greg Rogers of the accounting firm of Rogers Financial Services and Sean Kim of the accounting firm of Paxton, Miller, & Kim CPAs, LLC, for their time and expertise in reviewing the tax chapters. Thanks must also go to Professor James A. R. Nafziger of Willamette University School of Law, who has written extensively in the field of international issues affecting Art Law, for his help in obtaining material; and to Professor Zhou Lin, who translated the second and fourth edition of this work into Mandarin and currently teaches an Art Law course at the Intellectual Property Center of China Academy of Social Science in the People's Republic of China, for the information he provided. We would also like to thank Nathaniel Monsour, Esq., for his help in proofing this manuscript.

Professor Murray thanks Sally Gu, J.D. Candidate at the University of Michigan Law School, for her research supporting the Copyright, Moral and Economic Rights, and Right of Publicity chapters.

I am grateful for the introduction written by Livingston Biddle, former head of the National Endowment for the Arts. The arts need more men like Mr. Biddle, and today it is quite clear that the Endowment would benefit greatly from his skill. I am also extremely honored by the very kind words of The Honorable Marybeth Peters, the former U.S. Register of Copyrights.

I am grateful for the support of my children and grandchildren. My son, Robert, has been very helpful with technology issues, and my daughter, Colleen, has been extremely creative with her graphic design skills. Her husband, Rudy, a soon-to-be lawyer who has recently joined our law firm, has been very helpful with research. I am also grateful to my grandson, Brian for his personal assistance and the newest member of my family, my granddaughter Athena, for her cheerfulness.

My late sister, Candace DuBoff Jones, J.D., Northwestern School of Law, Lewis & Clark College, 1977; my late father, Rueben R. DuBoff; and my late mother, Millicent Barbara DuBoff, all provided me with the inspiration to create works such as this.

I valued my mother-in-law Cumi Elena Crawford's faith, trust, and inspiration, which helped me create this project. Finally, I would like to express my sincere gratitude and acknowledge the contribution to this project by my partner in law and in life, Mary Ann Crawford DuBoff. Without her, this fifth edition of Art Law in a Nutshell would never have become a reality.

OUTLINE

INTRODUCTION TO THE FIFTH EDITION V
INTRODUCTION TO THE FOURTH EDITION VII
INTRODUCTION IX
ACKNOWLEDGMENTS XI
TABLE OF CASES XXI

Chapter 1. Art: The Customs Definition 1
A. Historical 1
B. The Present Rule... 3

Chapter 2. Art: International Movement 9
A. The Problem 9
B. Controlling the International Movement of Art 17
   1. Export Restrictions... 17
   2. Import Restrictions.. 20
   3. Treaties.. 21
   4. Self-Regulation by Nongovernmental Organizations... 26
C. Sanctions for Vandalism and Theft 27

Chapter 3. Art: The Victim of War 33
A. The Problem 33
B. Judicial Solutions.. 36
C. Nonjudicial Solutions.. 42

Chapter 4. Art as an Investment 49
A. The Art Market 49
B. Investment Factors and Considerations 54
C. Methods of Acquisition 57

Chapter 5. Auctions 61
A. Auctions in General 61
B. Bidding.. 62
C. Bidding Tactics.. 64
D. Auctioning Problems..................................... 66

Chapter 6. Authentication 75
A. Establishing Authenticity 75
B. Art Experts 80
C. Scientific Authentication 86
D. Purchasers' Common Law Remedies Against Sellers 87
E. Warranties... 92
   1. Express Warranties 95
   2. Implied Warranties.................................. 98
   3. Disclaimers... 100
   4. Art Warranty Statutes 101
F. Fine Print and Multiples Legislation 103
G. Preventative Measures 106

Chapter 7. Insurance 111
A. Pros and Cons of Insuring 111
B. The Insurance Contract................................ 114
C. Recovery and Remedies 120

Chapter 8. Tax Problems: Collectors and Dealers... 127
A. Properly Characterizing Income 127
B. Deductions 130
C. Charitable Contributions 135
D. Estate Planning 140
E. Tax Shelters 144

Chapter 9. Tax Problems: Artists 151
A. Properly Characterizing Income 151
B. Deductions 156
C. Charitable Deductions 160
D. Estate Planning 162

Chapter 10. Aid to the Arts 167
A. Direct Aid 167
   1. Historical Development 167
   2. The National Endowment for the Arts 170
   3. Other Direct Aid 174
B. Indirect Aid... 176
   1. Percentage Allocation for Art 176
   2. Landmark Preservation 178

Chapter 11. The Working Artist 183
A. Places to Work and Sell 183
B. Galleries and Commissions 188
C. Working Conditions 194

Chapter 12. Copyright 199
A. Historical: Common Law, Copyright and Preemption 199
B. Scope of Protection 203
C. Statutory Subject Matter 209
   1. Original Work of Authorship 210
   2. Fixed in a Tangible Medium of Expression 212
   3. Other Requirements 214
D. Formalities 218
E. Duration 227
F. Infringement 231
   1. Elements of Infringement 231
   2. Remedies 234

    3. Fair Use 236
    4. Parody 239
    5. The Transformative Test 242

Chapter 13. Trademark 245
A. Introduction 245
B. Background 246
C. Federal Common Law Trademark 246
D. Federal Registration 252
    1. Principal Register 253
    2. Supplemental Register 255
E. Infringement 255
F. Dilution 259
G. State Trademark Laws 261
H. International Trademark Protection 263
I. Trade Dress 264
J. Conclusion 266

Chapter 14. Moral and Economic Rights 267
A. Moral Rights 267
    1. The Right to Create 269
    2. The Right of Disclosure 271
    3. The Right to Withdraw 273
    4. Name Attribution 273
    5. Integrity 277
    6. Excessive Criticism 284
B. Economic Rights 284

Chapter 15. Freedom of Expression 293
A. Censorship of the Arts 293
B. The First Amendment Framework 295
C. Symbolic Speech 301
D. Flag Desecration as Protest 306

OUTLINE

E. Obscenity 312
  1. From Roth to Miller 312
  2. Child Pornography 317
  3. An Alternative Approach to Regulation 322

Chapter 16. Museums **327**
A. Introduction 327
B. The Museum Organization 327
C. Trustee and Director Liability 333
  1. Mismanagement 335
  2. Nonmanagement 341
  3. Conflicts of Interest 342
D. Managing the Museum Collection: Acquisitions 348
E. Loans 354
F. Managing the Museum Collection: Deaccessions 357
G. Location of the Collection 365
H. Labor Relations 366
I. Codes of Ethics 369
J. Conclusion 370

Chapter 17. Right of Publicity **371**
A. Introduction 371
B. What the Right of Publicity Protects 372
C. Requirements of a Right of Publicity Claim 375
D. Commercial Speech and Advertising 377
E. Balancing Publicity Rights with Free Speech Rights 380
F. Fair Use 384

Photographs of Artwork **395**
INDEX 411

TABLE OF CASES

References are to Pages

A.V. ex rel. Vanderhye v. iParadigms, LLC, 243
AB Recur Finans v. Nordstern Ins. Co. of North America, 120
Abdul-Jabbar v. General Motors Corp., 374
Abercrombie & Fitch Co. v. Hunting World, Inc., 252
Abercrombie & Fitch Co. v. Moose Creek, Inc., 256
Abrams v. United States, 299
ACA Galleries, Inc. v. Kinney, 92
Airis v. Metro. Zoological Park & Museum Dist., 356
Ali v. Playgirl, Inc., 374
Allied Artists Pictures Corp. v. Rhodes, 202
American Booksellers Ass'n, Inc. v. Hudnut, 315
American Library Association, Inc., United States v., 321
Arrowpoint Capital Corp. v. Arrowpoint Asset Mgmt., LLC, 255
Art Masters Associates, Ltd. v. United Parcel Service, 120
Ashcroft v. American Civil Liberties Union, 320
Ashcroft v. Free Speech Coalition, 321
Attorney General of New Zealand v. Ortiz, 18
Attorney General v. Olson, 345
Authors Guild v. Google, Inc., 244
Autry v. Republic Productions, Inc., 273
Aymes v. Bonelli, 207, 209
Balog v. Center Art Gallery-Hawaii, Inc., 54
Barnes Foundation, In re, 336, 338, 339
Barnes v. Glen Theatre, Inc., 306
Bayer Co. v. United Drug Co., 252
Bella Lewitzky Dance Foundation v. John Frohnmayer, 172
Bill Graham Archives v. Dorling Kindersley Ltd., 243
Blanch v. Koons, 243
Board of Managers of Soho International Arts Condominium v. City of New York, 281
Boll v. Sharp & Dohme, Inc., 86
Bonnichsen v. United States, 15

TABLE OF CASES

Booth v. Curtis Publishing Company, 378
Boston Duck Tours, LP v. Super Duck Tours, LLC, 256
Bouchat v. Baltimore Ravens, Inc., 231
Bowers v. Baystate Technologies, Inc., 203
Brancusi v. United States, 2
Brandenburg v. Ohio, 300
Brennan's, Inc. v. Brennan's Restaurant, LLC, 256
Brockhurst v. Ryan, 193
Brookfield Commc'ns, Inc. v. W. Coast Entm't Corp., 250
Brooklyn Institute of Arts and Sciences v. City of New York, 323
Brooks v. Sotheby's, 73
Brown v. Entertainment Merchants Association, 317
Buckley v. Vidal, 284
Buffet v. Fersig, 277
C.B.C. Distribution & Mktg., Inc. v. Major League Baseball Advanced Media, L.P., 386, 391
Calvin Klein Cosmetics Corp. v. Parfums de Coeur, 248
Campbell v. Acuff-Rose Music, Inc., 237, 241, 242, 244
Carco v. Camoin, 271
Cardtoons, L.C. v. Major League Baseball Players Ass'n, 385
Cariou v. Prince, 243
Carol Wilson Fine Arts, Inc. v. Qian, 207
Carson v. Here's Johnny Portable Toilets, 373, 378
Carter v. Helmsley-Spear, Inc., 6, 207, 209, 279
Cecil v. Commissioner, 131
Chevron Chemical Co. v. Voluntary Purchasing Groups, Inc., 264
Christian Louboutin S.A. v. Yves Saint Laurent Am. Holdings, Inc., 264
Churchman v. Commissioner, 157
Chute v. North River Insurance Co., 119
Cleveland Creative Arts Guild v. Commissioner, 186
Coca-Cola Co. v. Alma-Leo U.S.A., Inc., 248
Comedy III Prods., Inc. v. Gary Saderup, Inc., 376, 386
Community Federal Sav. and Loan Ass'n v. Orondorff, 262
Community for Creative Non Violence v. Reid, 206, 207
Consmiller v. United States, 6
Corwin v. Walt Disney Co., 233
Cowgill v. California, 304

Crile v. Commissioner, 157
Cristallina S.A. v. Christie, Manson & Woods Intern., Inc., 72
Curphey v. Commissioner, 158
Custom Mfg. & Eng'g, Inc. v. Midway Servs., Inc., 256
Dallas Cowboys Cheerleaders, Inc. v. Pussycat Cinema, Ltd., 262
Dastar Corp. v. Twentieth Century Fox Film Corp., 256, 276
David Smith, Estate of v. Commissioner, 163
DC Comics v. Towle, 217
Dearborn Motors Credit Corp. v. Neel, 86
Dennis v. Buffalo Fine Arts Academy, 364
Detective Comics, Inc. v. Bruns Publications, 217
Diaz, United States v., 28
Dillinger, LLC v. Electronic Arts Inc., 374
Doe v. TCI Cablevision, 375, 386, 391, 392
Dole v. Carter, 44
Dr. Seuss Enters., LP v. Penguin Books USA, 243
Dreamwerks Prod. Grp., Inc. v. SKG Studio, 249
E. & J. Gallo Winery v. Gallo Cattle Co., 250
Echo Travel, Inc. v. Travel Associates, Inc., 248
Eden v. Whistler, 269
Eichman, United States v., 311
Eldred v. Ashcroft, 230
Elliott v. Virginia, 301
Elonis v. United States, 300
Enrique Bernat F., S.A. v. Guadalajara, Inc., 249
Erie, City of v. Pap's A.M., 306
Esperanza Peace and Justice Center v. City of San Antonio, 175, 323
Esquire, Inc. v. Ringer, 216
Ets-Hokin v. Skyy Spirits, Inc., 212
ETW Corp. v. Jireh Publishing, 256, 387, 391
Facenda v. N.F.L. Films, Inc., 373
Fair Wind Sailing, Inc. v. Dempster, 264
Federal Republic of Germany v. Elicofon, 39
Federal Trade Commission v. Magui Publishers, 103
Federated Department Stores, Inc. v. Gold Circle Ins. Co., 250
Feist Publications, Inc. v. Rural Tel. Serv. Co., 210, 211, 231

XXIV   *TABLE OF CASES*

Finley v. National Endowment for the Arts, 173
First Brands Corp. v. Fred Meyer, Inc., 264
First Covenant Church of Seattle v. City of Seattle, 180, 181
Fisher v. Dees, 239
Flaum v. Great N. Ins. Co., 124
Florsheim v. Travelers Indemnity Co. of Illinois, 115
Fort Wayne Books, Inc. v. Indiana, 324
Foster v. Lee, 207
Franklin Mint Corp. v. National Wildlife Art Exchange, Inc., 271
French v. Sotheby & Co., 72
Frick Collection v. Goldstein, 353
G. Heileman Brewing Co. v. United States, 7
Galerie Furstenberg v. Coffaro, 54, 266
Gary Friedrich Enterprises, LLC v. Marvel Characters, Inc., 207
Gates v. Central City Opera House Association, 196
Gaylord v. United States, 243
General Elec. Co. v. Alumpa Coal Co., Inc., 263
General Foods Corp. v. Mellis, 262
Georgia O'Keeffe Foundation (Museum) v. Fisk University, 334
Georgia O'Keeffe Museum v. County of Santa Fe, 329
Gilliam v. American Broadcasting Companies, 282
Gitlow v. New York, 299
Goldsboro Art League, Inc. v. Commissioner of Internal Revenue, 186
Gorton, State ex rel. v. Leppaluoto, 334
Gowans v. Northwestern Pacific Indemnity Co., 120
Graham v. John Deere Co. of Kansas City, 210
Graham, Estate of v. Sotheby's, Inc., 291
Grauer v. Deutsch, 281
Gross v. Seligman, 271
Guille v. Colmant, 274
Gund, Inc. v. Fortunoff, Inc., 248
Hahn v. Duveen, 81, 85
Halicki Films, LLC v. Sanderson Sales & Mktg., 217
Hamling v. United States, 314
Harney v. Sony Pictures Television, Inc., 212
Hart v. Elec. Arts, Inc., 376, 388, 392

TABLE OF CASES

Haughton Elevator Company v. Seeberger (Otis Elevator Company Substituted), 252
Hawaii Jewelers Association v. Fine Arts Gallery, Inc., 66
Heit v. Bixby, 342
Henley v. Dillard Dep't Stores, 374
Hill Aircraft & Leasing Corp. v. Simon, 96
Hoffman v. Capital Cities/ABC, Inc., 373
Hollinshead, United States v., 29
Home Legend, LLC v. Mannington Mills, Inc., 217
Hughes v. Design Look, Inc., 265
Hustler Magazine v. Falwell, 241
Hustler Magazine, Inc. v. Moral Majority, Inc., 241
Images International of Hawaii, Inc. v. Hang Ups Art Enterprises, Inc., 257
Inhale, Inc. v. Starbuzz Tobacco, Inc., 217
Island Insteel Systems, Inc. v. Waters, 246
JCW Investments, Inc. v. Novelty, Inc., 257
Jeanneret v. Vichey, 19
Jendwine v. Slade, 96
Ji v. Bose Corp., 376
Jysk Bed'N Linen v. Dutta-Roy, 248
Katz v. Google Inc., 244
Kehoe Component Sales Inc. v. Best Lighting Products, Inc., 256
Keller v. Elecs. Arts, Inc., 388
Kelley Blue Book v. Car-Smarts, Inc., 257
Kelley v. Chicago Park Dist., 278
Kellogg Co. v. Exxon Corp., 258
Kemper Ins. Cos. v. Federal Express Corp., 125
Kesel v. United Parcel Service, Inc., 125
Kienitz v. Sconnie National LLC, 244
Kieselstein-Cord v. Accessories by Pearl, Inc., 216
King-Seeley Thermos Co. v. Aladdin Industries, Inc., 252
Kirby v. Marvel Characters, Inc., 207
Kirtsaeng v. John Wiley & Sons, Inc., 235, 238
Klauber Bros., Inc. v. Target Corp., 217
Klayminc, In re, 257
Korn v. Elkins, 308
KP Permanent Make-Up, Inc. v. Lasting Impression I, Inc., 248
Kraut v. Morgan & Brother Manhattan Storage Co., 120
KSR Int'l Co. v. Teleflex Inc., 210

Kunstsammlungen Zu Weimar v. Elicofon, 40
Lackawanna Chapter of Ry. & Locomotive Historical
   Soc'y, Inc. v. St. Louis Cnty., 355
Lee v. A.R.T. Co., 238
Leibovitz v. Paramount Pictures Corp., 241, 242
Leigh v. Warner Bros., 212, 265
Letter Edged in Black Press, Inc. v. Public Building
   Commission of Chicago, 219
Lewin v. Richard Avedon Found., 207
Lewis v. Activision Blizzard, Inc., 207
Lindt v. Henshel, 71
Lubner v. City of Los Angeles, 282
Lucas v. South Carolina Coastal Council, 180
Madsen v. Women's Health Center, 300
Mandel v. Pitkowsky, 195
Martin v. City of Indianapolis, 6, 279
Marvel Characters, Inc. v. Kirby, 207
Massachusetts Museum of Contemporary Art Found., Inc.
   v. Büchel, 274
Masses Publishing Co. v. Patten, 298
Mattel, Inc. v. Walking Mountain Productions, 246
Mazer v. Stein, 215
McClain, United States v. (McClain I), 29
McClain, United States v. (McClain II), 30
McCrady v. Roy, 193
Menzel v. List, 37
Merchants Fire Assurance Corp. v. Lattimore, 124
Merck Eprova AG v. Gnosis S.p.A., 246
Midler v. Ford Motor Co., 373
MikLin Enterprises, Inc. v. N.L.R.B., 368
Miller v. California, 313
Miller v. Columbia Broadcasting System, Inc., 213
Miller's Ale House, Inc. v. Boynton Carolina Ale House,
   LLC, 247
Mirage Editions, Inc. v. Albuquerque A.R.T. Co., 238
Mississippi State University Alumni, Inc. v.
   Commissioner, 332
Montana v. San Jose Mercury News, Inc., 380
Morris v. Guetta, 244
Morris v. Young, 244
Morse v. Frederick, 305
Moseley v. V Secret Catalogue, Inc., 261

TABLE OF CASES

Musto v. Meyer, 212
Namath v. Sports Illustrated, 379
National Endowment for the Arts v. Finley, 173
Navajo Nation v. U.S. Dept. of Int., 15
NCAA Student-Athlete Name & Likeness Licensing Litig., In re, 388
Neri v. Monroe, 244
New York Times Co. v. Sullivan, 299
New York v. Ferber, 317
Newcombe v. Adolf Coors Co., 374
Newport Harbor Art Museum v. NEA, 172
Nola Spice Designs, L.L.C. v. Haydel Enterprises, Inc., 212
North Jersey Media Group Inc. v. Pirro and Fox News Network, LLC, 244
O'Brien, United States v., 302
Olivotti & Co., United States v., 2
Olson v. National Broadcasting Co., 217
Oracle Am., Inc. v. Google Inc., 212
Orient Ins. Co. v. Dunla, 124
Oriental Fin. Grp., Inc. v. Cooperativa de Ahorro y Credito Oriental, 258
Osborne v. Ohio, 319
Owens-Corning Fiberglas Corp., In re, 248
Palazzolo v. Rhode Island, 180
Paramount Pictures Corp. v. Davis, 271
Park 'N Fly, Inc. v. Dollar Park & Fly, Inc., 247
Pasternack v. Esskay Art Galleries, Inc., 70
Patterson v. Colorado ex rel. Att'y Gen. of Colo., 298
Penn Central Transportation Co. v. New York City, 178
Pennzoil-Quaker State Co. v. Miller Oil & Gas Operations, 258
Perfect 10, Inc. v. Amazon.com, Inc., 243
Perry, United States v., 1
Phillips v. Pembroke Real Estate, Inc., 6, 278
Pillsbury Co. v. Milky Way Productions, Inc., 262
Pinocchio's Pizza Inc., 250
Pitchfork Ranch Co. v. Bar TL, 67
Plaza Equities Corp. v. Aetna Casualty and Surety Co., 118
Pom Wonderful LLC v. Hubbard, 247
Pope v. Illinois, 314

XXVIII TABLE OF CASES

Power v. Barham, 96
Princess Paley Olga v. Weisz, 39
Prouty v. National Broadcasting Co., 282
Pushman v. New York Graphic Society, Inc., 205
Qualitex Co. v. Jacobson Products Co., 264
R.A.V. v. City of St. Paul, Minnesota, 300
Radich v. New York, 309
Radich, People v., 309
Radich, United States ex rel. v. Criminal Court of City of New York, 309
Range Road Music, Inc. v. East Coast Foods, Inc., 231
Rearden LLC v. Rearden Commerce, Inc., 256
Redmond v. New Jersey Historical Soc., 352
Reed Enterprises v. Clark, 316
Reno v. American Civil Liberties Union, 320
Repp v. Webber, 233
Republic of Austria v. Altmann, 40
Respublica v. Oswald, 296
Rice v. Fox Broadcasting Co., 217
Rodrigue v. Rodrigue, 203
Rogers v. Grimaldi, 375, 385
Rogers v. Koons, 231
Romm Art Creations Ltd. v. Simcha International, Inc., 265
Rosciszewski v. Arete Associates, Inc., 202
Rosen v. Spanierman, 97
Rosetta Stone Ltd. v. Google, Inc., 259
Roth v. United States, 312
Ryan v. Editions Ltd. West, Inc., 202
Safeco Ins. Co. of America v. Sharma, 122
Salinger v. Colting, 243
Sam Francis Foundation v. Christies, Inc., 291
Sanchez v. Stein, 275
Satava v. Lowry, 212
Schacht v. United States, 304
Schenck v. United States, 299
Schultz, United States v., 32
Scotch Whiskey Ass'n v. Majestic Distilling Co., Inc., 246
Scott, People ex rel. v. George F. Harding Museum, 334
Seattle, City of v. First Covenant Church of Seattle, Wash., 180
Selle v. Gibb, 233

TABLE OF CASES   XXIX

Seltzer v. Green Day, Inc., 243
Seltzer v. Morton, 86
Seng-Tiong Ho v. Taflove, 212
Serra v. United States Gen. Servs. Admin., 278
Sheldon v. Metro-Goldwyn Pictures Corp., 210
Shulman v. Group W Prods., Inc., 384
Simeonov v. Tiegs, 386
Singer v. Nat. Fire Ins. Co. of Hartford, 118
Singleton v. Dean, 233
Skidmore v. Led Zeppelin, 232
Smyer, United States v., 28
Society of Jesus of New England v. Boston Landmarks Com'n, 181
Sony Corp. of Am. v. Universal City Studios, Inc., 237
Spence v. Washington, 305, 308
Spirits Int'l, N.V., In re, 249
Standard Oil Co. v. Clark, 199
Stanley v. Georgia, 320
Starbucks Corp. v. Wolfe's Borough Coffee, Inc., 259
Steinway & Sons v. Robert Demars & Friends, 263
Stern v. Lucy Webb Hayes Nat. Training School for Deaconesses and Missionaries, 341
Stewart v. Abend, 237
Stone v. Rullo Agency, 118
Stromberg v. California, 302
Sturdza v. United Arab Emirates, 203
Suntrust Bank v. Houghton Mifflin Co., 241
Swanstrom v. Ins. Co. of N. Am., 117
Texas v. Johnson, 311
The Prosecutor v. Ahmad Al Faqi Al Mahdi, 42
Tillamook Country Smoker, Inc. v. Tillamook County Creamery Ass'n, 250
Tinker v. Des Moines Independent Community School District, 304
Tobin v. United States, 104
Tobin, United States v., 104
Toho Co., Ltd. v. William Morrow & Co., Inc., 217
Trade-Mark Cases, In re, 246
Travis v. Sotheby Parke Bernet, 83
Trinity Evangelical Lutheran Church v. City of Peoria, 181
Tunick, Inc. v. Kornfield, 94

TABLE OF CASES

Two Pesos, Inc. v. Taco Cabana, Inc., 264
Ty, Inc. v. GMA Accessories, Inc., 232
United Artists Theater Circuit, Inc. v. City of Philadelphia, 180
University of Alabama Bd. of Trustees v. New Life Art, Inc., 258
Urbont v. Sony Music Entertainment, 207
Vaad L'Hafotzas Sichos, Inc. v. Krinsky, 207
Vail Associates, Inc. v. Vend-Tel-Co., 248
Vanier v. Ponsoldt, 65
Vargas v. Esquire, Inc., 276
Various Articles of Obscene Merchandise, Schedule #1303, United States v., 315
Varsity Brands, Inc. v. Star Athletica, LLC, 217
Virginia v. Black, 301
Visual Arts and Galleries Ass'n v. Various John Does, 251
Von Rosen, People v., 307
Von Saher v. Norton Simon Museum of Art at Pasadena, 42
Wal-Mart Stores, Inc. v. Samara Brothers, Inc., 265
Walnut & Quince Streets Corp. v. Mills, 177
Walt Disney Productions v. Air Pirates, 217
Weiner King, Inc. v. Wiener King Corp., 250
Weisz v. Parke-Bernet Galleries, Inc., 70, 91
Welding Servs. Inc. v. Forman, 248
West Virginia State Board of Education v. Barnette, 302, 372
White v. Kimmel, 221
Whitney v. California, 299
William J. Jenack Estate Appraisers and Auctioneers, Inc. v. Rabizadeh, 69
Williams, United States v., 321
Winkworth v. Christie Manson and Woods Ltd., 28
Wisconsin v. Mitchell, 301
Wolff v. Smith, 192
Wright Hepburn Webster Gallery, Ltd., State v., 77
Wrightsman & Wrightsman v. United States, 131
Zacchini v. Scripps-Howard Broadcasting Co., 381
Zalewski v. Cicero Builder Dev., Inc., 212

ART LAW
IN A NUTSHELL®

FIFTH EDITION

CHAPTER 1
ART: THE CUSTOMS DEFINITION

A. HISTORICAL

The term art has many meanings, depending on the context in which it is used. In the law, some of the most important and well developed definitions are articulated in the customs cases. This is because most works of art may enter the United States duty free. In deciding what qualifies as art for the purposes of determining tariff rates or exemptions on imports, the courts have focused on the appearance of the object, the occupation of the person producing it, the purpose for which the object is made, and, if the object is editioned or serialized (like prints or bronze sculptures), the method of execution or number of pieces in the edition or series. The definitions that emerge reflect not only the policies underlying the tariff laws, but also the changing nature of art and the emergence of new art forms and media.

Early customs cases restricted the definition of art to the fine arts, as distinguished from the useful mechanical and industrial arts. In *United States v. Perry*, 146 U.S. 71 (1892), the United States Supreme Court held that stained glass windows containing effigies of saints and other representations of biblical subjects for use in a church could not be admitted duty free as fine art. While the court noted that the stained glass windows were artistic in the sense of being beautiful and that the windows required a high degree of artistic merit for their production, they, nevertheless, were classified as decorative and industrial. The court stated that Congress extended its special favor to the fine arts alone, which the court defined as works "intended solely for ornamental purposes, and including paintings in oil and water, upon canvas, plaster, or other material, and original statuary of marble, stone or bronze." Excluded from the definition were "[m]inor objects of art, intended also for ornamental purposes, [which] are susceptible of an indefinite reproduction of the original; objects of art, which serve primarily an ornamental, and incidentally a useful, purpose . . . ; and objects primarily designed for a useful purpose, but made ornamental to please the eye and gratify the taste. . . ."

Another requirement of the early customs cases was that the item be representational. In *United States v. Olivotti & Co.*, T.D. 36,309, 7 U.S. Cust. App. 46, 30 Treas. Dec. 586 (1916), for example, the court held that sculpture was confined to imitations of natural objects, chiefly the human form, represented in their true proportions. Later cases, however, recognized the evolution of abstract art. In *Brancusi v. United States*, T.D. 43,063, 54 Treas. Dec. 428 (Cust. Ct. 1928), Brancusi's *Bird in Flight* was held to be sculpture and thus entitled to duty-free entry. The court recognized that "[w]ithout the exercise of rather a vivid imagination, it bears no resemblance to a bird, except, perchance, with such imagination it may be likened to the shape of the body of a bird." However, the court stated it was necessary to recognize the existence and influence of "a so-called new school of art, whose exponents attempt to portray abstract ideas rather than to imitate natural objects." Instead of the representational test enunciated in *Olivotti*, the court articulated a more liberal definition: *Bird in Flight* qualified as fine art because it was to be used for purely ornamental purposes, it was beautiful and symmetrical in outline, and it was the work of a professional sculptor. See page 395 for a photograph of this sculpture, which is also known as *Bird in Space*.

The full implications of the liberal position adopted in *Brancusi* were not realized for almost 30 years. Until the 1958 Amendments to the tariff laws, courts continued to struggle with many subtle and somewhat arbitrary distinctions between art and non-art. These distinctions often penalized innovative forms. For instance, under the earlier laws, many importers of artworks were subjected to custom duties because the works were not executed in any of the media specifically enumerated in the statutes. In later years, as artists continued to experiment in different media, the courts seemed to become dissatisfied with the narrow view.

B. THE PRESENT RULE

In response to the emergence of new art media, the Tariff Act of 1930 was amended by legislation in 1958. The amendments allowed free entry to art works "in other media," works for certain narrowly defined commercial uses, as well as those specifically enumerated. The customs definition of art was modified to comply with international law when the Harmonized Schedule was adopted in 1988. See https://www.usitc.gov/tata/hts/index.htm (the current 2016 Harmonized Tariff Schedule). The Harmonized Schedule incorporates internationally established product definitions to which all major U.S. trading partners subscribe. By using this uniform descriptive scheme for all goods, not just art, that move through international trade, goods classifications are more accurate, and tracking of imports and exports is more efficient.

Since the 1958 amendments, most art objects have been allowed free entry without litigation, but occasionally artwork is still duties because of the media or method in which it was executed. For example, the tariff schedule does not allow free entry to articles made by stenciling, photocopying, or other mechanical processes, or to painted or decorated manufactured articles, such as vases, cups, plates, screens, cases, trays, chests, etc. In addition, because it apparently is believed that a large number of reprints or castings is indicative of commercialism rather than artistic creation, prints are duty free only if they are hand pulled from plates, stones, or blocks etched, drawn or engraved with hand tools. The 1958 amendments restricted duty-free entry of limited edition sculpture to the first 10 replicas. The Harmonized Schedule, however, now allows the first 12 castings of sculptures and statuary. Under the Harmonized Schedule, the definition of art remain narrow—only "fine art" is exempt from import duties. The position of the customs service regarding the definition of art is generally consistent with earlier rulings. The following categories are exempt from import duties as works of art: (a) original paintings and drawings, (b) collages and decorative plaques, (c) original prints, engravings and lithographs, (d) sculptures and statuary, (e) postage stamps, (f) collectors' pieces, and (g) antiques.

Another requirement for duty-free entry is that the work must be the product of an artist, rather than an artisan. Under the 1958 amendments, a sculpture could be admitted duty free only if it was the work of a "professional" sculptor. In determining whether a person was a professional sculptor, the courts tended to place great emphasis on the individual's credentials; thus, a graduate of a course in sculpture from a recognized school of art or an artist with works exhibited in public at an exhibition limited to the fine arts likely would have been considered a professional sculptor. Similarly, one who was recognized by his or her peers or by art critics also would have been considered an artist for customs purposes. See CLA–2: R.R.V.C.S.C. 061949 TL, May 19, 1980. Under the Harmonized System, the professional status requirement now applies only to sculptors working in ceramics. However, the customs service continues to differentiate between an artist who creates an original work and an artisan or craftsperson for the purpose of ascertaining originality. A work is the product of an artist rather than an artisan only when the creator leaves the paths of his or her trade and, as a result of a mental concept, constructs something original that appeals to the artistic eye and mind. In other words, an artist works from inspiration and skill. Thus, whereas professional productions of an artist may include work done by assistants under the artist's supervision, the work must reflect the artist's exercise of his or her own aesthetic imagination and conception. A similar process is used under the United States Visual Artists Rights Act (VARA), 17 U.S.C. § 106A, to determine if a sculptor or other artist has enough "recognized stature" to come under the protection of this moral rights law. See *Phillips v. Pembroke Real Est., Inc.*, 459 F.3d 128, 129–30, 133, 134 (1st Cir. 2006); *Carter v. Helmsley-Spear, Inc.*, 71 F.3d 77, 83 (2d Cir. 1995); *Martin v. City of Indianapolis*, 982 F. Supp. 625, 631 (S.D. Ind. 1997), *and* 4 F. Supp. 2d 808 (S.D. Ind. 1998), *aff'd*, 192 F.3d 608 (7th Cir. 1999); See also Massachusetts Art Preservation Act, Mass. Gen. Laws Ann. ch. 231, § 85S(f). (VARA is discussed *infra* in Chapter 14, "Moral and Economic Rights").

Original paintings, executed solely by hand, appear to enjoy special treatment for customs' purposes as they are presumed to be executed by professional artists. The only important consideration under the customs regulations is whether the painting was executed wholly by hand, rather than with the aid of any mechanical device.

The final requirement of the customs' definition of art is that the work must not be an item of utility or made for commercial uses. The question of utility is often a matter of degree. As the court noted in *Consmiller v. United States*, T.D. 32,585, 3 U.S. Cust. App. 298, 301, 22 Treas. Dec. 983 (1912), whereas two small figures carved on a marble mantel piece did not make the mantel a work of art, it was possible that "the inspiration of a sculptor might be so chiseled on a marble mantel that the identity and especially the utilitarian nature of the latter would be practically forgotten in the motif and artistic beauty of the sculptural work." *Id.* at 301. However, the majority of courts are more conservative and hold that if the work has any functional characteristics, it is precluded from being classified as a work of art. Certain objects are considered to be utilitarian by nature, for example, vases, plates, chests, and the like. This is so even though they are executed by noted creators such as Fabergé or Cellini. However, when a set of decorated beer steins was imported into the United States, it was classified as ornamental because the size, composition, and decoration of the mugs made it clear that they were chiefly for display rather than for regular use. *G. Heileman Brewing Co. v. United States*, USITR, 14 CIT 614 (Ct. Int'l Trade 1990).

Even if the work is otherwise a work of art because of its purely aesthetic characteristics, it still may not be eligible for duty-free entry if it is imported for a commercial or industrial use, such as reproduction on the cover of a magazine, use as a prop in an advertisement, or if the work is commonly produced in mass quantities for a large market. This disqualification probably results from the belief that the commercial art market is limited and that the imported piece might displace one created by an American artist; thus, a customs duty is imposed on art imported for commercial purposes to make it less economically desirable. In determining what is a commercial purpose, courts focus on the reason the items were imported rather than on the intent of the artist in creating them and, where the reason for importation is ambiguous, on the chief use in the hands of the ultimate recipient.

Thus, the technical definition of art adopted by Congress and interpreted by the courts for customs' purposes reflects political and economic concerns that are divorced from aesthetics. There are other legal contexts in which art is defined using more aesthetic considerations, such as in copyright law (See Chapter 12 *infra*). It, therefore, is important to determine the context in which the term "art" is used when attempting to develop a definition.

CHAPTER 2
ART: INTERNATIONAL MOVEMENT

A. THE PROBLEM

Art acts as a goodwill ambassador, creating an understanding of, interest in and admiration for the people of the country of its origin. Movement of art internationally also broadens tastes and sensibilities, eliminates parochialism, and promotes international understanding; yet, countries also have an interest in retaining and protecting their national treasures. The availability of cultural property within any country enhances the national conscience, fosters community pride, and contributes to local scholarship. The prevention of looting, theft, and destruction of art and archaeological evidence is also important in order to preserve individual works of art and to maintain the association of art and cultural property within its historical and geographical milieu.

Many countries thus have placed limits on international art trade by adopting regulations on the import and export of art and on the disposition of cultural artifacts. Yet, in so doing, countries must reconcile the international demand for art and artifacts with the need for their protection. Regulations that are too restrictive merely encourage black market activity, and the failure to provide for legitimate cultural exchange merely hampers international accord. The task of balancing national and international interests thus poses difficult problems for nations and for individuals concerned with the availability and protection of art.

For centuries, the international art market functioned virtually without any effective legal, moral, or ethical constraints. As a result, much valuable art work was pillaged or destroyed. Traffic in pre-Columbian antiquities, for example, has stripped Central America of countless cultural artifacts and has seriously hindered the efforts of archaeologists to unravel the mysteries of ancient civilizations. Not only do the pre-Columbian articles lose much of their archaeological significance when removed from their sites, but many artifacts wind up in private collections to which scholars have no access. Many artifacts available to scholars often are of little historical value since they are mere fragments that have been wrenched out of their archaeological context. In order to remove large stone slabs called "stelae," ornately carved with figures and hieroglyphs, for instance, looters use techniques ranging from severing the stone with chainsaws to heating the stone with fire and then pouring water on it until it shatters. After this treatment, the hieroglyphs, which are of major importance in analyzing the Mayan language, become indecipherable.

The cost of properly protecting cultural property and conserving archaeological sites is so great that few nations can afford it. Theft poses a continuing problem—the value of fine art stolen each year is estimated to be between $5 billion and $8 billion. Kris Hollington, *After Drugs and Guns, Art Theft is the*

Biggest Criminal Enterprise in the World, Newsweek.com (July 22, 2014 at 10:09 A.M.), available at http://www.newsweek.com/2014/07/18/after-drugs-and-guns-art-theft-biggest-criminal-enterprise-world-260386.html; FBI Art Crime Team—Art Theft Site, https://www.fbi.gov/investigate/violent-crime/art-theft. In Italy, for instance, churches containing priceless articles are often unguarded, and museums, as well as private collections, are inadequately protected. See Judith Harris, *Preying on Italian Churches*, Artnews.com (Nov. 12, 2014 at 9:30 A.M.), available at http://www.artnews.com/2014/11/12/art-theft-in-italian-churches/; Alexander Forbes, *Three Paintings Stolen from Italian Castle*, ArtNet News (Aug. 27, 2014), available at https://news.artnet.com/art-world/three-paintings-stolen-from-italian-castle-86880.

Pollution and industrial progress also present serious threats to the preservation of cultural property. In Greece, the Parthenon and other Greek monuments have suffered more destruction from industrial fumes than they have from the past four centuries of weathering. In the United States, when the Tennessee Valley Authority began constructing the Tellico Dam and Reservoir Project in 1967, archaeologists were forced to race bulldozers to excavate Indian archaeological sites before the area was submerged.

Archaeological excavations also can suffer when international tensions are involved. Trouble arose over excavations in Jerusalem in the early 1970s when the Israelis were accused of destroying property of historical and cultural significance to the Arabs. This alleged destruction of property led to a lengthy dispute, principally between Israel and Jordan, concerning the legality and propriety of the Israeli excavations. In response, the UNESCO General Conference in 1974 adopted two resolutions rejecting an Israeli request to be included in UNESCO's European group and proposing to withhold assistance from Israel in the fields of education, science and culture.

Even when cultural antiquities are removed legally from their country of origin, tremendous controversy may result. One example is the episode of the Elgin Marbles, which occurred in 1779 and which continues to be controversial today. Lord Elgin, England's envoy extraordinaire to Constantinople, obtained permission from the Turkish government first to sketch, then later to remove, marble sculptures from the Parthenon. Elgin originally planned to use the marbles to decorate his mansion in England, but after personal economic reversals, he presented them to the British government for purchase. The debates in the House of Commons in 1816 were heated, but ultimately the House of Commons approved the purchase and the marbles were placed in the British Museum.

In 1983, the Greek government formally requested that the marbles be returned to Greece, and in 1984, the British government refused to do so. As a result of the furor, the term "Elginism" became synonymous with the pillage of art treasures. The Greek government, unhappy about the loss of a part of its cultural heritage, continues periodically and regularly to demand the return of the Elgin marbles. The arguments against their return range from the assertion that they can be viewed by more people if they remain in England to the accusation that the Greeks cannot properly preserve their antiquities.

In 2006, a German university agreed to return a segment of the Parthenon to Greece. This is the first time any institution has voluntarily returned any piece of the Parthenon and may put pressure on the British Museum to return the Elgin marbles. Greece has continued to take steps to recover the marbles, and in 2016 sought assistance from the United Nations. *Greece looks to UN for help reclaiming the Elgin Marbles*, The Telegraph (May 9, 2016 at 12:39 A.M.), available at http://www.telegraph.co.uk/news/2016/05/08/greece-looks-to-un-for-help-reclaiming-the-elgin-marbles/. See page 396 for examples of the Elgin Marbles in the British Museum.

The problem of possible destruction upon the return of native art poses difficult conflicts for museums and collectors. One especially acute situation occurred in 1978 when the Zuni Indian tribe requested the return of a Zuni War God acquired by the Denver Art Museum in 1953. Under Zuni law, no person can own gods such as these, since they are tribal property, and only tribal members are permitted to see them. After much deliberation, the museum trustees issued a release, stating:

> The museum has held the object in good faith for over 25 years, exhibiting, publishing and protecting it for the benefit of the public

throughout the world. Should the museum donate the object to the Zunis, it will be placed in an outdoor setting subject to the hazards of the natural elements of windblown sand, intense heat, cold, and certain, and in fact intentional, deterioration and destruction. New War Gods are produced annually to succeed and supplement their predecessors; they are intended to "eat themselves up." The possibility of theft also exists. The Zunis have outlined plans to increase security measures at the several shrines which are near public roads, but acknowledge that a large number of more remote shrines also exist and are largely unprotected. The return of the object will assure its ultimate destruction.

Nevertheless, the trustees voted in 1979 to return the object to a suitable shrine in New Mexico under appropriate security conditions. In 1991, the Zuni Tribe acknowledged that the war gods statues known to have been in the hands of museums and collectors finally had been returned and restored, and were at peace. Michael Haederle, *War Gods Are Finally at Peace: Culture: After 13 years, Zuni Indians have reclaimed the last of 67 religious statues known to have been in the hands of museums and collectors*, Los Angeles Times (Aug. 12, 1991), available at http://articles.latimes.com/1991-08-12/news/vw-381_1_war-gods.

In 1990, Congress reversed 80 years of government policy that promoted the discovery and institutionalization of Indian remains and artifacts for study and display by enacting the Native American Graves Protection and Repatriation Act (Pub. L. No. 101–601 (codified at 25 U.S.C. Chapter 32)). The Repatriation Act facilitates the return of human remains, funerary objects, and other sacred objects held in the collections of publicly-funded museums and universities by returning a great deal of authority over ancient Indian art and artifacts to the tribes. In addition, the Act makes illegal the purchase or sale of human remains or associated funerary objects and restricts artifact hunting. For a succinct summary of the enactment and operation of the Archaeological Resources Protection Act (ARPA), 16 U.S.C. § 470cc, and the Native American Graves Protection and Repatriation Act (NAGPRA), 25 U.S.C. §§ 3001–3013, see *Navajo Nation v. U.S. Dept. of Int.*, 819 F.3d 1084, 1088–89 (9th Cir. 2016).

A recent controversy involved the *Kennewick Man*, whose 9,000-year-old skeleton was discovered along the banks of the Columbia River in 1996. Northwest Native American tribes consider the bones sacred and want to bury them, but scientists want to study the skeleton, which is one of the oldest, most complete skeletons found in North America. The Ninth Circuit ruled that because there is no evidence connecting the remains with any existing tribe, scientists are free to study the *Kennewick Man*. *Bonnichsen v. United States*, 367 F.3d 864, 868 (9th Cir. 2004).

Museums also can face difficult conflicts when they unwittingly acquire art that is claimed to belong to someone else. In 1963, the Dumbarton Oaks Museum was presented with an assemblage of sixth-century Byzantine silver acquired by one of its founders from a Greek antique dealer. Within a year, Dumbarton Oaks learned that this silver was part of a large treasure of liturgical silver known as the *Kumluca Treasure* from the Antalya region of Turkey. In the late 1960s the Turkish government made fruitless requests both to Dumbarton Oaks and to the United States government for the return of the Treasure. In 1981, the Turkish Minister of Culture retaliated by barring individuals affiliated with the museum from working on archaeological excavations in Turkey, and threatened to extend the ban to other American institutions if the art pieces were not returned.

More recently, Italy indicted Marion True, curator of the Paul Getty Museum, on criminal charges involving the acquisition of 42 antiquities prosecutors alleged were removed from the country illegally. According to Italian court documents, the Getty had acquired at least 52 items that were looted or originated from smugglers. The court documents named additional allegedly looted objects at the Metropolitan Museum of Art in New York, the Museum of Fine Arts in Boston, the Princeton University Art Museum, and the Cleveland Museum of Art. As a result, the Metropolitan agreed to return six antiquities from its collection to Italy, subject to Italy providing long-term loans of other artifacts. The Metropolitan's agreement to voluntarily return works has sparked something of a trend among museums and institutional collections that continues in the 2010s. Hugh Eakin, *The Great Giveback*, N.Y. Times (Jan. 26, 2013), available at http://www.

nytimes.com/2013/01/27/sunday-review/the-great-giveback.html?_r=0.

B. CONTROLLING THE INTERNATIONAL MOVEMENT OF ART

1. EXPORT RESTRICTIONS

Many concerned nations have attempted to solve the problems presented by the international movement of art by adopting laws to control the flow of cultural property in and out of their geographical boundaries. Most nations encourage the export of contemporary art by living artists, but the vast majority of countries have enacted some form of export restrictions for other cultural property. A few countries have no restrictions on art exports.

Of the countries that do restrict exports, some utilize screening, or selective, prohibitions; others utilize across-the-board, or complete, prohibitions. The screening regulations allow the government of the country of origin to decide whether a particular work of art should be allowed to leave its borders. Under English law, for example, a license must be obtained to export any object more than 100 years old and valued at over £8,000 (sterling), which either was created in Britain or was imported into Britain at least 50 years prior to the date export is desired. The determination of whether to grant a license is made in each case depending on the object's close connection with English history and national life, its aesthetic importance, and its significance for academic study.

Because this type of selective restrictions system results in a fair representation of the exporting nation's art being on the international market, the system encourages cultural intercourse among nations and tends to discourage illicit traffic in art. By contrast, complete prohibition systems tend to be much less successful. In Mexico, for example, the government imposed a complete restriction on the export of pre-Columbian art in 1972. The consequence of this government action was the escalation of black market operations to epidemic proportions. Apparently, when a nation dams up the legal channels of commerce, pressure builds up, deflecting the stream to clandestine outlets and resulting in a complete loss of legal control over the market.

Export restrictions are typically enforced by criminal sanctions or by provisions for forfeiture. Unless an object can be prevented from leaving the country, however, forfeiture provisions are only a partial solution to the problem of recovery of the object. In some cases, an article must be seized by the government before it is considered forfeited and returned to its rightful owner. For example, in *Attorney General of New Zealand v. Ortiz*, [1984] 1 A.C. 1 (H.L. 1983), the New Zealand government tried to recover in an English court an historic article which had been illegally exported without a certificate from the New Zealand government and which had subsequently been sold to the defendant. The court refused to order the return of the object, interpreting the New Zealand export statutes to provide that forfeiture to the New Zealand government was not automatic upon export but, rather, was to take effect only upon seizure by the New Zealand customs or police. Thus, only upon seizure could the New Zealand government acquire title to the article, although once seized, the statute provided that the forfeiture to the crown would relate back to the date of the illegal exportation.

Between private parties, export laws may be used to annul the sale of an illegally exported work of art based on the breach of an implied warranty of title, Uniform Commercial Code (U.C.C.) § 2–312. This issue was raised but left undecided in *Jeanneret v. Vichey*, 693 F.2d 259, 266–67 (2d Cir. 1982). The plaintiff, Marie Louise Jeanneret, a professional art dealer, purchased a Matisse painting from the defendants, Anna and Luben Vichey. In 1970, the Vicheys brought the painting to the United States from Italy. When Mme. Jeanneret discovered that the Vicheys had not obtained an export license or a permit from the Italian authorities, she claimed, among other things, that the Vicheys had breached the implied warranty of title to the painting. The court declined to decide this issue in the absence of any guidance from the New York courts, and the case was remanded for a new trial. The court did note in support of Mme. Jeanneret's claim that the painting probably could not be sold to any reputable dealer or auction house. It was also noted, however, that so long as Mme. Jeanneret or any subsequent purchaser from her did not bring the painting back into Italy, it could not be confiscated and that neither she nor a subsequent purchaser would be liable to the Italian government.

2. IMPORT RESTRICTIONS

Another means of national control of the international movement of art is the use of import barriers. Generally, there are few legal restrictions on the importation of works of art, although a few countries have set up economic barriers in the form of import duties. It is, nevertheless, common for art and antiquities to be exempt from duties. For example, Brazil and Israel exempt antiquities from customs duty since these objects do not pose a financial threat to domestic artists. As discussed in Chapter 1, *supra*, the United States also exempts most works of art from customs duties.

A few countries unilaterally refuse to admit art illegally exported from another country. The United States law, 19 U.S.C. §§ 2091–2095 *et seq.*, is an example of this type of legislation, which covers pre-Columbian monumental or architectural sculptures or murals. Importation of Pre-Columbian Monumental or Architectural Sculpture or Murals, 19 U.S.C. §§ 2091–2095. The legislation permits the country of origin to recover the property in question, but since there is little incentive for a nation to unilaterally ban the import of illegally exported art, some countries, like Israel and New Guinea, promise to return illegally exported items only if the country of origin has a reciprocal provision. While these laws cannot properly be termed treaties, they operate in a similar fashion.

3. TREATIES

As a means of regulating the international movement of art, treaties have the disadvantage of requiring extensive international negotiations for their creation and modification. Yet, unlike reciprocal import provisions, which can place a nation in the position of having to return illegally exported art before determining whether the country of origin of the returned piece will grant similar cooperation, treaties are preexisting agreements that clearly indicate the signatory nation's policy and intent.

There are several bilateral treaties which prohibit the importation of art that has been illegally exported from another country and provide for the return of this illegally exported art. In addition, some bilateral treaties, such as the extradition treaty between the United States and Mexico, Treaty Signed at Mexico City May 4, 1978, 31 U.S.T. 5059, T.I.A.S. No. 9656, provide for the extradition of persons suspected or convicted of violating one country's antiquities laws. Many bilateral treaties also provide important mechanisms for cultural exchange. The Treaty of Cooperation Providing for the Recovery and Return of Stolen Archeological, Historical and Cultural Properties between the United States and Mexico, for example, promotes joint archaeological activity and exchange of antiquities. See Treaty of Cooperation Providing for the Recovery and Return of Stolen Archaeological, Historical and Cultural Properties between the

United States and Mexico, https://eca.state.gov/files/bureau/treaty01.pdf.

Multilateral treaties can accomplish many of the same objectives on a larger scale. Some, like the Organization of American States' San Salvador Convention on the Protection of the Archeological, Historical and Artistic Heritage of the American Nations, http://www.oas.org/juridico/english/treaties/c-16.html, are limited regional efforts. One of the major shortcomings of any treaty, but especially regional treaties with few members, is that they bind only their members, thus leaving other outlets open to black marketeers. Moreover, the San Salvador Convention adopts the extreme position of presuming that all importation shall be considered unlawful, except when the state owning cultural property authorizes its exportation for the purpose of promoting knowledge of national cultures. A further article of this Convention provides that regulations on ownership of cultural property shall be governed by domestic legislation, thus affirming the extremely restrictive position of many countries that have declared that cultural property belongs to the government of the country of origin. The Mexican Antiquities Laws of 1897, 1934 and 1970, Ley Sobre Monumentos Arqueologicos, Diario Oficial de 11 de mayo de 1897, XIV Anuario de Legislacion y Jurisprudencia (1897); 82 Diario Oficial 152, 19 de enero de 1934 (1934); 303 Diario Oficial 8, 16 de diciembre de 1970 (1970). See also related enactments of 58 Diario Oficial 7, 31 de enero de 1930 (1930); 312 Diario Oficial 16, 6 de mayo de 1972 (1972), for example, provide that certain defined archaeological monuments are national property which must be registered and which may be exported only with express state authorization.

Other multilateral treaties are more comprehensive. The UNESCO Convention on the Means of Prohibiting and Preventing the Illicit Import, Export and Transfer of Ownership of Cultural Property, http://www.unesco.org/new/en/culture/themes/illicit-trafficking-of-cultural-property/1970-convention/, for example, is a global effort. Yet, early drafts of the UNESCO Convention failed to provide for legitimate cultural exchange and, therefore, were opposed by the United States. Ultimately, however, the UNESCO Convention explicitly recognized that "the interchange of cultural property among nations for scientific, cultural and educational purposes increases the knowledge of the civilization of Man, enriches the cultural life of all peoples and inspires mutual respect and appreciation among nations." Thus, instead of focusing on national patrimonies, the Convention emphasizes international interests in cultural property, whose proper protection and use demand international cooperation.

The earliest signatory nations to the UNESCO Convention were primarily art-exporting countries such as Ecuador, Cameroon, Mexico, Egypt, and Brazil, which caused some critics to doubt the effectiveness of the treaty, but in 1983, President Reagan signed the enabling legislation (the Convention on Cultural Property Implementation Act), making the United States a participant in the

Convention, although U.S. compliance extends only to material stolen from another party to the treaty. Now 131 countries are party to this treaty. http://www.unesco.org/eri/la/convention.asp?ko=13039&language=e.

The enabling legislation directs the Secretary of the Treasury, in consultation with the Director of the United States Information Agency, to promulgate a list of protected objects of archaeological or ethnological interest and imposes import restrictions on objects illegally exported from other countries party to the treaty. Articles that are not accompanied by a certificate or other documentation from the country of origin, certifying that the exportation was not illegal, are subject to seizure and judicial forfeiture and are to be offered for return to the country of origin if that country bears the expenses of returning them. However, even without a certificate, an article may be imported if the importer furnishes satisfactory evidence that the article was exported from the country of origin 10 years or more before the date of entry into the United States and that neither the importer nor any related person contracted for or acquired an interest in the article more than one year from the date of entry. Entry without a certificate also is allowed if the article was exported before the list of protected archaeological or ethnological materials was promulgated.

Articles of cultural property are treated slightly differently than archaeological or ethnological materials. Articles of cultural property stolen from a museum, religious, or secular public monument or similar institution may not be imported into the United States, but where an article is imported by one who establishes valid title, the article will not be forfeited unless the country of origin pays the owner just compensation for it. Furthermore, if valid title cannot be established but the article was purchased for value and without knowledge or reason to believe it was stolen, the article will not be forfeited unless the country of origin pays the owner the amount that was paid for the article, or unless the United States establishes that the country of origin would return an article from an institution in the United States without requiring the payment of compensation as a matter of law or reciprocity.

In 2001, UNESCO adopted the UNESCO Convention on the Protection of the Underwater Cultural Heritage, http://www.unesco.org/new/en/culture/themes/underwater-cultural-heritage/2001-convention/official-text/, designed to help protect history found in shipwrecks and other underwater sites. At the same time, it adopted a new international ethical standard, the Universal Declaration on Cultural Diversity, http://portal.unesco.org/en/ev.php-URL_ID=13179&URL_DO=DO_TOPIC&URL_SECTION=201.html, which requires its members to combat illicit traffic in cultural property. Only a handful of countries have become signatories to this treaty.

UNIDROIT drafted a Convention on Stolen or Illegally Exported Cultural Objects, which was opened for signature in 1995. http://www.unidroit.org/instruments/cultural-property/1995-convention.

This treaty, signed by more than 37 countries, http://www.unidroit.org/status-cp, provides for a three-year period after the location of a stolen cultural object becomes known, during which the country of origin may make a claim for restitution, limited by a 50-year statute of repose from the time of theft. Special allowances are made for objects belonging to a monument, archaeological site, or public collection, in which cases the claimants are subject to only the three-year statute of limitations. Illegally exported cultural items are treated similarly. A state may declare that claims are subject to a limitation of 75 years or longer for stolen cultural objects but not for illegally exported items. When a request for return is made, the court of the state addressed is to order the return of the object if the requesting state establishes that the illegal removal impairs the preservation of the object or its content, the integrity of a complex object, the preservation of information, or the ritual use of the object by a tribal or indigenous community. In either case, a bona fide purchaser for value who employed due diligence may be entitled to compensation. The United States is not a party to this treaty.

4. SELF-REGULATION BY NONGOVERNMENTAL ORGANIZATIONS

Museums and other institutions can also self-regulate in order to prevent some of the difficulties that arise from the illicit international art trade. In addition to influencing treaty agreements and national legislation, organizations such as the International Council of Museums, the Society of

American Archaeology, the International Association of Art, the International Council of Monuments and Sites, and the International Centre for the Study of the Preservation and Restoration of Cultural Property provide important nongovernmental regulatory policies. Agreements between institutions encouraging short-and long-term loans of their holdings, for example, help to control the illicit acquisition of artifacts and cultural property. Parties to such agreements may additionally be required to adopt restrictive acquisition policies and to comply with strong ethical codes. While some resistance to such agreements exists, the nongovernmental organizations provide an important mechanism to control the illicit international movement of art. Though most museums reject claims that cultural property should be repatriated, there are notable exceptions. The Michael C. Carlos Museum at Emory University returned a mummy to Egypt and the Hermitage returned a rare copper bowl to Kazakhstan.

C. SANCTIONS FOR VANDALISM AND THEFT

In addition to regulating the import and export of illegally obtained art, many countries also regulate the manner in which cultural artifacts are first obtained. In the United States, the Antiquities Act of 1906, 16 U.S.C. §§ 431–33, prohibits vandalism by requiring that a permit be obtained before any excavation of cultural artifacts is conducted on federal lands. Although the law was held unconstitutionally vague when the government attempted to apply it to two-year-old Apache ceremonial masks in *United States v. Diaz*, 499 F.2d 113 (9th Cir. 1974), other circuits have upheld the constitutionality of the statute. *United States v. Smyer*, 596 F.2d 939 (10th Cir. 1979).

Moreover, in 1979, Congress passed a more stringent archaeological protection law, the Archaeological Resources Protection Act of 1979, Pub. L. No. 96–95, 93 Stat. 721 (codified at 16 U.S.C. §§ 470aa–470mm), which avoids the vagueness problems of the 1906 statute. The Native American Graves Protection and Repatriation Act, enacted in 1990 and discussed in Section A of this chapter, goes further, restricting the trade of artifacts excavated after November 16, 1990, from government or tribal lands and limiting access to Indian sites. The Repatriation Act's provisions restrict the acquisition and sale of Indian artifacts that are illegally excavated from federal lands or tribal lands and ban the purchase or sale of human remains or associated funerary objects regardless of when they were excavated, unless permission is granted by the lineal descendant or by the appropriate tribe. Violators of the Act are subject to fines and imprisonment.

Another means of regulation is through the use of local conversion laws and theft statutes, usually part of a country's general scheme of property and criminal law, to control the procurement and disposition of domestic and foreign art. The determination of who owns property that is stolen, however, frequently depends on the construction of foreign laws. In *Winkworth v. Christie Manson and*

Woods Ltd., [1980] 1 ER (Ch) 496, [1980] 1 All ER 1121, for example, it was held that where the plaintiff's art was stolen from him in England, taken to Italy, and subsequently sold to the defendant, Italian law should be applied to determine who had title to the art. The court relied on the *lex situs* rule, which provides that the validity of a transfer of movable property is governed by the laws of the country where the property is situated at the time of the transfer. Similarly, in *United States v. Hollinshead*, 495 F.2d 1154 (9th Cir. 1974), the court held that defendants who conspired to procure pre-Columbian artifacts in Guatemala and to sell them in this country violated the National Stolen Property Act, 18 U.S.C. §§ 2314–15, which prohibits the transportation in interstate or foreign commerce of any goods worth $5,000 or more with knowledge that the goods were "stolen, converted or taken by fraud." The court's decision was based on its finding that Guatemalan law makes all pre-Columbian artifacts the property of the Guatemalan government and requires the government's approval to remove them from its territory. There was ample evidence to demonstrate that the defendants knew that it was contrary to Guatemalan law to remove the stela they had conspired to import and that they knew that the stela was stolen. See page 397 for a photograph of the stela taken by Dr. Ian Graham prior to its removal from the Guatemalan jungle.

A similar situation was presented in *United States v. McClain* (*McClain I*), 545 F.2d 988 (5th. Cir. 1977), *reh'g denied*, 551 F.2d 52 (5th Cir. 1977). In *McClain I*, five individuals were convicted for violating the

National Stolen Properties Act after they sold Mexican pre-Columbian antiquities to an undercover agent for the Federal Bureau of Investigation. While the antiquities had not been stolen in any conventional sense, they had been exported from Mexico in apparent violation of Mexico's laws. According to the prosecution, these statutes vested title to all pre-Columbian artifacts in the Mexican nation. However, the court held that Mexico had only unambiguously declared that all pre-Columbian art belonged to the state by an enactment of May 6, 1972. Unlike the *Hollinshead* case, where the prosecution introduced sketches of the stela and an archaeologist testified that he had observed the piece *in situ* after the effective date of the Guatemalan law, the prosecution in *McClain I* had failed to present evidence that the antiquities had been removed from Mexico after 1972.

McClain I was reversed and remanded to determine, among other things, the date the artifacts were exported from Mexico. At the new trial, the defendants were convicted again, and they again appealed. In *United States v. McClain (McClain II)*, 593 F.2d 658 (5th Cir. 1979), *cert. denied*, 444 U.S. 918 (1979), a different panel of the court of appeals upheld the conspiracy count but reversed the convictions for a substantive violation of the National Stolen Property Act. The court held that although Mexican experts had testified that since 1897 Mexico had considered itself the owner of all pre-Columbian artifacts, it had failed to express that position in its statutes with sufficient clarity to survive translation into terms understandable by and binding upon

American citizens through the National Stolen Property Act. The application of Mexican law via the federal statute, therefore, was held a violation of due process and a violation of the notice requirements of the Fifth Amendment.

However, the court intimated that the conviction would have been affirmed if the government had relied on either of two other theories in the case. First, in 1934 and 1972, Mexico declared its ownership in all monumental works of art and all movable works of art found in or on such monuments. Individuals were given an opportunity to register pieces in their private collections in order to establish their individual ownership. Items not registered were presumed to belong to the state. Thus, the court suggested, proving that the works in question were not registered and were removed from Mexico after 1934 would have resulted in a conviction. Second, in 1972, the Mexican government unambiguously declared itself to be the owner of all pre-Columbian art "whether known or unknown" within its geographic borders. Hence, establishing the fact that the defendants removed the works from Mexico after this date would likewise have resulted in a conviction. The government chose to rely instead on the earlier Mexican law of 1897, which was patently unclear.

More recently, the Second Circuit held that the National Stolen Property Act applies to property stolen from a foreign government where that government asserts actual ownership of the property pursuant to a valid patrimony law in the case of a

New York City art dealer, Frederick Schultz, charged with conspiring to receive stolen Egyptian antiquities. *United States v. Schultz*, 333 F.3d 393 (2d Cir. 2003), *cert. denied*, 540 U.S. 1106 (2004).

The problems presented by the international movement of art and artifacts are being resolved on the national and multinational levels. As one example, in January 2015, thirty-five individuals were arrested and 2,289 cultural artifacts were seized, in a multi-country, international operation supported by Europol to prevent the theft and trafficking of European cultural property. Europol, *European Police Arrest 35 and Recover Thousands of Stolen Cultural Artefacts* (Jan. 28, 2015), available at https://www.europol.europa.eu/content/european-police-arrest-35-and-recover-thousands-stolen-cultural-artefacts. Many countries have recognized the importance of their cultural properties and have taken steps to protect their treasures. The biggest cultural property arrest of 2016, in the UK, was of fourteen men linked to an organized crime gang, who were arrested and convicted of plotting to steal rhino horn and Chinese artefacts worth up to £57 million in a series of museum smash and grabs, and auction house raids. See Peter Walker, *Gang's £57m haul put the Hatton Garden robbers in shade . . . their expertise less so*, The Guardian (Feb. 29, 2016 at 13:34 EST), available at https://www.theguardian.com/uk-news/2016/feb/29/chinese-artefacts-fourteen-men-convicted-british-museums-rhino-horn. The methods used to accomplish the conservation differ in many respects, and only time will tell which is the most effective.

CHAPTER 3
ART: THE VICTIM OF WAR

A. THE PROBLEM

Conquering armies have plundered defeated countries from the earliest times. Homer, in the *Odyssey*, catalogues many of the treasures collected from the sack of Troy, though it was the Romans who first glorified the plunder of art. Art of an invaded country is taken not only for its pecuniary value, but also as a talisman of wartime prowess. In Rome, masterpieces from Greece, Egypt, and Asia Minor were acquired, not for their intrinsic worth, but as symbols of Roman strength. Similarly, in the pre-World War II period and in the war itself, the Germans seized the art of other countries in order to make these priceless items available to the superior race; at the same time, countless pieces of post-Impressionistic works were destroyed as "degenerate."

Art and cultural property have also been used as war game pawns and destroyed in the midst of technological warfare. In Asia, when the Pol Pot regime relocated large segments of the urban population to the countryside, refugees scratched messages into the columns and walls of the Angkor Wat shrine in the hope that separated family members might find each other. Soldiers and villagers took sanctuary at the shrine in the belief that its sacredness would deter attack, but their belief was ill founded; the Angkor temples are now scarred by bullet holes as well as willful defacement and desecration. Islamic artifacts were removed by the Iraqis from the Kuwaiti National Museum during the Persian Gulf War. Fortunately, most were returned after hostilities ended, thanks chiefly to United Nations pressure. In Kosovo, more than 100 churches and monasteries have been damaged since 1999. Afghan art, including ancient Buddha statues, were destroyed by the Taliban, and Iraq's National Museum of Antiquities was pillaged in 2003 after U.S. troops entered Baghdad.

More recently, the Arab Spring and post-Arab Spring unrest and revolutions in Egypt, Libya, Iraq, and Syria have caused widespread destruction and looting of works of cultural and archeological heritage. Joris Kila, *Heritage Destruction in the Mediterranean Region*, Association for Research into Crimes Against Art (ARCA) (May 14, 2016), available at http://art-crime.blogspot.com/2016/05/heritage-destruction-in-mediterranean.html (discussing the destruction of works of cultural and archeological heritage in the Arab Spring and post-Arab Spring unrest and revolutions in Egypt, Libya, Iraq, and Syria); United Nations Security Council, *Security Council Urged to 'Stop the Madness' as Terrorists Trample Cultural, Religious Diversity of Middle East* (Mar. 27, 2015), available at http://www.un.org/press/en/2015/sc11840.doc.htm (same—broadening the discussion to include Bahrain, Yemen, and Turkey). This includes both collateral damage from fighting, shelling, and bombardment, to looting and theft, to direct destruction of artifacts and monuments by Da'esh (also referred to as ISIL or

ISIS) in Syria and Libya. Kila, *supra*; UN Security Council, *supra*; 3 Silvia Perini and Emma Cunliffe, *Towards a Protection of the Syrian Cultural Heritage: A summary of the national and international responses (Sept 2014–Sept 2015)*, available at http://fr.unesco.org/syrian-observatory/sites/syrian-observatory/files/Towards-a-protection-of-the-Syrian-cultural-heritage_Vol3.pdf (describing the efforts to protect and restore the archaeological and cultural heritage of Syria affected by the civil war). This situation should be of particular concern to all citizens of the world because these countries are recognized as containing the locations of several of the cradles of world civilization, and their importance to mankind's development of language, government, religion, culture, and history cannot be overstated.

One of the earliest attempts at setting limits on the destruction of art and other cultural property in wartime was the Lieber Code, General Orders No. 100: The Lieber Code—Instructions for the Government of Armies of the United States in the Field, prepared by Francis Lieber, promulgated as General Orders No. 100 by President Lincoln, 24 April 1863, available at http://avalon.law.yale.edu/19th_century/lieber.asp, a set of United States Army field regulations. The code allowed seizure of art objects in only a few situations where the works could be removed without injury, and established that their ultimate ownership was to be settled by the ensuing peace treaty. It was not until the Conventions of the Hague of 1899, Hague Convention on the Laws of War: Convention with respect to the Laws and Customs of War on Land (Hague II) (July 29, 1899), available at http://avalon.law.yale.edu/19th_century/hague02.asp, and 1907, Hague Convention on the Laws of War: Convention with respect to the Laws and Customs of War on Land (Hague IV) (Oct. 18, 1907), available at http://avalon.law.yale.edu/20th_century/hague04.asp, however, that the first formal international guidelines were established. The Conventions still sanctioned the taking of booty, which had long been allowed under the international rules of war as the taking of supplies and materials necessary to support an invading army. The seizure or destruction of private property, including the property of institutions dedicated to religion, charity, education and the arts and sciences, defined as plunder, was made illegal. These rules were acceded to by all the major powers, but with the advent of the major global conflicts in the 20th century (World War I and World War II), they proved largely ineffectual as preventative measures.

B. JUDICIAL SOLUTIONS

The problem of returning or compensating the owners of destroyed, confiscated, or stolen art and other cultural property in the aftermath of war required judicial solutions. After World War I, the task of sorting out confiscated and lost private property was assigned to a Mixed Claims Commission under the Treaty of Berlin, which was signed by the United States, and a Mixed Arbitral Commission under the Treaty of Versailles, which was signed by the other Allies. Under the terms of these treaties, Germany accepted full responsibility for causing all damage and loss which occurred as a result of the War, although since German resources were insufficient to provide compensation for all losses, restitution was limited to the civilian population. Damages could be collected only where the losses were susceptible to reasonably exact monetary measurement and where Germany's acts were the proximate cause of the loss.

These commissions had no authority to adjudicate disputes over title between private parties. Cases determining the ownership of property lost or stolen during war had to be decided in the civilian courts. Thus, in *Menzel v. List*, 267 N.Y.S.2d 804 (Sup. Ct. N.Y. Cnty. 1966), *modified by* 279 N.Y.S.2d 608 (App. Div. 1st Dep't 1967), *rev'd,* 246 N.E.2d 742 (N.Y. 1969), the court had to determine whether the Menzels could reclaim their Marc Chagall painting, which they had abandoned when they fled Brussels in the face of the oncoming Nazis during World War II. The painting had been seized by the Nazi-Göring-Rosenberg group, sold on the international art market, and ultimately acquired by the Perls Gallery. The gallery was unaware of the work's past history and purchased it in good faith. The piece was ultimately bought by List in whose possession the Menzels rediscovered it. After unsuccessfully demanding return of the work, the Menzels sued, and the court was placed in the unenviable position of having to determine which of two innocent parties should bear the loss.

The defendant was ordered to either return the work or pay its value to the original owners, the Menzels, but since there is an implied warranty of title which is part of every sales transaction, the defendant was able to shift the loss back to the gallery. The court rejected the gallery's defense that it was a bona fide purchaser for value, taking the painting free of any claims, since the Nazis, who had originally taken the painting, were thieves. The principle is basic in the law, the court stated, that a thief conveys no title as against the true owner.

The court also rejected the gallery's claim that it acquired good title under the Act of State Doctrine. This doctrine rests on four factors:

(1) The taking must be by a foreign sovereign government;

(2) It must be within the geographic boundaries of that government;

(3) The foreign government must be extant and recognized by the United States at the time of the suit; and

(4) The taking must not violate any treaty obligations.

The court held that since none of these factors were met, the gallery could not have acquired good title. The seizures were made by the Nazi party, not by a foreign sovereign government. Since the Belgian government was still in existence when the painting was seized, the seizure in Belgium was not made within the geographic boundaries of the offending government. Moreover, the United States had not recognized the Nazi party, and the taking was in violation of the terms of the Hague Convention of 1907.

The opposite result is reached when a revolution has occurred within a country and the plaintiff seeks redress in a jurisdiction that has recognized the new revolutionary government. In *Princess Paley Olga v. Weisz*, [1929] 1 KB 718, (1929) 5 ILR 95 (CA), the widow of the Grand Duke of Russia sued the purchaser of property she had abandoned when she fled the country during the Russian Revolution. The Soviet government had seized the property, declaring all property of those who fled Russia to be nationalized and the property of the state. The English court refused the plaintiff recovery, holding that the Russian decrees were acts of state, the validity of which cannot be challenged by an English court. Thus, the Soviet Union conveyed good title when the property was sold to the purchaser.

Special problems arise when governments attempt to litigate the title to works looted from them during war. Thus, in *Federal Republic of Germany v. Elicofon*, 358 F. Supp. 747 (E.D.N.Y. 1970), *aff'd*, 478 F.2d 231 (2d Cir. 1973), *cert. denied*, 415 U.S. 931 (1974), the Weimar Art Collection, an agency of the German Democratic Republic (East Germany), sought to recover two Albrecht Dürer paintings that had been stolen from the Castle Schwartzburg during World War II. At the time the suit was commenced, the United States government did not recognize East Germany, and the case was, therefore, dismissed. It was held that the plaintiff lacked standing to adjudicate claims in American courts under the separation of powers doctrine. The judiciary cannot constitutionally accord recognition to governments that have not been recognized by the executive.

Subsequently, in 1974, the U.S. President recognized the East German government, and the suit was recommenced. This time it was held that the Weimar Art Collection had standing, and the evidence adduced at trial supported its allegations that the paintings were indeed stolen. *Kunstsammlungen Zu Weimar v. Elicofon*, 536 F. Supp. 829 (E.D.N.Y. 1981), *aff'd*, 678 F.2d 1150 (2d Cir. 1982).

The U.S. Supreme Court held that a U.S. court has jurisdiction over a lawsuit involving several paintings by Gustav Klimt, which were in a Vienna museum. Maria Altmann sued the Republic of Austria to recover those paintings, which she alleged were taken from her family by the Nazis. The court held that the Foreign Sovereign Immunities Act, which allows for certain civil suits against foreign governments, applies retroactively. Altmann and the Austrian government agreed to have the case submitted to an Austrian arbitration court, which recently held that the paintings are Ms. Altmann's rightful property. *Republic of Austria v. Altmann*, 541 U.S. 677 (2004). Two Egon Schiele paintings, known as *Portrait of Wally* and *Dead City III*, on loan to New York's Museum of Modern Art were seized by Manhattan District Attorney Robert Morgenthau after the heirs of Lea Bondi Jaray contended that the paintings had been taken from him by the Nazis. *Dead City III* was subsequently returned to Vienna.

The lawsuit regarding the *Portrait of Wally* ultimately was settled in 2010, with the estate of Lea Bondi Jaray receiving $19 million in compensation from the Leopold Museum in Austria, and the painting being returned to the Leopold Museum. See Thomas R. Kline, *Portrait of Notoriety*, Wall Street Journal (Jul. 27, 2010 at 12:01 A.M.), available at http://www.wsj.com/articles/SB10001424052748703 294904575385543744550822; Catherine Hickley & Zoe Schneeweiss, *Leopold Pays $19 Million to Keep Schiele's 'Wally'*, Bloomberg (July 21, 2010 at 7:54 A.M.), available at http://www.bloomberg.com/news/articles/2010-07-21/vienna-s-leopold-pays-19-million-to-keep-schiele-s-wally-.

More recently, the heir of Jacques Goudstikker is pursuing an extended litigation to recover two 16th century works, *Adam* and *Eve* by Lucas Cranach the Elder. The lawsuit tells an increasingly familiar tale of a Jewish art collector and gallery owner, forced to flee and leave behind his collection, including the two Cranach works, because of the Nazi invasion of the Netherlands. The works were personally selected for confiscation by Hermann Göring, and displayed at one of his mansions. Later, after the war, the works were delivered to an Allied collection point for stolen art, and in 1946, the Allied Forces returned the pieces and the rest of the Goudstikker Collection to the Dutch government so that the artworks could be held in trust for their lawful owners. The Dutch government, however, refused to return the paintings to the heir, claiming that the transfers at the time Goudstikker fled the Nazi invasion were voluntary. A further wrinkle in the case is that another claimant, George Stroganoff Scherbatoff, interjected himself into the dispute, claiming that the paintings had originally been illegally confiscated by the Soviet Union in 1927, and then sold them off at auction to Goudstikker in 1931. The lawsuit that arose has for now dealt with procedural issues, *Von Saher v. Norton Simon Museum of Art at Pasadena*, 754 F.3d 712 (9th Cir. 2014) (carefully recounting the long factual and procedural history of the case up to 2014), *cert. denied*, 135 S. Ct. 1158 (2015), but may actually proceed to trial.

A new avenue of prosecution for destruction of cultural property in wartime may be emerging—namely, a war crimes prosecution in the International Criminal Court (ICC) in The Hague. In 2015, Ahmad Al Faqi Al Mahdi was charged in the ICC with war crimes of directing attacks against historic religious monuments and buildings, including nine mausoleums and one mosque in Timbuktu, Mali. *The Prosecutor v. Ahmad Al Faqi Al Mahdi*, ICC–01/12–01/15 (Int'l Crim. Ct.). On June 1, 2016, the court announced that the trial of Al Mahdi would begin on August 22, 2016. *Al Mahdi Case* (*The Prosecutor v. Ahmad Al Faqi Al Mahdi*, ICC–01/12–01/15), charges confirmed, case committed to trial to open on August 22, 2016, available at https://www.icc-cpi.int/mali/al-mahdi.

C. NONJUDICIAL SOLUTIONS

Because of these questions of jurisdiction, standing, and conflicts of laws, the courts are not always able to resolve adequately the problems of lost, stolen, and confiscated property that arise in the aftermath of war. Sometimes nonjudicial solutions are more effective. For example, after World War II, catalogues of lost or stolen art were prepared by various countries and circulated among dealers and collectors in an endeavor to locate the works and have them returned to their rightful owners. It was expected that political pressure would prove to be as effective as the threat of litigation in persuading individuals who realized they possessed looted or stolen works to return them.

During World War II, numerous objects were held for safekeeping by the United States government. In fact, there was a branch of the military charged with responsibility of cataloguing and properly caring for captured enemy treasures. The vast majority of these works were returned shortly after the armistice. Some pieces, however, were not returned until political pressure was brought to bear. For example, as a result of efforts by German artists whose works were seized during World War II by the United States because it feared the art might glorify Nazism, President Carter signed legislation in 1978 permitting the return of some of the 9,000 seized pieces. Pub. L. No. 95–517, 92 Stat. 1817 (1978). Similarly, return of treasures from the Wawal Castle in Krakow, which had been transported to Canada for safekeeping, was initially refused by the Canadian government on the grounds that the present Polish government was not the same as the government that had originally sent the works to Canada. Ultimately, bowing to pressures from private individuals, the Polish government, and the United Nations, the treasures were returned.

A situation similar to the Canadian possession of Poland's art treasures was presented in *Dole v. Carter*, 444 F. Supp. 1065 (D. Kan. 1977), *mot. for inj. pending app. denied*, 569 F.2d 1109 (10th Cir. 1977), involving Hungary's *Holy Crown of St. Stephen*. The crown, given to the first King of Hungary by Pope Sylvester II in approximately 1000 A.D., was of extraordinary historical and cultural significance to the people of Hungary. Just prior to the Soviet occupation of Hungary after World War II, the crown and the coronation regalia were sent to the United States for safekeeping, but when President Carter tried to return the regalia to the People's Republic of Hungary in 1977, Senator Robert Dole (R. Kansas) sued to enjoin the return on the grounds that the President's action, taken without the advice and consent of the Senate, violated Article II, Section 2, of the Constitution. That provision confers on the President the power "by and with the Advice and Consent of the Senate, to make Treaties, providing two-thirds of the Senators present concur."

The district court rejected Senator Dole's argument. No evidence was presented to support the Senator's contention that negotiators of the Paris Peace Treaty had agreed to hold the regalia until Soviet troops withdrew from Hungary. The agreement to return the regalia was in itself too insubstantial to be an Article II treaty, and since a President may recognize a foreign government without obtaining Senate approval, the President's unilateral action was held constitutional. The court of appeals affirmed, although for a different reason—that the return of the Hungarian crown represented a nonjusticiable political question. See page 398 for a picture of the *Crown of St. Stephen*.

Also bowing to political pressure, the government of Austria agreed to auction some 8,000 artworks and other unclaimed objects looted by the Nazis from Austrian Jews. The auction, held in 1996, was organized by the Jewish Community of Vienna and grossed over $14.5 million. Most of the proceeds were retained by the Jewish Community for charitable purposes, though 12 percent was given to groups representing non-Jewish victims of Nazism in Austria.

As these situations suggest, the best medicine for the problems of art lost or stolen during war is prevention, and aside from doing away with wars altogether, the only means of preventing the damage or looting of art during war is by treaty. Thus, in 1954, the Convention of The Hague reconvened for the purpose of reestablishing the principles that had been neglected during the two World Wars. The provisions agreed to by the contracting parties allow for total protection of the cultural properties of any nation, either from the ravages of war or from the pillages that occur during times of peace. The Convention for the Protection of Cultural Property in the Event of Armed Conflict, done at The Hague (May 14, 1954), available at http://portal.unesco.org/en/ev.php-URL_ID=13637&URL_DO=DO_TOPIC&URL_SECTION=201.html, prohibits the confiscation of any work of art, regardless of ownership, mobility, or location. The destruction of a work of art to obtain war materials is expressly forbidden. More importantly, the Convention also establishes the means of protection by calling for a limited number of refuges to shelter movable cultural property. It also extends immunity to immovable cultural properties, such as monuments, except in exceptional cases of unavoidable military necessity. Enforcement is primarily dependent upon the assurances given by each participating nation, although the participants may call on UNESCO for assistance in carrying out the terms of the Convention and in resolving problems.

The effectiveness of these designated means of enforcement has not yet faced a severe test, though as noted in Section A of this chapter, cultural property and artworks continue to be stolen, damaged, and destroyed during war; and, of course, all mankind hopes that the occasion for such a test will not arise. One provision of the Convention that has received a great deal of criticism is the provision allowing for withdrawal of immunity of cultural property on the grounds of exceptional cases of military necessity. According to Professor Stanaslaw Nahlik of the Jagellonean University of Krakow, Poland, one of the individuals involved in drafting the treaty, the provision was included only because the United States and England said they would not become parties to any convention without such a provision. Since neither country has yet become a signatory, it has been suggested that the military necessity exception should be removed.

Art and the owners of art have suffered for centuries at the hands of countries at war. The loss of private and cultural property is not likely ever to be completely prevented, and thus the task of adjudicating those losses will necessarily fall on the courts. To the extent that countries can agree on the conduct of armies and the disposition of art during war, then so much the better. In the meantime, courts will have to decide questions of ownership and loss within the confines of existing international policy and law. In addition, political pressures will have to be used where possible to inhibit pillage and destruction of cultural property or to aid in the return of works of art to individuals or nations that are victims of expropriation.

CHAPTER 4
ART AS AN INVESTMENT

A. THE ART MARKET

Throughout the centuries, the wealthy have always collected works of art, not only for their own enjoyment but also with the underlying knowledge that art can be exchanged or upgraded as the buyer's wealth increases. Although the concept of purchasing art purely for investment purposes was originally greeted with horror, today it is safe to say that investing in art has achieved the status of respectability. Some investment advisors encourage their clients to purchase art as a hedge against inflation and as a complement to a traditional investment portfolio. In addition, art also provides intangible dividends, such as the aesthetic enjoyment of the piece and an opportunity for personal contact with the artist and with others knowledgeable about art.

As an investment vehicle, art appears to perform well in inflationary times. This seems to be the result of a belief among some that art is more valuable than money or stocks. The devaluation of currency in the United States and Europe in the early 1970s, for example, resulted in panic buying in the art market and substantial increases in the value of many works of art. *Pick's World Current Report* analyzed price trends in 1975 and concluded that the best hedge against inflation was French Impressionist paintings. They rose an astonishing 230 percent, whereas the Dow Jones averaged a mere 38 percent increase. In periods of deflation, on the other hand, investors seek a return in terms of money rather than in property held for appreciation. More recent research by wealth management companies has shown these trends remain true. As a result, some investment advisors counsel their clients to put no more than 10 percent of their assets, exclusive of real estate, into tangible investments, including art. Although many experts believe that a diversified portfolio of good art can beat the stock market, others believe a money market account offers higher returns.

As art prices continue to set records, new art funds and investment companies continue to appear. There are also indexes to help investors track the fluctuating art prices, such as the Mei/Moses Fine Art Index. According to the Mei/Moses Index, over the past half century, art has kept pace with stocks measured on the Standard and Poor's Index, and during the last decade, art has outperformed stocks. Despite fears that the attacks of September 11, 2001, would cause the art market to crash, prices on the art market have soared. In 2004, Picasso's *Boy with a Pipe* sold for $104,000,000, shattering the record for an auctioned painting, previously set by Van Gogh's *Portrait of Dr. Gachet*, which sold for $82,500,000 in 1990. Prices have continued to rise, and in 2015, the record for an auctioned painting was broken by Picasso's *Les femmes d'Alger (Version 'O')*, which sold for $179,365,000. In 2016, concerns have arisen over what Britain's exit from the European Union ("Brexit") will mean for the art market. Some worry about the effects of uncertainty and the fall in value of the pound. Others believe that, as after September 11, 2001, the art market will remain a safe harbor in the turmoil of the financial markets.

Knowing what to buy, how much to acquire and when and where to purchase it is the key to any successful investment. Every investor should thus learn as much as possible about the art market. In the art market, corporations, banks, museums, individual collectors, and art funds comprise the bulk of the purchasing community, and each group influences the market in accordance with its tastes and purchasing patterns.

The art market is largely unregulated. Unlike more traditional forms of investment, which are regulated by statute and policed by administrative agencies, there is no comprehensive body of statutes specifically designed to prohibit manipulative or deceptive practices in the art market. Some states have enacted consumer-oriented statutes that are applied to a limited extent in the art market (see Chapter 6, *infra*), but none are as comprehensive as the federal and state securities laws. The question arises, therefore, whether these laws, designed to regulate the trading of securities, can be applied to art.

The Securities Act of 1933 requires an issuer of securities to file a registration statement with the Securities and Exchange Commission (SEC) before securities may be issued. The law also requires the issuer to prepare a detailed prospectus disclosing all material facts of the offering. These documents aid the potential investor in making an informed decision by disclosing all relevant information about the security in question. A "security" is defined by Section 2(1) of the 1933 Act as "any note, stock . . . [or] investment contact." Items such as self-improvement courses in a pyramid sales context and a portfolio of rare coins have been held to be securities. These holdings are mainly based on an expectation of profit and the inducement of the investor to enter into the arrangement by the seller's representations of wealth to be made. Yet, in 1979 the SEC concluded that promoters who assembled $10,000 artwork portfolios for investment were not subject to the 1933 Act's registration requirements, even though the investors had the option of having the promoter retain and maintain the portfolio for a fee. [1979] Sec. & L. Rep. (BNA) No. 514, at C1 (Aug. 1, 1979).

In addition to the 1933 Act registration requirement for original issues, the Securities and Exchange Act of 1934 regulates the trading of securities in the so-called "after market," that is, after the securities have been issued. One particularly important regulation under the 1934 Act is the SEC's Rule 10(b)(5), which provides:

> It shall be unlawful for any person, directly or indirectly, by the use of any means or instrumentality of interstate commerce, or of the mails . . . ,
>
> (a) To employ any device, scheme, or artifice to defraud,

(b) To make any untrue statement of a material fact or to omit to state a material fact necessary in order to make the statements made, in the light of the circumstances under which they were made, not misleading, or

(c) To engage in any act, practice, or course of business which operates or would operate as a fraud or deceit upon any person, in connection with the purchase or sale of any security.

Courts have interpreted Rule 10(b)(5) as requiring a standard of conduct far more exacting than the minimum standard required to avoid being guilty of common law fraud, which standard may loosely be thought of as fairness under the circumstances, but thus far there have not been any reported cases considering whether Rule 10(b)(5) should be applied to the purchase or sale of art itself. Art investment funds are subject to the anti-fraud provisions of the securities laws, though many art investment funds avoid increased SEC regulation by meeting the definition of private investment vehicles. A fund qualifies as a private investment vehicle if it limits its offerings to fewer than 100 "accredited" investors or to fewer than 500 "qualified" investors. Art fund managers themselves must register as investment advisors with the SEC if either they engage in significant leveraging and securities trading strategies, or the art fund exceeds the $150,000,000 threshold for "assets under management," which is rare. Art fund managers may also need to register if required by state laws. Even with this lack of regulation, an investor in a private investment fund may have more protection than an individual art purchaser, since, unlike galleries, auction houses and individual sellers, art fund managers have a fiduciary duty to their investors.

Some purchasers and competitors have attempted to invoke the Racketeer Influenced and Corrupt Organizations Act (RICO). In *Galerie Furstenberg v. Coffaro*, 697 F. Supp. 1282 (S.D.N.Y.1988), the court held that a competitor which held exclusive rights to certain drawings and etchings by Salvador Dali was injured by, and thus had standing to sue under RICO a gallery that marketed and sold counterfeit Dali works. Another case involving counterfeit Dali prints, *Balog v. Center Art Gallery-Hawaii, Inc.*, 745 F. Supp. 1556 (D. Haw.1990), held that in the Ninth Circuit, a civil RICO action accrues upon discovery of the injury, rather than at the time of the injury.

B. INVESTMENT FACTORS AND CONSIDERATIONS

Because the art market is largely unregulated and because it has many unique characteristics which may be traps for the unwary, collectors of art should carefully evaluate their art investments. Investing in art is a speculative undertaking; at best, it is a gamble; and like any investment, the higher the risk, the higher the potential return. Art is also not a particularly liquid investment. It is difficult to sell artworks on short notice, and a year or more may be needed for a work to sustain a sufficient increase in value so that a profit may be realized. Dealers take commissions from between 10 and 50 percent, so the piece must appreciate substantially before the seller can obtain a return on his or her initial investment. Additionally, the seller of a work of art does not have the advantage of simply picking up the telephone and reaching a buyer; rather, the seller must find a customer or dealer willing either to make an outright purchase or to accept the work on consignment. Further, it is difficult, if not impossible, to obtain an accurate estimate of artwork that is being held as an investment, since the actual market value is determined only when the work is sold. Prior to sale, the estimated value is based on recent sales of similar works, which may not always be available. Thus, trying to gauge the fluctuation in value of an art collection would require employing experts and be quite expensive and time-consuming.

Some categories of art do better than others. While most experts agree that collectors should simply buy what they like, it is important that the prospective purchaser learn as much as possible about the particular type of art prior to acquiring it. In addition to developing a general understanding of art and the art market, the collector should review local dealer prices and catalog and auction sales prior to making any purchase. Most money in the art market is made either by capitalizing on established trends or by taking big risks. Investment advisors consistently recommend against purchasing most works in the middle range, that is, works that are neither the best nor the least expensive in any given category of art.

There are several other factors individuals should consider before purchasing any work of art. Collateral costs, such as the costs of maintenance, insurance, security systems, and proper air conditioning and humidity controls, must be estimated, although the collector should note that these costs can be reduced by loaning the work to a museum for display. Tax consequences of a later sale should also be considered if the collector anticipates reselling the work at a profit.

One way of financing art investments is buying art on installment. This method of purchasing art is available in nearly every gallery in the United States. Some use installment buying just as they would buying on margin on the stock market; their motive is quick profit from the resale of an object as soon as its price rises.

Another method of financing art is taking out a loan using the art as collateral. Due to the continued strength of the art market, increased numbers of collectors and dealers are using art as collateral for loans. Some of the major lenders for art include US Trust (the private bank arm of Bank of America), Citi Private Bank Art Advisory and Finance, Emigrant Bank Fine Art Finance, JP Morgan Chase, ArtAssure, Art Capital Group, Goldman Sachs, Willstone Management, Christie's, and Sotheby's. Such lending programs are often combined with art advisory services.

C. METHODS OF ACQUISITION

Works of art can be procured at auctions, from galleries, directly from living artists, and even from Costco, which began selling fine art in 2003. However, many artists have contractual obligations to sell their works only to specific galleries. Buying from a reputable dealer may give the collector certain advantages, such as knowledgeable advice, approval periods, payments by installment without interest, comfortable surroundings conducive to browsing, and a large collection from which to choose. Some dealers provide the option of exchanging a particular work for another executed by the same artist. A dealer may even guarantee to take back any work at a specified percentage of its value, ranging from 80 to 100 percent in some cases, provided the work has not sustained damage and another purchase is made.

Dozens of online galleries sprang up in the late 1990s, but when the Internet bubble burst, many of these sites folded. Recently, a second wave of investors is taking on the Internet market. While online sales still make up less than 10 percent of the art market, many lower priced works are sold through Amazon, Art.com, Artsy, 1stDibs and other online venues. Sotheby's has partnered with eBay to live-stream its auctions, and Christie's offers a number of online-only auctions.

The investor should be aware that many art galleries are no longer enclaves of silent prestige that let the forces of the market determine an artist's reputation and price range. Some galleries use sophisticated marketing and public relations techniques, such as taking potential clients to the artist's studio, engineering sales to the "right" buyers, and circulating rumors that the artist's work is becoming scarce. While successful marketing can boost the demand for a particular artist's work, the investor should be sure to verify the reputation and worth of a particular artist's work with others knowledgeable about the market. When making a selection, it is imperative to the buyer that the dealer write the full particulars of the work, including the name of the artist, school, medium, year executed, and any other pertinent information, into the bill of sale; then, if it is discovered that the work is not what it was purported to be, the dealer is obliged to take the article back and make a full refund.

Many investors utilize consultants to assist them in making acquisitions, and, as the art market has grown, the ranks of so-called art advisors has swelled. The roles and fees of corporate art consultants vary; services include counseling, collection evaluations, procurement, and installation. Most work on commission, but some bill a fixed rate per project or an hourly rate. Concerns have arisen over the lack of any certification process for these "experts."

Instances of fraud in the sale of art rarely come to light, but when they do, they can be spectacular. In 2010, art dealer Larry Salander pled guilty to 30 counts of grand larceny and fraud for stealing more than $120 million. Salander confessed to selling artwork he didn't own and selling fractional shares of a painting that added up to more than 100 percent.

He also pocketed money that was owed artists on consignment sales. He used this money to fund his lavish lifestyle, flying on private planes and splitting his time between a townhouse he owned near the Metropolitan Museum of Art and a 66-acre estate in Millbook, New York, complete with a tennis court, swimming pool, and baseball diamond. Salander's victims included John McEnroe and Robert De Niro. As pointed out above, there are no reported decisions recognizing the applicability of the Rule 10(b)(5)'s securities fraud provisions to art; yet, cases like this one may warrant its application or, better still, may contribute to the development of some new statute tailored to meet the needs of art investors.

In addition to concerns about fraud, art investors should be aware that sellers generally have no fiduciary obligation to buyers (no matter how close the relationship is or how disproportionate the parties' expertise) and thus are not required to make full disclosure to potential buyers, or even avoid making a secret profit. See for example, *MAFG Art Fund, LLC v. Gagosian,* 2014 NY Slip Op 30321(U) (Sup. Ct), *affirmed in part and modified in part,* 123 A.D.3d 458, 998 N.Y.S.2d 342 (1st Dep't 2014), *leave to appeal denied,* 25 N.Y.3d 901, 7 N.Y.S.3d 273, 30 N.E.3d 164 (2015). Billionaire Robert Perelman sued Larry Gagosian and his gallery, accusing them of concealing material information, as well as "undervaluing works when purchasing them, overvaluing them when selling them, and pocketing the substantial differential." The court held that, despite the parties' long-term working relationship and friendship, no fiduciary duty was owed and that

Perelman should have conducted due diligence research.

CHAPTER 5
AUCTIONS

A. AUCTIONS IN GENERAL

There are three basic forms of conveyance in a free market economic system. The first form, with which the individual consumer is probably most familiar, is fixed pricing, in which the buyer may choose either to accept or reject the price designated by the seller. This form is most efficient in minimizing transaction costs but has the disadvantage of being a take-it-or-leave-it system. The second form, private negotiation, on the other hand, allows the parties to determine a mutually acceptable price, but the potential costs of advertising or contracting through an agent to find a buyer may be significant.

When several buyers are attracted at the same time and compete with each other for a desired piece, the transaction is an auction, which is the third form of conveyance and the largest single secondary art market. Like private negotiation, auctions also have fairly high transaction costs since it is necessary to attract numerous competitors to the proposed sale. Most auction houses recover their costs by requiring the seller to pay a commission, and some require the buyer to pay a surcharge as well. The system of gathering all interested buyers together to set the price by competitive bidding is especially useful for art transactions since each art object is subject to radical fluctuations in its market price. These fluctuations occur because the value of art stems not only from the cost of the materials used but also from its aesthetic appeal, the artist's present status, the availability of similar works, and anticipated appreciation based on performance of the artist's other works. Auctions are effective mechanisms for measuring the value of these kinds of intangibles. Thus, appraisals for insurance frequently are based on auction catalogues. Auctions are important even for nonparticipants because, simply stated, auctions establish prices.

While traditional auctions are still the most common, telecast sales and cyber-auctions are increasing in popularity. Online auctions and live streamed auctions appear to be the wave of the future. Sotheby's has partnered with eBay to live-stream its auctions, and Christie's offers a number of online-only auctions. Because auctions take many forms and many complex tactics for influencing prices are used, the novice should exercise extreme caution before participating in an auction.

B. BIDDING

In competitive bidding, an offer may be either disclosed or undisclosed. In disclosed bidding, potential buyers openly compete in an attempt to outbid one another. Generally, the bidding is oral, but raised cards or paddles may also be used. In undisclosed bidding, sealed or secret offers are submitted without knowledge of the other competitors' bids. Secret offers may be conveyed by writings, complicated hand signals, or whispers. The auctioneer then compares the bids without disclosing the amount or the identity of the bidder. Undisclosed bids have some disadvantages, most notably the fact that auctions involving them are very time-consuming to conduct, and sealed bids have the additional disadvantage that each bidder has only one chance to bid. A combination of disclosed and sealed bidding is frequently used. In this situation, individuals who cannot attend an auction submit sealed bids in advance, authorizing the auctioneer or an identified agent to interpose bids on behalf of the absentee up to a designated price.

The form of bidding varies from place to place, but there are three particularly common techniques: the ascending bid, or English method, most frequently used in the United States; the descending bid, or Dutch method; and the simultaneous bid, or Japanese method. In the English method, the auctioneer first solicits a bid; if there is no response, he or she will suggest an opening bid which is lowered until adopted. The auctioneer then either allows free bidding or guides the bidding by calling out the next acceptable bid, and each bid is successively higher. The final, unchallenged high bidder is awarded title to the property upon payment. In the Dutch method, the auctioneer announces an opening figure and then lowers the price until someone enters a bid. Unlike the English method, the first, rather than the last, bidder obtains the article. In the Japanese method, in contrast to the other two bidding methods, the pieces are not displayed prior to the auction. Immediately after display of each piece for the first time, the bids are entered using hand signals that designate specific amounts or sealed bids handed to the auctioneer. The auctioneer then determines who offered the highest bid during the short interval permitted for bid entry, and the seller may either accept the highest offer or withdraw the piece while stating the reasons for doing so.

C. BIDDING TACTICS

These bidding techniques permit the auctioneer, sellers, and purchasers to employ various tactics to influence prices. Some of these are legitimate, such as the auctioneer's dress, voice, personality, demeanor, and comments about the items to be sold. Auctioneers may also orchestrate the order in which the items are introduced in order to establish the tempo of the bidding. Other techniques are not legitimate. For example, the auctioneer may recognize phantom bids, sometimes trapping an excited bidder into bidding against him-or herself. This is known as "bidding off the chandelier." This practice is illegal in many places, but occurs so frequently that professional buyers often seat themselves in a far corner of the room in order to survey the bidding competition. The auctioneer may also arrange to place a confederate in the audience who bids solely to encourage high bids. In England, this practice is called "puffing"; in America it is called "shilling" or "shill" bidding. The practice is considered a criminal conspiracy. In addition, under the Uniform Commercial Code § 2–328, where the auctioneer knowingly receives a bid on the seller's behalf without notice to the other bidders that the seller may participate, the buyer may void the sale or take the goods at the price of the last good faith bid prior to the completion of the sale. The buyer loses the right to these remedies, however, by accepting the contract with knowledge of the sham bidding. See *Vanier v. Ponsoldt,* 251 Kan. 88, 833 P.2d 949 (Kan. 1992). In 2000, the online auction house eBay canceled a sale for $135,805 of an abstract painting which seemed to be the work of Richard Diebenkorn, contending that the seller had violated its rules by shill bidding. Three men were eventually indicted for taking part in a bidding ring that cost hundreds of buyers a total of $450,000. More recently, three of Mastro Auction's executives were sentenced to prison for shill bidding and selling bogus sports memorabilia, with terms ranging from 12 to 57 months.

Occasionally, bidders will be interested in having pieces sell for high prices. For example, an individual owning a large collection of a particular artist's work may want to have high prices paid for other works by the same artist. Collectors and dealers may, therefore, use many of the same tactics used by auctioneers to keep bidding active. Usually, however, bidders who actually intend to purchase employ various strategies to keep prices low. They may make disparaging remarks about the item on sale, or they may interrupt a rapidly spiraling bid sequence by creating a diversion. Bidders with limited resources may strategically avoid bidding on small items, hoping the competition will purchase them and commit all of their available money. If the presence and interest of a known dealer or collector would spark excessive bidding, the collector may use an agent to buy the piece. Bidders may also participate in joint buying schemes, in which a group of buyers sends only one bidder to an auction. These arrangements may be legal where they are designed simply to alleviate the inconvenience of attending or to reduce transaction costs, but where buyers make secret agreements not to compete with each other with a specific intent to depress prices, known as "ring" formation, the agreements probably violate the American antitrust laws and are illegal in England as well.

D. AUCTIONING PROBLEMS

Many states require auction houses and auctioneers to be licensed. The licensing requirement is intended not only to protect against fraudulent auctioning techniques, but also to raise revenue and prevent the use of an auction for the disposal of stolen goods. Problems occasionally arise, however, in determining what constitutes an auction for licensing purposes. In *Hawaii Jewelers Association v. Fine Arts Gallery, Inc.*, 51 Haw. 502, 463 P.2d 914 (1970), for example, the defendants argued that, although sales were conducted by competitive bidding, the sales were not auctions because the defendant's money-back guarantee gave the buyer the right to return any article for any reason within 30 days. This procedure, it was argued, conflicted with the definition of an auction in the U.C.C., which states that a sale by auction is complete when the auctioneer so announces by the fall of the hammer. The court held that this distinction was not controlling. All other indicia of an auction were present, so the 30-day guarantee was either an option given the successful bidder to return the goods and get a refund or a continuing offer by the defendants to repurchase the goods for a period of 30 days from the date of the sale. The defendants, therefore, were enjoined from conducting auctions until they obtained a license.

Most states also have attempted to regulate the conduct of auctions. Two areas in particular that have prompted legislative action are the concepts of "reserve" and "procedures" for withdrawing goods or bids. The reserve concept was first introduced in England in an attempt to combat "illegal rings." The reserve price is a threshold price, customarily kept secret by the auctioneer, which must be reached before the goods can actually be sold. Section 2–328 of the U.C.C. expressly provides that all auctions are presumed to be with reserve unless otherwise expressly stated. In an auction with reserve, goods may be withdrawn at any time before the auctioneer announces the completion of the sale. Thus, the goods may be withdrawn, for example, when the minimum amount designated by the seller, the reserve price, is not bid.

In auctions without reserve, on the other hand, any bid by a potential buyer is an acceptance of the auctioneer's offer of the goods; thus, U.C.C. § 2–328 provides that the auctioneer may not withdraw the goods in an auction without reserve unless no bid is made within a reasonable time. Furthermore, in an auction without reserve, it has been held that an auction house may not adopt a minimum increment bidding policy. In *Pitchfork Ranch Co. v. Bar TL*, 615

P.2d 541 (Wyo. 1980), the Wyoming Supreme Court stated that an increment policy has the effect of rejection of the highest bid, which violates the seller's unconditional offer to sell to the highest bidder in an auction without reserve. Of course, whether or not the auction is with reserve, the bidder may withdraw the bid at any time before the fall of the hammer.

Proponents of secret reserve prices argue that the system protects sellers against boycotts and collusive bidding practices such as rings. Some attempts have been made, however, to force disclosure. New York City auction houses are now required to inform bidders that there is a reserve but are not required to disclose the amount.

Another problem area is the disclosure of ownership. Customarily, auctioneers and auction houses merely act as selling agents; however, the auction house may own some of the items to be auctioned. If the auction house is considered the seller in this situation, failing to disclose that fact in an auction with reserve would appear to violate U.C.C. § 2–328(4), which permits bidding on one's own goods only if other bidders are given notice that this right is reserved. Removing an item from the auction block because the reserve price has not been met could be interpreted as the auction house bidding on its own property.

In 1974, there was an unsuccessful attempt to pass legislation to prevent this situation by requiring disclosure of ownership. The auction houses opposed the requirement, arguing that it discriminated against them and favored dealers, because sellers who preferred to keep their identity undisclosed would sell their property through a dealer rather than at public auction. In an apparent effort to forestall other regulatory legislation, some auction houses, such as Sotheby's, adopted a policy of disclosing which pieces were owned by the auction house and which pieces were being sold pursuant to a reserve. In 1987, auction regulations were amended to conform to current conditions. The City of New York Administrative Code requires disclosure of any auction house interest in an auction item and whether there is a reserve price on the object.

Auction houses may guarantee that a seller will make at least a certain minimum amount by arranging for a third party to purchase the work for that price if it does not sell for more at the auction. The guarantor is paid a cut of the proceeds above that guarantee—sometimes even when the guarantor is the purchaser. This is generally not disclosed to the bidding public. This means the sales price disclosed by the auction house may be inaccurate, because the real price is the sales amount less the payment back to the guarantor. Another concern with this type of arrangement is that it may cause guarantors to bid just to drive up the sales price.

It is common practice that when an auction house acts as a disinterested third party agent for a seller, the identity of the seller is not disclosed. The New York Court of Appeals held in *William J. Jenack Estate Appraisers and Auctioneers, Inc. v. Rabizadeh*, 22 N.Y.3d 470, 982 N.Y.S.2d 813, 5 N.E.3d 976 (2013), that disclosure of only the auctioneer's name is sufficient for statute of frauds purposes, and that the seller's name may be kept anonymous. However, the fact that the seller is not disclosed raises the problem of whether the auctioneer warrants the authenticity and title of the property sold in such cases. In *Weisz v. Parke-Bernet Galleries, Inc.*, 67 Misc. 2d 1077, 325 N.Y.S.2d 576 (Civ. Ct. N.Y. City 1971), *rev'd*, 77 Misc. 2d 80, 351 N.Y.S.2d 911 (Sup. Ct. App. Term 1974), the New York trial court held that buyers of a forged painting reasonably relied on the gallery's representation that the named artist created the work. The trial court suggested that auction houses could protect themselves by conspicuously disclaiming such warranties. The appellate division reversed. The court noted that one of the factors entering into competition among bidders is the variable value of paintings depending upon the degree of certainty with which they can be authenticated and stated that "[The purchasers] will not now be heard to complain that, in failing to act with the caution of one in circumstances abounding with signals of *caveat emptor*, they made a bad bargain." Where there is fraud or misrepresentation by the auctioneer, on the other hand, the buyer may recover. In *Pasternack v. Esskay Art Galleries, Inc.*, 90 F. Supp. 849 (W.D. Ark. 1950), an auction house representative advised the plaintiff that a lot of jewelry was worth approximately $46,000 and urged the plaintiff to bid on it, agreeing to resell the jewelry at a subsequent auction with the profit from the resale to be split between the two parties. In fact, the jewelry was worth only $11,000, and the plaintiff's $14,000 auction purchase was rescinded.

Where the goods involved in an auction transaction are stolen, most states hold the auctioneer liable for conversion, even if the auctioneer did not have actual or constructive knowledge of the theft. If the auctioneer acquired the goods as a result of fraud on the part of the seller, however, the auctioneer who sells them without notice of the defect may not be liable for conversion. The requirement of notice is met if the auctioneer had actual knowledge of the fraud or if the circumstances were such as to put a reasonable person on notice to inquire further. These rules tend to discourage theft and require the auctioneer to verify the seller's title, while absolving the auctioneer from liability for defects beyond his or her control.

Disputes as to title occasionally arise where one party successfully bids for the work and another person actually pays the sales price. In *Lindt v. Henshel*, 306 N.Y.S.2d 436, 254 N.E.2d 746 (N.Y. 1969), the plaintiff, Mrs. Bulova, bid for a Brancusi sculpture, but her husband paid for it. After the couple's separation and Mr. Bulova's death, his executrix donated the piece to the Guggenheim Foundation. The court held that the sculpture still belonged to Mrs. Bulova. Mrs. Bulova contracted to purchase the piece at the time her bid was accepted by the auctioneer. The source from which she obtained the funds to pay for it was immaterial. Since Mrs. Bulova had already undertaken to purchase the sculpture, the court stated, Mr. Bulova's payment of her obligation was either a gift or a loan to her, and, in his will, Mr. Bulova had discharged her from any indebtedness.

Since the auctioneer's acceptance of a bid creates a contractual obligation, the auction house may maintain an action to recover its damages if the bidder fails to pay. The nature and extent of the damages can be complex, however. In *French v. Sotheby & Co.*, 470 P.2d 318 (Okla. 1970), it was noted that under U.C.C. § 2–703, a seller may elect either to seek recovery for nonacceptance (§ 2–708) or, in a proper case, the price (§ 2–709), or to resell the item and hold the defaulting party liable for damages (§ 2–706). In *French*, the auction house elected not to resell the goods but, rather, to seek recovery of the price. The auction house, however, could not establish that it met the requirements of Section 2–709: that the goods were accepted, that they were lost after the risk of loss had passed to the buyer, or that the seller was unable to resell them at a reasonable price. Further, because the auction house had sought recovery only under Section 2–709, the court declined to award recovery for nonacceptance under Section 2–708. This pleading error by the auction house was unfortunate. Had it alleged damages under Section 2–708, the auction house probably would have been entitled to the difference between the market price and the unpaid contract price, plus any incidental damages, less expenses saved because of the resale.

The seller may also seek damages from the auction house. In *Cristallina S.A. v. Christie, Manson & Woods Intern., Inc.*, 117 A.D.2d 284, 502 N.Y.S.2d 165 (1st Dep't 1986), the consignor of works of art sued Christie's and its auctioneer for a failed auction. Cristallina contended that the auctioneer's selection of paintings did not have auction appeal, that the auctioneer negligently failed to provide the seller with material information concerning the auction value of the paintings, that Christie's presale estimates provided the public with contradictory advice, and that the auctioneer violated auction house policy by recommending reserves higher than the highest presale estimates. The court held that these claims should not have been dismissed on summary judgment, and one week into the trial, Cristallina and Christie's reached an undisclosed out-of-court settlement.

Disputes between auction houses and bidders may arise over the terms of the arrangement between the parties. Often, these terms are contained only in auction catalogs, and there is no formal agreement. In *Brooks v. Sotheby's*, No. 13–cv–02183 RS, 2013 WL 3339356 (N.D. Cal. July 1, 2013), the court enforced a forum-selection clause in the auction catalog, holding that the buyer who sought to avoid application of that clause had received reasonable notice of the clause and that he would have had a "large incentive" to review the terms of sale for such an expensive item as a $96,000 painting.

In 2000, Sotheby's and Christie's, which together dominate the worldwide auction market, settled class action lawsuits for antitrust violations on behalf of United States buyers and sellers that alleged price fixing for $512,000,000 and a similar suit on behalf of buyers and sellers outside the United States for $40,000,000. Sotheby's also pled guilty to price fixing after a Department of Justice investigation and paid a $45,000,000 fine. A. Alfred Taubman, principal owner of Sotheby's, was convicted of conspiring with Christie's to fix fees charged to auction house sellers, sentenced to one year in prison, and fined $7,500,000. Christie's and its chief executive Christopher Davidge were granted conditional amnesty from prosecution by the government, as they agreed to cooperate with the government in the investigation.

As the problems discussed above indicate, novices should be cautious when participating in auctions. Although licensing requirements and the practices of reputable auction houses provide some protection, the complexities of auctioning tactics and procedures make auctions potential traps for the unwary. Auctions do, however, provide important information to nonparticipants about prices and demand for art. Thus, a basic understanding of how auctions work and their potential pitfalls is important to anyone involved in the art market.

CHAPTER 6
AUTHENTICATION

A. ESTABLISHING AUTHENTICITY

The emergence of art as an investment has stimulated an increase in art forgery. The Fine Art Expert Institute in Geneva says 70 to 90 percent of the artwork it examines is forged or misattributed. It recognizes that the authenticity of the works it is consulted about is already in question, but believes that up to 50 percent of art on the market may be fake. Other experts put the number at between 10 and 40 percent. The amount of money to be realized from a successful forgery can be substantial and no doubt serves as the major incentive to unscrupulous individuals. Since the value of an artwork is determined partially by aesthetic appeal and partially by the work's authenticity, it is of paramount importance to a purchaser that the piece's authenticity be ascertainable with a high degree of certainty. Clever and talented forgers often have made this determination extremely difficult, even for the experts.

A fundamental question is whether concern over authenticity is justified. Perception of art is a gestalt in which one perceives the visual beauty of a piece, as well as its age, originality, and position in the spectrum of artistic creation. A forgery disrupts this gestalt and may have economic repercussions as well. While the purchaser of a piece of forged art is injured most directly by not receiving the benefit of the bargain, there also are numerous secondary victims, such as art historians, who may be misled by an anomaly appearing in a forged work, and banks who may lend money, accepting forged art as collateral.

There are three general categories of forgeries: (1) fabrications deliberately created to be sold as the product of another artist, with an intent to deceive, including the forging of an artist's name, the work's documentation, or the entire work; (2) replicas, reproductions and copies, created without an intent to deceive, that are ultimately sold as originals due to misattribution or error, including works executed "from the school of" a famous artist, which are later sold as the work of the master; and (3) altered art, including embellishments, fragmentation of oversized pieces, completion of unfinished works, and excessive restorations.

Han Van Meegeren made a successful career by forging Vermeers and was discovered only when he himself disclosed the frauds in order to escape prosecution by the Dutch government for aiding the enemy during World War II. The art world, shaken by the news, refused to believe him until he created a "masterpiece" in his jail cell, proving that he had actually cheated the Germans. Sophisticated scientific techniques confirmed other "Vermeers" to be frauds.

Another notorious forger, David Stein, adopted the style of noted artists, forged their signatures and sold the works he created as authentic. Stein's skill was extraordinary, and he continued to work even while confined in prison, although his works bore the caption "Forgeries by Stein." An exhibition and sale of Stein's works was held despite legal attempts to block the show by the New York Attorney General. The Attorney General argued that an unscrupulous person could purchase a Stein, remove Stein's name, and add the signature of the artist Stein emulated. The court held, however, that the possibility of an intervening unlawful act was not sufficient to justify the issuance of an injunction. *State v. Wright Hepburn Webster Gallery, Ltd.*, 64 Misc. 2d 423, 314 N.Y.S.2d 661 (Sup. Ct. N.Y. Cnty. 1970), *aff'd*, 37 A.D.2d 698, 323 N.Y.S.2d 389 (1st Dep't 1971). Over half of Stein's works sold on the first night of the sale. The works of several other forgers, including John Myatt, Icilio Federico Joni, Wolfgang Beltracci, and Joseph Van der Veken, have been exhibited as acknowledged fakes.

In 1995, the British police uncovered a multimillion dollar forgery ring that faked works by artists such as Giacometti, Braque, Chagall, and Dubuffet. The forgeries were accompanied by detailed but fabricated provenances and sold through Christie's, Sotheby's, and Phillips auction houses. Recently, forgers have been retouching hundreds of works by minor European artists and putting the signatures of major Russian artists on them. The forgers have sometimes merely changed signatures and titles; other times, they have erased or repainted elements that do not "look Russian."

In 2013, federal prosecutors alleged that art dealers Glafira Rosales, Jose Carlos Bergantiños Diaz and Jesus Angel Bergantiños Diaz led collectors to spend more than $80 million on forged masterpieces, including those attributed to Jackson Pollock and Mark Rothko. Many of the works were sold through venerable art dealer Knoedler & Company, which had been in business for more than 165 years when it closed in 2011. The painter, a Chinese immigrant named Pei-Shen Qian, had been selling his work on the streets of New York before being recruited to assist with the fraud. Rosales pled guilty to wire fraud, money laundering and tax evasion. The Diaz brothers were arrested in Spain, and are to be extradited to the US, but the painter fled the country and is believed to be in China.

Federal and state antifraud statutes provide some sanctions against art forgery, but the penalties are slight compared to the potential profits that may be gained by creating and successfully disseminating fakes. In addition, these penal statutes all require proof of a fraudulent or criminal intent. This element is easily established in the case of the forger but is more difficult to prove when applied to the intermediate seller, who may merely suspect the spurious origin of the object or be totally ignorant of it. Were it not for the existence of civil penalties, sellers might even be tempted to remain ignorant about the authenticity of the pieces they sell.

Preventative measures aimed at making forgeries more difficult to pass off are by far the best protection for art purchasers. There are several precautions that can be taken to reduce the likelihood of acquiring a counterfeit piece. A prospective buyer should gain a familiarity with the style, period, and artist's peculiarities and compare the desired work with known forgeries, as well as with authentic pieces. Several museums have arranged to show collections of fakes as a service to the public in order to provide an opportunity to become acquainted with the most frequent stylistic errors of forgers. A careful buyer also should question the seller regarding the name of the artist, a description of the piece, the date of its execution, and the existence of historical records indicating the chain of ownership or the genuineness of the artist's signature.

If the artist is living, the buyer may request a certificate of authenticity and a bill of sale, both of which should accompany the piece whenever it is sold or transferred. The certificate of authenticity should include the name of the artist, the title of the work, the date and place of completion, a description of the subject matter, materials and media used, a statement of the rights reserved by the artist (see Chapter 14, *infra*), and, if possible, the artist's signature warranting that the piece is genuine. If the sale is made by a dealer and the author's signature is unobtainable, the seller may give the warranty of genuineness. Unfortunately, some artist foundations that had offered authentication boards or committees have dissolved those boards or committees, due to the prevalence of authentication lawsuits. For example, the authentication board of the Andy Warhol Foundation was dissolved in 2012 after it spent $7 million defending itself against a lawsuit brought by a collector after the Board refused to authenticate a portrait he owned. The authentication boards for works by Alexander Calder, Roy Lichtenstein, Jean-

Michel Basquiat and Keith Haring have also dissolved.

B. ART EXPERTS

In addition to relying on personal knowledge, the prospective purchaser may consult an art expert. Art experts fall into two general categories: stylistic and scientific. Stylistic authentication results from a subjective evaluation of the work by an art historian based on knowledge, intuition, and experience. Scientific authentication, on the other hand, results from an objective evaluation of the work based on the results of assorted scientific tests performed on the work.

The differences between these methods occasionally result in insoluble conflicts, particularly when the scientific data contradicts an expert's stylistic opinion. However, these two approaches are not mutually exclusive. If professional jealousies and ego can be overcome, one method can complement the other and lead to an even more accurate determination.

An art historian relies on a mental "data bank" to relate an object under study to other cultures, periods, and artists, and this, in itself, is a scientific approach. Of course, any data bank's reliability depends on the quality and amount of information that it contains. The comparison method, where the most minute details of a work are examined in conjunction with the details of authenticated works by what is believed to be the same artist, is the most useful and popular method.

A purchaser who employs an art expert to authenticate a piece and who later discovers that the work is not what the expert thought may be tempted to try to recover the loss from the expert. Not all "experts" are entirely scrupulous. The threat of time-consuming and costly litigation makes many honest experts reluctant to render opinions at all. Museum curators, potentially an excellent source of information for a prospective purchaser, are prohibited by most museums from giving opinions to outsiders. Many private experts refuse even to contradict blatantly incorrect reports of other experts for fear that litigation will result or that their own reputation may be compromised. It, therefore, is difficult, if not impossible, to have a newly discovered piece conclusively identified and authenticated. It is more common for experts to say that, based on the accumulated data, a work is more likely to have been created in a particular period by a particular artist than any other.

In a case that rocked the art world, *Hahn v. Duveen*, 133 Misc. 871, 234 N.Y.S. 185 (Sup. Ct. 1929), art expert Duveen settled out of court for $60,000 for statements he made about the plaintiff's painting. Duveen, a stylistic expert who had never actually viewed the painting, claimed that it had not been painted by Leonardo da Vinci and that the original was actually in the Louvre. The plaintiff Hahn alleged that her property rights had been violated when Duveen falsely and maliciously stated to a *New York World* reporter that the Hahn picture was not genuine. Hahn added that these statements caused her special damage by inducing the Kansas

City Art Museum to call off negotiations then in progress regarding the purchase of her picture. Duveen, on the other hand, contended that his First Amendment right of free speech would be destroyed if statements of opinion could not be made in good faith regarding a picture that was before the public for sale and that had been the subject of newspaper articles in America and France. This amounted to a "fair comment" defense by the defendant.

The fair comment defense has been broadened since the *Hahn* case. Fair comment or criticism on a matter of public interest is not actionable so long as the comment is not motivated by actual malice. The social values inherent in a free interchange of opinion far outweigh the injury that such a discussion might cause to a person in the public eye. As such, the essential elements of the fair comment defense are (1) that the publication is an opinion, (2) that it relates not to an individual, but to his or her acts, (3) that it is fair, namely, that the reader can see the factual basis for the comment and draw his or her own conclusion, and (4) that the publication relates to a matter of public interest or to anything submitted to the public, such as books, art exhibits, and musical performances. Thus, careful evaluators can protect themselves against possible defamation actions by confining their comments to those that are factually accurate and by relating their comments to criticism of the work, rather than criticism of the person, character, or professional competence of the artist. The expert thus should be protected even if the plaintiff's business reputation is injured, causing monetary loss.

There are, however, some limits to the fair comment defense. If the defendant's statements were made with actual malice, that is, with knowledge of their falsity or in reckless disregard of the truth, the fair comment defense cannot be sustained. Further, a professional critic should not be allowed to rely on the fair comment defense when the offending statement is based on conduct that does not meet the duty of care expected in the defendant's profession. Thus, although the defendant Duveen settled with Hahn, the fear instituted in art experts over the case may not have been justified. After all, Duveen was a stylistic expert who had never even viewed the piece in question. His conduct, therefore, was quite unprofessional, making his fair comment defense inappropriate.

A later New York case, *Travis v. Sotheby Parke Bernet,* Index No. 4290/79 (Sup. Ct. Nassau County 1982), further illustrates the importance of professional conduct by art experts. If an expert is less than thorough in the methods used to determine a work's authenticity or in making an appraisal, he or she may face a charge of professional negligence by a disappointed art buyer. On the other hand, a thoroughly professional evaluation resulting in an honest opinion should not subject the expert to liability, even though the opinion may be contrary to the belief and expectations of the party who hired the expert. In *Travis,* a first time fine art purchaser, who by his own admission knew nothing about art, acquired at an auction for $17,000 what he thought was a painting by Sir Joshua Reynolds. The buyer hoped for a high appraisal of the work, which he would then donate to the Metropolitan Museum of Art and thereby receive a charitable tax deduction. His plan was frustrated when the auction house's expert appraised the painting for only $30,000 (instead of the $200,000 hoped for) and indicated that, in her opinion, the painting was by Tilly Kettle, not Sir Joshua Reynolds.

The plaintiff-buyer then brought suit against the appraiser for negligence and slander of title, alleging that the appraisal caused him financial loss. The court disagreed and granted the defendant's motion for partial summary judgment, finding that the plaintiff had not submitted sufficient evidence to support a *prima facie* case on either charge. In his oral opinion, the judge acknowledged the difficulties facing an expert attempting to authenticate or appraise a work of art, stating that "what we are dealing with here has no objective standards. Each of the experts bases his opinion on his own personal aesthetic considerations and experience. . . . In short, we have experts making what they consider to be educated guesses about what transpired over two hundred years ago."

As to the negligence charge, the court felt that the appraiser had performed her job as adequately as could be expected under the circumstances. She had conducted in-depth research, referred to the standard texts and references, and spoken with the recognized authority on Reynolds' works. No more could be expected of her, and so her conduct was not negligent.

The court also could not find the necessary elements to support the slander of title claim. No one knows with absolute certainty who actually had painted the picture, so the requisite publication of a falsehood was doubtful, but even assuming the falsehood (that the painting was not Kettle's but Reynolds'), the added requirement of malice was found to be lacking. This was not a situation like the one in *Hahn v. Duveen* where the court said that whenever a man unnecessarily intermeddles with another's affairs with which he is wholly unconcerned, such officious intermeddling will be deemed malice and he will be liable for any special damages. Instead, the defendant here was invited to make the appraisal and was merely doing her job.

The *Travis* court was also hard pressed to find that the plaintiff had suffered any damages as a result of the alleged disparagement. The painting, as appraised, was worth considerably more than the amount the plaintiff had paid for it only six months earlier. Moreover, the museum was still willing to accept the painting, whether it was a Reynolds or a Kettle. The plaintiff appeared to suffer nothing more than unfulfilled expectations. Further, those expectations may not even have been reasonable since the work's authenticity as a Reynolds was openly in question before the time of the plaintiff's purchase.

More recently, an art expert was awarded nearly $21,400,000 in damages after bringing suit for malicious prosecution and abuse of process. (The trial court reduced the jury award to $11,300,000.) The expert, Steve Seltzer, was sued after he concluded that his own grandfather had created a painting bearing the name of a better known artist. The work's new owner sued, alleging that Seltzer knew his opinion about the painting was wrong and had damaged the painting's value to the point it could not be sold. See, e.g., *Seltzer v. Morton*, No. 05–378 (Mont. 8th Dist. Ct. Feb. 7, 2005), *app. filed*, No. 05–378 (Mont. 2005). Some experts attempt to limit their liability by obtaining a covenant against suit in the contract between themselves and a client. However, this type of provision is not favored by the law. Some jurisdictions have held such provisions void against public policy, as in *Dearborn Motors Credit Corp. v. Neel*, 184 Kan. 437, 337 P.2d 992 (1959), a case involving a contractual waiver of defenses in a retail tractor sale. Other jurisdictions strictly construe these kinds of covenants against the writer and give them only limited effect. See, e.g., *Boll v. Sharp & Dohme, Inc.*, 281 A.D. 568, 121 N.Y.S.2d 20 (1st Dep't 1953), *aff'd*, 307 N.Y. 646, 120 N.E.2d 836 (1954).

C. SCIENTIFIC AUTHENTICATION

There are many scientific methods that can be used to assist in authentication, often by determining the work's age and the materials used to create it.

These methods include radiocarbon age determination, thermoluminescent analysis, chemical analysis, obsidian hydration, fission tracks, infrared reflectology, dendrochronology, high performance chromatography, electron microscopy, Raman spectroscopy, potassium-argon dating, comparative analysis, reconstruction of manufacturing techniques, microscopic techniques, X-rays, X-ray diffraction, autoradiography, and even computer analysis for patterns such as fractals and mathematical "fingerprints" using statistics about the pressure of the drawing tool, orientation of the stroke, and the like. Even an artist's fingerprints and hairs stuck under paint can be used to help establish whether the work is authentic. These methods and others allow scientists to date the materials used in the works, as well as examine the external and internal structure of the works. While these tests may be feasible when a major work of art is involved, their costs will generally outweigh their utility in the case of minor acquisitions. Scientific methods were recently used to conclude that two deauthenticated Rembrandts owned by the Statens Museum for Kunst in Copenhagen were Rembrandt works after all. For three years, experts studied the work, using X-rays, infrared reflectography, dendrochronology, studies of the canvas thread count, ground, layers of paint, and the like. The museum has presented a full account of these studies at its exhibit called *Rembrandt? The Master and His Workshop*.

D. PURCHASERS' COMMON LAW REMEDIES AGAINST SELLERS

Artists who are victims of the sale of forgeries bearing their names have several potential remedies. As discussed in Chapter 14, *infra*, they may have a cause of action for a violation of right of privacy or may be able to bring an action for a false designation of origin under Section 43(a) of the Lanham Act, 15

U.S.C. § 1125(a), but what remedies are available to the purchaser of a counterfeit? A buyer who discovers that the painting purchased is worthless has not experienced any violation of privacy but has only lost the benefit of the bargain. Nor can an action be brought under the Lanham Act. Most courts hold that consumers have no standing to sue under Section 43(a), despite the broad language of the section, which provides for a private right of action by "any person who believes that he is or is likely to be damaged" and despite the fact that trademark law is intended to protect consumer's expectations.

Purchasers of counterfeit artworks do have some remedies against the seller, however. Special art legislation has been enacted in some states, allowing purchasers to recover from sellers of counterfeit art, and in some circumstances, the seller may be able to recover from a prior seller, if the prior seller can be found, for a breach of warranty. In addition, purchasers may be able to recover under common law tort and contract doctrines. Many of these doctrines overlap. For example, in *Weisz v. Parke-Bernet Galleries, Inc.*, discussed *infra*, a claim was brought on the basis of a breach of warranty, but the case was decided by the appeals court on the basis of the doctrines of fraud and mistake. Sellers and purchasers involved in disputes over a counterfeit work, therefore, need to be aware of the requirements of each of these theories and the interrelationships between them.

A possible purchaser's remedy is a tort action for fraud, which may result in either monetary damages or entitle the aggrieved purchaser to rescind the transaction. As a common law doctrine, the proof necessary to establish fraud varies from state to state, but typically it is necessary to prove that the defendant seller made a misstatement which (1) is related to a material matter of fact, (2) was made deceitfully with intent to induce reliance, (3) induced justifiable reliance, (4) as a result of which the plaintiff suffered damages. An action for fraud is thus most likely to be successful if the purchaser can show that the seller knew that a work was not created by the named artist but, nevertheless, stated that it was. In some circumstances, however, a purchaser can recover for fraud even if the misrepresentation was merely negligent. A negligent misstatement may be actionable if the defendant failed to exercise reasonable care in ascertaining the facts or if a dealer/seller failed to exercise the skill and competence required by his or her profession. Yet, since the vast majority of art fraud is extremely difficult to detect, even for experts, a cause of action based on a negligent misrepresentation ordinarily will be extremely difficult to prove.

Misrepresentation may be relied on as grounds for rescinding a contract. Depending upon local law, the proof necessary to establish misrepresentation may be quite similar to the proof required for fraud, but this is not always so. One frequently made distinction is that liability in tort arises only if the misrepresentation is both material and intended to deceive, whereas under contract law, a misrepresentation may make a contract voidable if it is either intended to deceive or is material. This is because tort law imposes liability in damages for misrepresentation, whereas contract law merely makes a contract procured by misrepresentation voidable; thus, the requirements in contract should be less stringent.

Since a statement about who authored a work of art is nearly always material to the sale, it is theoretically not necessary to show that the seller intended to deceive the purchaser in order to avoid the contract on the grounds of misrepresentation. However, where the seller of a counterfeit work has no intent to deceive, any statement made about the work's authorship is necessarily a matter of opinion, not a statement of fact. No person except one who actually viewed the artist create a work or the artist can say with absolute certainty that the artist created it. Thus, any seller who has no direct knowledge of the work's authorship but who states that a work is authentic is really saying, "From all the facts available to me, I think this work is authentic, but there is no way I can be sure of it." In this light, allowing the purchaser to void a contract simply because the purchaser failed to exercise his or her own independent judgment is unfair, unless the relationship between the seller and the purchaser is one of special trust and confidence or the purchaser reasonably believes that, as compared to her-or himself, the seller has special skill, judgment or objectivity with respect to the work of art being sold. See Restatement (Second) of Contracts, § 169 (1981).

Another potential remedy is the contract doctrine of mutual mistake. In order for the purchaser to void the contract, generally it is necessary to show that (1) the mistake was a basic assumption on which the contract was made, (2) the mistake had a material effect on the agreed-upon exchange of performances between the parties, and (3) the adversely affected party did not assume the risks of the mistake. A mistake by only one of the parties may allow the aggrieved party to void the contract too, but only if it can be shown, in addition to the three elements of mutual mistake, that the effect of the mistake is such that enforcement of the contract would be unconscionable or that the other party had reason to know of the mistake or his or her fault caused the mistake. In this case, the mistake really will amount to misrepresentation, duress, or some other wrongdoing on the part of the seller.

Where the seller of a forged work has no intent to deceive the purchaser, a claim based on mistake will be particularly vulnerable to the defense that the purchaser assumed the risk of the lack of authenticity. This was the case in *Weisz v. Parke-Bernet Galleries, Inc.*, 77 Misc. 2d 80, 351 N.Y.S.2d 911 (Sup. Ct. App. Term 1974), *rev'g* 67 Misc. 2d 1077, 325 N.Y.S.2d 576 (Civ. Ct. N.Y. City 1971). The plaintiffs purchased at auction two paintings believing them to be by Raoul Dufy, but the paintings later turned out to be forgeries with little commercial value. The appellate court stated:

> Since no element of a willful intent to deceive is remotely suggested in the circumstances here present the purchasers assumed the risk that in judging the paintings as readily identifiable,

original works of the named artist, and scaling their bids accordingly, they might be mistaken.... They will not now be heard to complain that, in failing to act with the caution of one in circumstances abounding with signals of *caveat emptor*, they made a bad bargain.

While this holding narrowly applies only to works sold at auctions, it could be said to apply to any sale of art. In fact, in *ACA Galleries, Inc. v. Kinney*, 552 Fed. Appx. 24 (2d Cir. 2014), the court held that the buyer, ACA, was not entitled to rescission of its purchase of a forged Milton Avery painting based on the doctrine of mutual mistake, because it "chose . . . to accept the risk that the painting was a forgery." According to the court, the buyer knew it had limited knowledge about the painting and had the opportunity to have it authenticated by the Milton & Sally Avery Arts Foundation, but chose not to do so until after the purchase was completed.

Since art forgeries are so prevalent in today's market, most buyers know or should know that there are risks in purchasing a work of art. Thus, absent some fraud or wrongdoing on the part of the seller or some special relationship of trust and confidence, it will be extremely difficult for the purchaser to hold an innocent seller liable under the common law theories of mistake or misrepresentation.

E. WARRANTIES

Another potential remedy against the seller of a counterfeit work of art is an action for breach of warranty. Unlike a tort action for fraud, a breach of warranty action is based upon concepts akin to strict liability. No fault on the part of the seller is required; the plaintiff need only prove that there was a warranty, that the goods failed to conform to the warranty, and that the plaintiff suffered a loss as a result. Moreover, unlike contract actions based on misrepresentation or mistake, the aggrieved purchaser in a warranty action can recover damages rather than simply electing to void the contract.

A codification of commercial law which has been adopted by every state (though only in part by Louisiana) is the Uniform Commercial Code. Article 2 of the U.C.C. deals with goods, which include works of art. (Note: Although Louisiana has not adopted Article 2, its civil code covers the sale of goods).

A warranty action under the U.C.C. allows for recovery of the difference between the value of the defective goods the purchaser actually received and the value of the goods had they been as warranted. See U.C.C. § 2–714(2). This measure of damages is the same as the measure of damages in most states for fraud and gives the purchaser the benefit of the bargain where he or she paid a below-market price. By contrast, a rescission of the contract for common law misrepresentation or mistake has the effect of allowing the purchaser to recover only out-of-pocket losses, the difference between the value of the defective goods and the contract price the purchaser actually paid. Note, however, that Section 2–608(1)(b) allows a buyer to rescind a transaction when acceptance "was reasonably induced . . . by the difficulty of discovery before acceptance. . . ." The fact that a work of art is a good forgery and undiscovered should be sufficient to satisfy the criteria of this section. The comments to the statute point out that revocation of acceptance under Section 2–608 and damages for breach may both be available to an aggrieved purchaser. It should also be noted if the specious character is discovered before acceptance, then Section 2–601 provides that a purchaser may refuse acceptance.

Tunick, Inc. v. Kornfield, 838 F. Supp. 848 (S.D.N.Y. 1993), which involved a dispute over a Picasso print with an alleged forgery of Picasso's signature, held that a seller's right to substitute conforming goods for nonconforming tender rejected by the buyer does not apply to art prints because every print is a unique piece of art.

Because the U.C.C. allows a purchaser who discovers a forgery after acceptance to recover damages that give him or her the benefit of the bargain, a breach of warranty action appears to be a promising vehicle for an action by a purchaser of a specious work against an innocent seller. Yet, there are several potential pitfalls to the use in this context of warranty statutes designed to regulate ordinary commercial sales. For this reason, several states have enacted warranty legislation that applies solely to art fraud. In the absence of such legislation, however, purchasers may try to recover their losses from sellers on the basis of warranty.

1. EXPRESS WARRANTIES

There are basically two types of warranties: express warranties and implied warranties. Under U.C.C. § 2–313, express warranties arise from (1) any affirmation of fact or promise made by the seller to the buyer which relates to the goods and becomes part of the basis of the bargain, and (2) any description of the goods that is made part of the basis of the bargain. An express warranty is not limited to representations written into the contract. Express warranties can arise from representations made in extrinsic materials, such as advertisements or catalogues, provided the buyer can demonstrate that he or she had personal knowledge of the representation and that the representation was a basis of the bargain. An express warranty may also arise from a seller's oral statements, even if the contract itself is within the statute of frauds. Furthermore, since an express warranty is not limited to the contract's terms, it may arise even after the contract has been made.

The drafters of the U.C.C. expressed the belief that all the statements of the seller become a part of the basis of the bargain, thus giving rise to an express warranty, unless good reason is shown to the contrary. Despite this sweeping language, a buyer must be careful to distinguish between an affirmation of fact or a promise, which creates a warranty, and a mere opinion, or "puffing," which does not. The distinction is often difficult to make, and the determination is properly left to the trier of fact. In the case of works of art, it has been suggested in *Jendwine v. Slade*, 170 Eng. Rep. 459 (1797), and *Power v. Barham*, 111 Eng. Rep. 865 (1836), that where old works of art are involved, an assertion as to their genuineness was necessarily a matter of opinion, whereas with more contemporary works, such an assertion might be more properly received as a statement of fact. Yet, it can also be argued that given the uncertainties of establishing authenticity, even for experts, both buyer and seller can be expected to have an opinion about the genuineness of any work of art, and thus no express warranty can ever be created on this basis. Another approach is to examine the facts particular to each case, focusing on the relative ambiguity of the statement, the respective levels of expertise of the parties, whether the statement was written or oral, and the context of the statement, including whether the seller said anything that might indicate that he or she was expressing an opinion and whether the seller said anything that might suggest to a reasonable buyer that the buyer should be on guard.

Another difficulty in applying warranty law to sales of counterfeit art is defining the meaning of "any description of the goods which is made part of the basis of the bargain," found in U.C.C. § 2–313(1)(b). In a non-art example, it has been held that a description of an airplane as "Aero Commander, N-2677B, Number 135, FAA, Flyable" created an express warranty that the plane would qualify for full certification by the Federal Aviation Administration. *Hill Aircraft & Leasing Corp. v. Simon*, 122 Ga. App. 524, 177 S.E.2d 803 (1970). However, a statement that a work of art is a "Rembrandt painting" is subject to several interpretations. The phrase might mean that the work was painted by Rembrandt, but it also might mean that it was merely painted "in the manner of" or "from the school of" Rembrandt. Because of its inherent imprecision, such a statement, therefore, may not constitute an express warranty that Rembrandt created the work unless the purchaser can show by proof of trade usage that the meaning of the phrase is sufficiently definite or that a fake work would not be acceptable in the trade under that description.

The price paid for a work might also be used to affect the claimed warranty. Thus, a purchase price which is commensurate with the amounts paid for authentic Dutch masters should support the position that the purchaser believed the Rembrandt was authentic. On the other hand, an extremely low price would likely put reasonable people on notice that the Rembrandt painting transaction is too good to be true, and, therefore, it is improbable that an authentic old master is being sold.

The statute of limitations applicable to a cause of action for breach of warranty was at issue in *Rosen v. Spanierman*, 894 F.2d 28 (2nd Cir.1990). Plaintiffs had received the painting *The Misses Werthheimer* as a gift. It had been purchased from defendant's gallery in the 1960s. The sales invoice said "this picture is fully guaranteed by the undersigned to be an original work by John Singer Sargent." Plaintiff's claim was dismissed, as New York's U.C.C. § 2–725 contains a four-year statute of limitations, which begins to run at the time of sale.

2. IMPLIED WARRANTIES

The U.C.C. also provides for the implied warranties of title, merchantability, and fitness for a particular purpose. The first warranty, the warranty of title, is implied under U.C.C. § 2–312 in every contract for the sale of goods, but is of little utility to the purchaser of a forged work of art. This warranty is breached if the seller does not have good title or the right to convey the item in question. Thus, a stolen or looted work of art would be subject to reclamation by its true owner, and its buyer should have a cause of action for breach of the implied warranty of title. Yet, for the purchaser of counterfeit works of art, this section does not provide a basis for recovery.

A second type of implied warranty is the implied warranty of merchantability, found in U.C.C. § 2–314, which provides that "unless excluded or modified, ... a warranty that the goods shall be merchantable is implied in a contract for their sale if the seller is a merchant with respect to goods of that kind." The implied warranty of merchantability has ordinarily been used by consumers as a vehicle for redress for personal injury or property damage caused by defective goods, but some decisions have applied this implied warranty to situations involving only the loss of a bargain. Still, the warranty of merchantability applies only when the work is purchased from a "merchant." Section 2–104 defines a merchant as "a person who deals in goods of the kind or otherwise by his occupation holds himself out as having knowledge or skill peculiar to the practices or goods involved in the transaction. . . ." Thus, sales by art dealers and most auction houses would fall within this section, but sales by ordinary individuals usually would not.

The implied warranty of merchantability is breached whenever the goods sold do not meet any one of the requirements of merchantability specified in Section 2–314(2). Three of the six requirements are potentially useful in the sale of a counterfeit work of art. Paragraph (a) provides that in order to be merchantable, the goods must "pass without objection in the trade under the contract description." Comment 2 elaborates: "[G]oods delivered under an agreement made by a merchant in a given line of trade must be of a quality comparable to that generally acceptable in that line of trade under the description or other designation of the goods used in the agreement." Paragraph (c) provides further that merchantable goods must be "fit for the ordinary purposes for which goods are used." Paragraph (f) requires that the goods must "conform to promises or affirmations of fact made on the container or label if any." Provided that a buyer can demonstrate that a work of art does not conform to its description, that the purchaser's investment or aesthetic purposes are compromised by the forgery, or that a signature on a work or on its frame is tantamount to a promise or affirmation of fact, the buyer may be able to argue that the implied warranty of merchantability has been breached.

Section 2–315 of the U.C.C. provides a third implied warranty—that of fitness for a particular purpose, which also may be applicable to art sales. To establish a breach of warranty for a particular purpose, three requirements must be met. First, the seller must know of the buyer's particular purpose. Second, the seller must know, actually or constructively, that the buyer is relying on the seller's skill and judgment. Finally, the buyer must actually rely on the seller's skill. Comment 2 defines "particular purpose" as a purpose that is specific and peculiar to the nature of the buyer's business and distinguishes it from "ordinary purpose," which is governed by Section 2–314, the implied warranty of merchantability. A purchaser motivated by ordinary investment potential or a collector is unlikely to satisfy the particular-purpose requirement. On the other hand, a purchaser who is trying to obtain a particular piece or complete a specific collection will likely fall within the coverage of this warranty.

3. DISCLAIMERS

Both implied warranties and express warranties may be disclaimed by the seller. Indeed, it is quite common for many dealers and auction houses to place legends in their catalogues disclaiming liability for a breach of warranty. This is a major defense to actions based on a breach of warranty, which makes this remedy unavailable in many situations. Yet, in order to be effective, disclaimers still must meet the requirements of U.C.C. § 2–316.

A disclaimer of an implied warranty of merchantability is valid only if it specifically mentions the word "merchantability." The disclaimer may be oral, but if it is written, it must be conspicuous. An implied warranty of fitness for a particular purpose may also be disclaimed, but it cannot be oral; it must be conspicuous and in writing, though the language need not specifically mention the words "fitness for a particular purpose."

Express warranties are much more difficult to disclaim. Comment 1 to Section 2–316 points out that the difficulty is designed to protect buyers from unbargained-for and unexpected disclaimers that are inconsistent with the terms of an express statement of fact. Thus, under the U.C.C., the trier of fact must decide in each case whether the express warranty and disclaimer can be construed in such a way as to be consistent with each other. Negation or limitation of an express warranty is inoperative to the extent that the construction is unreasonable. Yet, this provision, when applied to cases involving the sale of counterfeit works of art, is far from satisfying to the victimized purchaser. A statement of authorship of a work of art is frequently quite ambiguous, thus making it likely that a disclaimer will be upheld.

4. ART WARRANTY STATUTES

Recognizing the difficulties of interpreting and applying the U.C.C.'s warranty and disclaimer provisions to art fraud, some states have enacted laws dealing specifically with art warranties. The New York legislature approved a bill in 1966 which provides that any art merchant who sells a work to a nonmerchant buyer creates an express warranty if, in describing the work, he or she identifies it with an author or authorship. N.Y. Arts & Cult. Aff. Law

§§ 13.01 to 13.21. This New York law recognizes that consumers rely upon art merchants' experience, education, and skill in designating pedigree. Therefore, art dealers are prohibited from asserting that their attribution of authorship was only their judgment, not an affirmation of fact. This law also creates a presumption that statements as to authenticity become part of the basis of the bargain and refuses even to permit puffing by the seller to induce the buyer to purchase a questionable work. Furthermore, to negate an express warranty of authenticity of authorship, a disclaimer must be conspicuous, written, and contained in a provision separate and apart from the language creating the warranty, "in words which would clearly and specifically apprise the buyer that the seller assumes no risk, liability or responsibility for authenticity of the authorship." The New York law also affords the purchaser greater protection than U.C.C. § 2–316(1) by providing that the disclaimer of an express warranty will be ineffectual if it is shown that the piece was counterfeit.

Michigan enacted a similar statute in 1970, Mich. Comp. Laws § 19.410 *et seq.*, as did Florida in 1990, West's F.S.A. §§ 686.501 to 686.506 and Iowa in 1991, Iowa Code 715B.1–B2. While the Michigan, Florida, Iowa and New York statutes go far in protecting the art consumer, they do have some limitations. First, they apply only in transactions between a merchant seller and a nonmerchant purchaser. The Michigan statute does define an art merchant to include an auctioneer who sells art at public auction, as well as the auctioneer's consignor or principal, but it does not appear to apply to collectors who do not sell through an auctioneer. Second, the statutes apply only to written representations. Third, the statutes apply only to sales made in New York, Iowa, Florida, and Michigan. An attempt in the late 1960s to enact similar legislation in Illinois, for example, was unsuccessful partly because legislators felt that the U.C.C. adequately covered the situation. Yet, as previously discussed, the warranty and disclaimer provisions of the U.C.C. leave many unanswered questions when art forgeries are involved.

F. FINE PRINT AND MULTIPLES LEGISLATION

Fine prints and limited edition sculptures have become popular for a variety of reasons. These include reasonable cost and the many new techniques available to create prints and sculptures. This popularity has been accompanied by an increasing number of questionable pieces entering the market. There are several ways in which the purchaser of a print can be duped. If a plate is not canceled or destroyed after the edition is completed, unscrupulous individuals may reuse it. The signature of an artist may be forged on an unsigned print. Copies of an authentic print may be made by unauthorized individuals. In at least one notorious situation, blank paper was signed by the artist, shipped into the United States and the artwork was later affixed to the paper by a mechanical process. See *Federal Trade Commission v. Magui Publishers*, Civ. No. 89–3818RSWL(GX), 1991 WL 90895 (C.D. Cal.1991).

Similarly, there are numerous problems that can arise with editioned sculptures. Unauthorized pieces can be made, restrikes may be sold as original works, molds may not be destroyed after the edition is complete, and posthumous copies may be passed off as done by the artist. In a curious case, thieves of a purported Remington sculpture attempted to defend their criminal prosecution on the ground that the piece they stole was a forgery. *United States v. Tobin*, 576 F.2d 687 (5th Cir.1978), *cert. denied sub nom. Tobin v. United States*, 439 U.S. 1051 (1978).

Several states have enacted statutes to regulate the fine print and multiple market. These states include California, Georgia, Hawaii, Illinois, Iowa, Maryland, Michigan, Minnesota, New York, North Carolina, Oregon, South Carolina and Wisconsin. West's Ann.Cal. Civ. Code §§ 1740 to 1745; O.C.G.A. §§ 10–1–430 to 10–1–437; H.R.S. § 481F; 815 I.L.C.S. § 345; Iowa Code 715B; Md. Code, Com. Law §§ 14–501 to 14–505; Mich. Comp. Laws § 19.409; Minn. Stat. Ann. § 324; N.Y. Arts & Cult. Aff. Law §§ 15.01 to 15.19; O.R.S. 359.300 to 359.315; S.C. Code 1976, §§ 39–16–10 to 39–16–50; Wisc. ATCP 117.01 to 117.25. These fine print and multiple disclosure statutes create specific rights and remedies on the part of the purchaser of a limited edition when it turns out to be more widely disseminated than the purchaser had a reasonable right to expect. While all of the statutes apply to editioned prints, only New York, California, Georgia, Iowa, Michigan and Wisconsin apply the statutes to other art created in multiples such as limited edition sculptures.

All of these state laws require the disclosure of certain information to accompany the item when sold on a certificate, invoice, or receipt. The information to be disclosed is specifically stated in each statute and generally includes the following: (1) the name of the artist and the year printed or cast; (2) whether the edition is limited (although the term "limited" usually is not defined); (3) the present status of the plate or mold; (4) if the work has more than one edition, the edition of this work and sizes created of the edition; (5) whether the edition is posthumous or a restrike, and if so, whether the plate or mold has been reworked; and (6) the name of the workshop or foundry (if any) where the edition was printed or cast. Most of the statutes also require information on the medium or process used, such as whether the print is an etching, engraving, woodcut, lithograph, or if the seller does not know. In the case of sculpture, the material used must be disclosed. In some states, disclosure requirements further include the source of the artist's name on the multiple (whether signed or stamped) and provide that unless disclosed, the number of multiples described as being in a limited edition shall constitute an express warranty that no additional numbered multiples of the same image have been produced.

If the edition is limited, further disclosures are required, including the maximum number of releases, broken down into signed and unsigned, the number of proofs allowed, and the total edition size.

Some states impose a liability for "knowingly" offering prints or multiples for sale without the required disclosures, whereas New York and Oregon impose strict liability. All the statutes have a disclaimer provision, allowing the seller to disavow any knowledge of information required to be disclosed. However, the disclaimer must be stated "specifically and categorically" with regard to each detail.

All the statutes provide that a person violating the disclosure requirements shall be liable for the amount of consideration the purchaser paid and allow for interest from the date of purchase (except for Wisconsin, which allows the purchaser to recover twice the damages and reasonable attorneys' fees and costs). In the case of a willful violation, the purchaser can recover up to three times the purchase price, although Hawaii allows recovery of up to three times the purchase price or $1,000, whichever is greater.

G. PREVENTATIVE MEASURES

The most impressive suggestion for protecting purchasers of fake or forged art is the establishment of an art registry. This would prevent the sale of forgeries by enabling purchasers to easily verify the authenticity of works of art. There are a variety of possible cataloguing methods. Living artists could file a certificate of authenticity, a photograph of the work, and the name of the first purchaser with a central registry. This central registry could be patterned after the automobile licensing system. As an alternative, the artist could place his or her signature or distinctive design on the creation, followed by the number of a special code impressed in a color of the spectrum with a high atomic weight. Archives of the artist's designs would then be kept. A variation of this method might be to use the artist's fingerprints on the painting, preserved by a chemical treatment.

The fingerprinting of art need not be confined to contemporary artists. Works of art themselves possess unique characteristics which may be identified. Therefore any work of art—contemporary, old, or ancient—can be catalogued. The owner could file a certified copy of the piece's certificate of authenticity with a central registry.

Several art registry systems have been established. In England, two policemen developed a grid fingerprinting method and incorporated it into an existing, centralized file of artworks known as the International Art Registry. In connection with the Bicentennial Celebration, the U.S. government established a registry for paintings created in or before 1914.

Another method of dealing with the problem of fakes and forgeries is to establish certification marks which may be used to identify authentic works and to impose penalties for the mark's improper use. The Indian Arts and Crafts Board, which is a branch of the U.S. Department of the Interior, has done this for Native American arts and crafts by adopting a certification mark that can be used only by Native Americans to identify their work. Penalties are imposed for violation of the statute. 25 U.S.C. §§ 305–305(c). The law provides that the board should assist Native Americans, their tribes, and associations with registration of their own certification marks. Unfortunately, since its enactment in 1935, this law has never been enforced. Alaska has adopted a similar form of legislation for its Native peoples. A.S. 45.65.010 to 45.65.1070.

Much more work needs to be done. Until the federal legislature recognizes the scope of the problem by appropriating funds for a complete up-to-date registry and enacting federal art warranty laws with substantial penalties for their breach, *caveat emptor* ("let the buyer beware") must be the byword for the art purchaser in most circumstances.

An alternative to legislation is for the art community to police itself. There have been some modest attempts to accomplish this among French and American art dealers. A code of ethics formulated and rigidly enforced by the members of the art dealing community would be helpful in stemming the tide of forgers. One method which could be effective for dealer self-policing is the creation of a nongovernmental licensing association. This would enable the art community to clean its own house and thus aid the purchasing public. Such a plan has been substantially followed by the Indian Arts and Crafts Association. The organization has a fairly rigid code of ethics, which it enforces, and it encourages members to display copies of this private organization's signet, as well as the ethical standards. Similarly, the Art Dealers Association of America has adopted an ethical code; yet, not all dealers are members.

The notoriety which accompanies the discovery that an alleged masterpiece is actually a forgery tends to frighten would-be art purchasers. A legislative response to this problem might offer aggrieved collectors a remedy, but a prophylactic approach to the problem could be more effective. To the extent purchasers feel that their acquisition is authentic because the work has a well-documented provenance, the art market will likely realize an economic benefit.

CHAPTER 7
INSURANCE

A. PROS AND CONS OF INSURING

It is impossible to eliminate all the risks of owning art, even when the most rigorous safeguards are employed. Expensive, complex alarm systems usually discourage amateurs but may intrigue or even challenge an ingenious professional burglar. Artists, collectors, dealers, and museums frequently must transport pieces for display or inspection by potential purchasers, thereby creating risks of loss and theft that might not otherwise exist. Fires, floods and earthquakes also pose threats to the safety of collections. One way of guarding against these possible economic losses is to have insurance.

The question of whether to insure can be most important to the owner or guardian of a collection. While premiums on fine arts policies are generally lower than those fixed for many other types of insurance, they can still be substantial. Premiums for large collections may be particularly high since insurance companies will usually add a loading factor reflecting a potential increase in the risk of theft. Premiums have risen as the number of art thefts has risen. According to the FBI, each year, $5 billion to $8 billion worth of artwork is stolen worldwide. Trafficking in stolen art is as lucrative and pervasive as trafficking in drugs, weapons and counterfeit goods. At best, only 10 percent of stolen works are ever recovered (some experts put the figure as low as two percent). In many cases, insuring against these risks is simply not worth the cost. Art collectors thus rarely insure for the full value of their collections, since losses due to theft and fire rarely wipe out an entire collection and since radical fluctuations in the value of art make it costly and difficult to periodically inventory, appraise, and reevaluate insurance coverage. While most large museums in the United States do have insurance against theft and damage, many museums, particularly in Europe, insure against fire and water damage—but not against robbery. An example is the Munch Museum in Oslo from which *The Scream* was stolen in August of 2003 (it was recovered two years later). Some museums choose not to insure for the value of the work but, rather, to buy a policy that covers the cost of art recovery experts.

Some institutions insure only works that are loaned out to others, and sometimes the lending institution will loan works only on condition that the receiving institution insures the works. Yet, traveling exhibits frequently are very costly to insure, since moving works between locations involves higher risks than if the works remain in one place. Some exhibits, however, may be eligible for insurance coverage through the National Endowment for the Arts' Arts and Artifacts Indemnity program. See 20 U.S.C. § 971. This program, authorized by Congress in 1975, was intended to make possible foreign exhibits by providing insurance that otherwise might be prohibitively expensive. Foreign shows traveling in the United States are eligible for the federal indemnity, as are United States shows traveling abroad if they are part of an exchange with the foreign country. The indemnity under the Act provides broad coverage, agreeing to pay for any item that is lost, destroyed, stolen, or suffers damage from any external cause, except wear and tear. Nuclear and war risks, as well as terrorism coverage, excluded under most other policies, are also covered. There is a $1.8 billion dollar aggregate loss limit and a deductible based on a sliding scale depending on the value of the exhibit and the amount of other insurance that usually is covered by a private carrier. Thus, it is possible for museums to insure many traveling exhibits that otherwise would not be made available for viewing.

Some fiduciaries and guardians of a collection may have no choice over whether or not to maintain insurance. Some trust instruments specify that insurance must be maintained, and some courts hold that a failure to insure is a breach of fiduciary duty where a loss would destroy a trust designed to produce income. In such cases, the failure to maintain insurance could subject the trustee to personal liability.

Where a choice of whether to insure is available, the institution or individual can evaluate the options by making a few simple calculations similar to those made by insurance companies. First, determine the present replacement cost of all items in the collection. Then ascertain the annual premium that would be charged on this amount and speculate on the likelihood of a loss and its probable magnitude. If losses are not likely to occur or only minimal damage would be sustained, then the collector will probably be better off setting aside an amount equal to the annual insurance premiums and becoming his or her own insurer. If, on the other hand, the risk is high and the damage would be great, insurance is definitely advisable. In the case of irreplaceable masterpieces, however, many museums and collectors prefer to spend the money that might otherwise go to insurance premiums on efforts to prevent loss or damage, such as fire and theft prevention.

B. THE INSURANCE CONTRACT

Once the decision to purchase insurance is made, the collector must decide what kind of coverage to obtain. While the insurance company and the insured are free to negotiate any contract they wish so long as it does not violate a statute or public policy, today individualized policies are rarely used. Instead, standard policies have been developed to cover common situations, and riders are used to cover slight variations.

The insurance agreement contains all the elements of a private contract. The parties must be competent to contract as determined by state law, and there must be legal consideration and mutuality of agreement. In an insurance contract, the parties must agree to the subject matter of the insurance, the type of risk insured against, the persons insured, the amount and duration of the risk, and the premiums due.

SEC. B THE INSURANCE CONTRACT

Agreement is evidenced by the standard contract principles of offer and acceptance. Generally, an application for insurance is considered to be the offer. Since acceptance must be only within the terms of the offer, the issuance of a policy which varies from the application will be considered to be a counteroffer. Technically, the insured must, therefore, assent to the variation or else no contract will be formed. Yet, notwithstanding this general rule, oral binders of insurance and initial orders are frequently incomplete in that they do not specify all the terms of the contract. In such cases, courts may imply the usual terms to prevent a failure of the formation of the contract. In other cases, unexpected terms of a policy may be attacked on the grounds that they were outside of the reasonable expectations of the insured. The courts are not in agreement on the question of whether the insured has an obligation to verify the policy's terms. Some courts impose a positive duty on the insured to read the policy, with the result that he or she may be estopped by negligence from asserting that a particular term is unenforceable. In *Florsheim v. Travelers Indemnity Co. of Illinois*, 75 Ill. App. 3d 298, 30 Ill. Dec. 876, 393 N.E.2d 1223 (1st Dist. 1979), the insured was unable to enforce her claim in court due to a provision in the policy requiring suit to be brought within one year of the loss. She claimed that she was unaware of this provision and had expected the insurance company to settle after she produced additional proof that the damage to her Vasarely painting was due to a spill of turpentine rather than an inherent defect. However, the court held that she was charged with notice of the policy contents and could not rely on the insurer to inform her of her duties. Other courts refuse to impose such harsh results and require an insurer to call the insured's attention to any variations in the policy before those variations can be enforced.

Public policy prohibits the issuance of an insurance policy to persons who do not possess an insurable interest in the item to be insured. The reason for this rule is to discourage gambling and to minimize the temptation for the insured to cause the loss insured against. The interests designated as insurable include a property right, a contractual right, a potential legal liability, and a factual expectation of damage. The individuals who have such interests include bailees, executors, administrators, guardians, trustees, remaindermen, stockholders, lessors, and lessees. The insurable interest must always exist at the time of the loss and, in some states, must also exist when the policy is created.

In interpreting an insurance contract, courts rely on a number of standard canons of construction. The intent of the parties is generally considered to be revealed by the words of the policy in their customary meaning to an ordinary untrained person. Specific clauses take precedence over general ones, and typed, handwritten, or stamped provisions take precedence over standard form provisions. If the language of the policy, considered as a whole, is susceptible to two reasonable and different interpretations, the court may consider extraneous information. The court will scrutinize the circumstances surrounding the transaction, the situation of the parties, and the coverage the insured intended to obtain. Specifics which may be considered include premium size, customs in the trade, and the sophistication of the parties. Generally, ambiguities are resolved in favor of the insured. Although an insured may not rely on a patently absurd interpretation, when an agent of the insurer interprets the policy for the insured, the insurer is estopped from denying the coverage promised.

One area that causes many interpretation problems is the existence of exclusions and limitations within the insurance contract. A personal household policy, for example, typically excludes any property which pertains to the business of the insured. For many collectors, this can present unexpected problems. A dealer or collector who sells part of his or her collection will find that all the remaining pieces are classified as pertaining to his or her business and are, therefore, ineligible for protection under a personal household policy. Collectors may also find that particular types of uses will be excluded. In *Swanstrom v. Ins. Co. of N. Am.*, 100 F. Supp. 374 (S.D. Cal. 1951), for example, recovery was denied under the insured's personal policy for artwork which was part of his personal collection but which had been displayed in his restaurant for a significant period of time. On the other hand, when the insured was an interior decorator who planned to loan pieces from her personal collection to a customer in order to illustrate her proposals for the customer's offices and the pieces were stolen from the insured's car while she was transporting them for this purpose, the court held that they were personal property and allowed recovery under the insured's personal policy. *Singer v. Nat. Fire Ins. Co. of Hartford*, 110 N.J. Super. 59, 264 A.2d 270 (1970).

Some types of policies will not cover artwork unless it is specifically mentioned in the insurance contract. This can be done either by identifying the artwork as a class within the clause that specifies the property covered or by separately scheduling the items, that is, including an itemized list of the pieces in the insured's collection. Such foresight will result in higher premiums but, in the long run, may avoid the loss of money and time in litigation.

In *Stone v. Rullo Agency*, 40 A.D.3d 1185, 834 N.Y.S.2d 588 (3d Dep't 2007), the court held that the plaintiff, who testified he never read the insurance policy, was nevertheless bound by its provisions excluding replacement coverage for "articles of art or rarity that cannot be duplicated." This problem could have been avoided had Mr. Stone scheduled the items and paid the necessary additional premium.

In comprehensive or all-risk policies, any type of loss or damage to the insured property will generally be covered, but even these types of policies may have exclusions and limitations. Thus, recovery was denied in *Plaza Equities Corp. v. Aetna Casualty and Surety Co.*, 372 F. Supp. 1325 (S.D.N.Y. 1974), when a large metal sculpture collapsed. Although the policy was designated an all-risk policy, it specifically excluded loss "directly attributable to error, omission or deficiency in design, specifications, workmanship or materials." Some courts will deny recovery for this type of loss even in the absence of a specific exclusion. When a gemstone insured under a comprehensive policy cracked because of an inherent defect, the court in *Chute v. North River Insurance Co.*, 172 Minn. 13, 214 N.W. 473 (1927), denied recovery. It held that the insurance contract was not a warranty of the quality and durability of the property insured but, rather, was a simple indemnity against loss or damage from fortuitous and extraneous circumstances. If the parties had intended to cover damage due to inherent defects, the court reasoned, they would have specifically written that coverage into the policy.

In fire policies, a distinction is often made between fires that are hostile and those that are friendly. A fire burning in a stove or a lamp is considered a friendly fire, and damage caused by these fires as a result of negligent management is considered outside the scope of the policy. Thus, damage caused by smoke from a lamp that is turned up too high or from a defective stove or furnace is not recoverable, as long as the fire remains confined to the place it is supposed to be. When the fire escapes to someplace other than its intended confines, however, a friendly fire may become hostile. Thus, when a chimney fire causes damage, the insurer must pay the loss. A friendly fire may also become hostile if it burns out of control.

An indemnity contract does not make the insurer liable to pay for all remote consequences of the insured event. Rather, the insurer is liable only for consequences that are immediate and within the terms of the contract. If an individual is insured for fire damage to his or her house and possessions, the insurance company is not obligated to pay for fire damage to a neighbor's house that occurs because the insured's house caught on fire. However, in *Gowans v. Northwestern Pacific Indemnity Co.*, 260 Or. 618, 489 P.2d 947 (1971), the court held that the insurance company must reimburse an individual insured for theft for a reward that led to the recovery of the stolen property. Ransoms have also been held recoverable. See *Kraut v. Morgan & Brother Manhattan Storage Co.*, 381 N.Y.S.2d 25, 343 N.E.2d 744 (N.Y. 1976). However, in order to prevent collusion between the insured and the alleged thief, many insurance policies require the insured to obtain approval of any ransom offer from the insurer. In addition, some policies provide that any disclosure of ransom coverage by the insured is grounds for cancellation, since disclosure of such coverage would make the insurance company quite vulnerable.

AB Recur Finans v. Nordstern Ins. Co. of North America, 130 F. Supp. 2d 596 (S.D.N.Y. 2001), concerned misdelivery of a painting by a bailee. The court determined that the mistaken delivery was, in fact, covered, as it resulted in a loss to the bailor.

C. RECOVERY AND REMEDIES

If a loss occurs, the amount of recovery will be primarily dependent upon the terms of the insurance contract. In a "valued" policy, the amount of recovery will be predetermined and, absent fraud or mistake, is conclusive upon the parties. In *Art Masters*

Associates, Ltd. v. United Parcel Service, 566 N.Y.S.2d 184, 567 N.E.2d 226 (N.Y. 1990), a gallery shipped six original Erte paintings via UPS to Art Masters. The gallery paid UPS an additional $2.25 in order to insure the paintings for $999.99. When the package was lost, Art Masters sued UPS for $27,000, the actual value of the paintings. The court held that UPS was not required to indemnify Art Masters for more than the declared value of the package. In an "open" or "unvalued" policy, the insured is indemnified for the full current worth of the property up to a specified policy limit. Many insurance policies also have what is known as a "co-insurance" clause. This clause requires the insured to carry insurance on the item for a certain percentage of the value (usually 80 percent). When a loss occurs and the required amount of insurance is in effect, the insured may recover the full amount of the loss up to the face value of the policy. Failure to carry the insurance at the required level makes the insured a co-insurer with the insurance company. Then the insurance company is not required to pay the full value of the policy but, rather, will be required to pay only a percentage based on the percentage of coverage to the actual value.

Determining the current worth of insured property creates many disputes. Insurance companies frequently require an appraisal of the item when insurance is first procured, but this does not necessarily mean that the insurer is bound to pay that amount since the appraiser is considered an agent of the insured and the amount merely suggestive. Many policies contain appraisal and arbitration clauses. These clauses provide procedures outside the courtroom for the resolution of disputes over value. The appraisers are required to determine the value of the items as claimed by the insured. Thus, the appraiser's award was overturned in *Safeco Ins. Co. of America v. Sharma*, 160 Cal. App. 3d 1060, 207 Cal. Rptr. 104 (2d Dist. 1984), when the appraisers valued 36 miniature paintings as an unmatched collection rather than as a matched set from the Bundi School, India, as the insured claimed. In other cases, if a suit is brought over the amount of recovery, proof of value usually becomes a battle between expert witnesses. If the proof is insufficient and the loss is total, some courts may allow only the original cost of the item. For coin collections, where the market value fluctuates radically, courts may allow recovery of a catalogue price rather than the fair market value.

If the loss is only partial, such as where a painting is damaged but not destroyed, the insurance company may apply a standard formula under which a flat percentage of the value of the property is offered for repairs and depreciation. Such a formula may not adequately compensate the owner of works of art, however, since the same amount of damage may affect the value of each piece in an art collection quite differently. A unique object may be repaired without diminishing its value, but damaged objects that are not original or unique may be virtually worthless. A better method of determining the amount of damage to a work of art is to have an expert evaluate each item individually.

SEC. C RECOVERY AND REMEDIES

If the amount offered by the insurance company is predetermined by a valued policy, the amount offered may be varied only if there was fraud or a mistake in the insurance contract. If the policy contains written errors, the usual contractual remedies of rescission and reformation may be available. Reformation is allowed only where the contract does not express the actual agreement of the parties. This agreement may be based on an oral contract or modification if no statute requires contracts of insurance to be in writing, but the discrepancy must in any event be material. Usually, reformation is not available if the mistake was unilateral, although some statutes authorize it if the other party knew or suspected there was a mistake. Courts also seem to require less proof of mistake for reformation of an insurance policy than they demand for reformation of other contracts, possibly due to the typically unequal bargaining positions of the parties, the extent of the insured's reliance, and the recognition that insurance contracts are classic contracts of adhesion. Nevertheless, the prudent collector should examine all documents carefully to assure that the policy properly reflects his or her intentions.

If a collector innocently insures a work of art that is discovered to be a forgery when a loss occurs and then recovers, as a result of the discovery, the lower value from the insurer, he or she may also be able to recover the excess insurance premiums paid based on the assumption that the work had a higher value. If, however, before the loss the piece was authenticated by an expert who was either mistaken or acting in collusion with the seller, the insured's remedy is against the expert, not the insurer. Thus, in *Orient Ins. Co. v. Dunla*, 193 Ga. 241, 17 S.E.2d 703 (1941), an insured tried to recover excess premiums paid to insure a pearl necklace which was worth substantially less than its insured value. Both parties believed that the necklace was worth $60,000, and the item was insured for this amount. Notwithstanding the mutual mistake by the parties as to the necklace's true value of $60, the court refused to order a refund of the insured's excess premiums. The court reasoned that if a loss had occurred prior to discovering the incorrect valuation, the company would have paid the insured value, and, thus, it had assumed that risk. Reformation of the policy and return of the excess premiums, the court stated, would be inequitable in such a case.

In *Flaum v. Great N. Ins. Co.*, 28 Misc. 3d 1042, 904 N.Y.S.2d 647 (Sup. Ct. Westchester Cnty. 2010), the court found that the discovery that a painting was a forgery did not result in a "physical loss" under the plaintiffs' insurance policy. They had purchased a "Renoir" painting for $50,000 and had it insured for $350,000. When an auction-house employee advised plaintiffs that the painting was a forgery, the insureds placed a $525,000 claim with their insurer for the "loss" of value of the painting.

A party who misrepresents the true value of an insured item may find that he or she is not covered at all. In such situations, the insurance contract may be rescinded, as it was in *Merchants Fire Assurance Corp. v. Lattimore*, 263 F.2d 232 (9th Cir. 1959). Lattimore had declared that the value of her unscheduled personal property was $9,950, although she knew it was really worth $36,500. The court voided the policy, citing the rule that each party to an insurance contract must in good faith communicate all material facts to the other party.

When a sponsor of a foundation that distributes fine art from Russia and the Ukraine had seven paintings shipped via UPS to California from Odessa, UPS advised an agent of the shipper that it must rely on the custom commission's valuation of $558 rather than the $60,000 that the shipper believed to be the approximate sales value of the paintings in the United States. When the packages were lost in transit, the shipper was able to recover only $558. The court held that even if UPS refused to insure the packages for more than $558, as the shipper's agent alleged, UPS had complied with applicable law by limiting available insurance to the value listed on the customs documents. The court further noted that the carrier had provided a fair opportunity to purchase greater coverage, though not up to the full value of the items. *Kesel v. United Parcel Service, Inc.*, 339 F.3d 849 (9th Cir. 2003). See also *Kemper Ins. Cos. v. Federal Express Corp.*, 252 F.3d 509 (1st Cir. 2001), *cert. denied*, 534 U.S. 1020 (2001), where the carrier limited coverage for "items of extraordinary value" to $500. In both cases, the courts noted that the shipper could have purchased additional coverage from a third-party insurer if desired.

While this chapter has focused on insuring the physical work of art, there is another insurance issue of importance to those in the art field. In many intellectual property infringement cases, defense is being tendered to the insurance company pursuant to the "advertising injury" clause of a general liability policy. Trademark infringement cases are often specifically identified in the insurance policy, but in some instances courts have ruled that patent and copyright infringements are covered by the advertising injury provisions as well. The insurance company in such a situation is thus required to defend the claim of infringement at its expense.

Obtaining an insurance policy that accurately reflects the circumstances and meets the needs of the party contracting for insurance is vital. When art is insured, it is especially important that the policy cover all the contingencies that may cause the work to be damaged, destroyed, or lost. Where a collector does not elect to self-insure, care in selecting and periodically updating the insurance policy is a vital aspect of protecting an investment in art.

CHAPTER 8
TAX PROBLEMS: COLLECTORS AND DEALERS

A. PROPERLY CHARACTERIZING INCOME

An individual about to engage in the purchase, sale, or other disposition of art should consider the potential tax consequences. Transactions involving works of art may be taxed under the income tax, gift tax, or estate tax laws. Since different rates and methods of reducing tax liability are available depending on how a particular transaction is structured, these different forms of tax should be analyzed before deciding on a particular method of acquiring or disposing of art. With a basic understanding of effective tax planning, a careful collector or dealer may be able to save a good deal of money.

The first step in determining income tax is identifying gross income. Section 61 of the Internal Revenue Code (IRC) defines gross income as "all income from whatever source derived." This is a broad definition, and it specifically encompasses "gains derived from dealings in property." The amount of the realized gain on the sale of a work of art is calculated by subtracting the "basis" of the item from the price received for it. Usually, the basis is the amount the seller originally spent to purchase the item; if, however, it was acquired as a gift, the basis generally will be the same as the donor's basis for the purposes of calculating gain, and if it was bequeathed, then the basis will be the fair market value of the item at the time of the decedent's death. With these and a few other exceptions, gain realized can be loosely thought of as profit on resale.

Usually, the amount of gain "realized" is "recognized," which means that the gain must be included in the taxpayer's gross income. There are a few important nonrecognition provisions, such as IRC § 1031, which provides for the nonrecognition of gains realized on the exchange of like-kind property held for productive use or investment; and § 1033, which provides for the nonrecognition of gains realized on the involuntary conversion of property destroyed due to theft, seizure, requisition, or condemnation. In these situations, no tax is due in the year of the gain; instead, the tax is postponed until a later transaction in which gain is recognized. Once gain is recognized, however, the gain is subject to taxation. The rate of tax is determined by whether the gain is characterized as either "ordinary income" or "capital gain." This characterization is important because capital gains are taxed at an effective rate that is lower than the rate for ordinary income. Whereas ordinary income may be taxed as high as 39.6 percent, capital gains are generally taxed at 15 or 20 percent, though the tax may be as high as 28 percent for certain types of property, and taxpayers in the lowest brackets, pay no capital gains tax. The gain on collectibles is taxed at the higher rate, that is, at 28 percent.

Net capital gain is defined by IRC § 1222 as the excess of net long-term capital gain (i.e., the excess of

SEC. A   PROPERLY CHARACTERIZING INCOME   129

long-term capital gain over long-term capital losses) over net short-term capital losses (i.e., the excess of short-term capital losses over short-term capital gains). Thus, depending on the taxpayer's other gains and losses, a capital gain generally occurs when he or she sells or exchanges, at a gain, a capital asset held for more than one year.

In order to have a capital gain, the taxpayer must sell or exchange a capital asset. A capital asset is defined by IRC § 1221 as "property held by the taxpayer (whether or not connected with his or her trade or business)," but excludes, among other things, stock in trade, inventory, and property held by the taxpayer primarily for sale to customers in the ordinary course of trade or business. Thus, dealers who are systematically engaged in buying and selling art generally cannot characterize their income on such sales as capital gains, because such transactions are basically sales of inventory.

One way of reducing taxes by spreading income is the installment method of accounting. If a collector sells a work for a negotiable note or other deferred payment obligation that is essentially equivalent to cash, the collector can report the income on an installment basis. Dealers cannot take advantage of this method, since it does not apply to the sale of inventory. For more information on the installment method, see Chapter 9, *infra*.

Collectors and dealers should be aware that, while this chapter focuses primarily on federal tax law, forty-three states levy individual income taxes, and nearly 5,000 jurisdictions in 17 states impose some type of local income tax.

B. DEDUCTIONS

Once income is characterized as ordinary income or capital gain, the taxpayer must determine how much of it is taxable. To do this, the taxpayer is permitted to deduct certain trade or business expenses ("above-the-line deductions") to arrive at adjusted gross income. Other itemized deductions ("below-the-line deductions") are subtracted from adjusted gross income to arrive at taxable income. Taxpayers have no constitutional guarantee of deductions; thus, if there is no specific legislation allowing them, there are no adjustments to gross income. For this reason, courts typically construe deductions as limited rights which only Congress may grant.

There are two categories of deductible expenses available to collectors and dealers: expenses for the production of income (IRC § 212) and business expenses (IRC § 162). The latter is used by taxpayers who carry on a "trade or business." The trade or business deduction is often more advantageous than the deduction for income-producing expenses, since income-producing expenses are sometimes deducted "below" the line from adjusted gross income and thus can be deducted only to the extent they exceed two percent of adjusted gross income, as well as the taxpayer's standard deduction (IRC § 63). In addition, income-producing expense deductions are disallowed under the alternative minimum tax, and claiming this type of deduction increases a taxpayer's chance of being audited.

In order to be deductible under IRC § 162 or § 212, the expense must be incurred in connection with a business or investment activity rather than for personal reasons. This distinction presents what may be one of the most complex classification problems in the entire tax field. It is extremely difficult to classify a particular transaction when the activity has characteristics of a hobby, such as collecting art. IRC § 183 provides that an activity is presumed to be engaged in for profit if the activity produced more income than deductions for three or more of five consecutive years, but where this presumption is not available, courts look at other factors.

Some courts have considered the nature of the enterprise and its financial success, such as in *Cecil v. Commissioner*, 100 F.2d 896 (4th Cir. 1939), where the court stated the test was that "the gross receipts must have substantial relation to the expenses of the operation, and the facts as a whole must exclude a finding that the enterprise was only a scheme for tax evasion." In *Cecil*, the expenses of maintaining and operating a museum were held deductible as trade or business expenses. On the other hand, in *Wrightsman & Wrightsman v. United States,* 192 Ct. Cl. 722, 428 F.2d 1316 (1970), the court held that expenses related to acquiring and maintaining a sizeable art collection were not deductible. Although there was evidence that the taxpayers invested in art because they were wary of other investment vehicles, that they kept meticulous records of their activities, and that much of their time was spent away from their residences in which most of the art was stored, the court focused on the facts that a great deal of the taxpayers' personal lives revolved around their art collection and collecting activities and that they made extensive personal use of their collection. The court recognized that there was an investment purpose to the taxpayers' activities but found that the taxpayers had not met their burden of proof to show that investment was their primary motive.

These and other factors now have been codified in the Treasury Regulations. Treas. Reg. § 1.183–2 provides that the factors relevant to whether an activity is engaged in for profit are as follows: (1) the businesslike manner in which the taxpayer carries on the activity; (2) the expertise of the taxpayer or his or her advisors; (3) the time and effort spent on the activity; (4) the expectation that assets used in the activity will appreciate; (5) the taxpayer's success in other activities; (6) the income and loss record of the activity; (7) the amount of occasional profits, if any, which are earned; (8) the taxpayer's income or capital from other sources; and (9) elements of personal pleasure or recreation. No one factor is considered determinative.

In addition to showing that an expense was not incurred for personal reasons, the taxpayer must show that the expense is "ordinary and necessary" and that it is a current expense rather than a capital investment. Generally, the "ordinary and necessary" requirement is open-ended and, under IRC § 162, specifically includes a reasonable allowance for salaries or other compensation, traveling expenses, and rentals. Because these types of expenditures create benefits only in the current tax year, they also are current expenses. However, § 263 disallows deductions for the cost of acquiring property whose useful life extends substantially beyond the close of the taxable year. These are capital investments, and since the cost of such investments represents a payment by the taxpayer for economic benefits that will accrue in the future, the deduction must be spread over the theoretical useful life of the property. Thus, expenses incurred to extend the useful life of capitalized property or to alter its function, such as the installation of heat and humidity controls in a building for art conservation purposes, cannot be deducted as current expenses but, rather, are added to the property's basis and then amortized over time. By contrast, simple repairs and maintenance, such as repairing a chipped frame on a painting, are deductible as current expenses. For many small businesses, however, an immediate deduction can be taken for certain capital expenses. In 2016, up to $500,000 of such purchases may be "expensed" for the year and need not be depreciated at all. Note that some states have set their own limits for immediate deductions instead of pegging them to the federal limit.

Losses are deductible when they are incurred in a trade or business, in any transaction entered into for profit, or as a result of fire, storm, shipwreck, other casualty, or theft. IRC § 165. If a work of art is otherwise considered a capital asset and is sold for a price which is lower than the original purchase price, the collector can claim the difference between what he or she paid for the piece and the amount for which he or she resold it as a capital loss. It should be noted that this capital gains treatment will only be available if the work was purchased as an investment rather than for personal enjoyment. This provision is especially important where, for example, the collector innocently purchases an art object that he or she later discovers is a worthless forgery. Capital losses are first used to offset capital gains in the year incurred. Any additional capital losses are deductible from ordinary income up to a maximum amount of $3,000 per year ($1,500 per year for married people filing separately), although any excess can be carried forward to the following taxable year. IRC § 1211 provides a formula to determine the exact amount of the deduction. The sale should be with complete disclosure regarding the work's authenticity in order for the taxpayer to avoid incurring liability for misrepresentation, breach of warranty, or the like. See Chapter 6, *supra*. All ordinary losses can be deducted from ordinary income dollar for dollar and, therefore, are more useful to the taxpayer than capital losses.

Taxpayers can deduct large casualty losses whether or not they occur in connection with a trade or business or investment activity. If a work of art is stolen and the taxpayer is not compensated for it by insurance or otherwise and the work is not used for a business purpose, he or she may deduct the entire amount of the loss except for the first $100 to the extent that this and other casualty losses exceed 10 percent of his or her adjusted gross income. To qualify, the taxpayer must prove that his or her property was taken illegally under the laws of the state where the taking occurred and that it was taken with criminal intent. Further information on casualty losses can be obtained from the Internal Revenue Service Publication No. 584, *Disaster and Casualty Loss Workbook*. On the other hand, if the taxpayer does receive insurance money as a result of a casualty loss and the property was insured for an amount greater than the taxpayer's basis, IRC § 1033 allows him or her to elect nonrecognition of the gain, so long as he or she reinvests the insurance proceeds within two tax years of the loss in property similar or related in service or use.

While not technically a deduction, another way collectors can save taxes is through laws exempting artwork from taxes in certain circumstances. Nevada passed a law in 2003 exempting "fine art for public display" from personal property taxes (NRS § 361.068).

C. CHARITABLE CONTRIBUTIONS

Collectors and dealers may take a deduction from adjusted gross income for works of art that they donate to certain qualified charitable organizations. In fact, as the value of art collections have gone up, owners reluctant to take a huge hit in capital gains taxes are choosing to donate to museums instead of selling. The aggregate amount of such deductions is governed by certain percentage limitations. Corporations may deduct a maximum of 10 percent of their taxable income. Individuals may deduct up to

50 percent of their adjusted gross income for contributions to churches, educational organizations, governmental units, and other defined organizations, but may deduct only 30 percent for contributions to other charities. Furthermore, contributors of capital gain property, such as artwork, are limited to a 30 percent deduction for contributions to churches, schools, and so forth (or alternatively, 50 percent, if deducting the tax basis of the property rather than the fair market value), but may deduct only 20 percent of contributions made to other charities. Some types of contributions are not deductible. Individuals asked to donate their time should know that no charitable deduction is allowed for the value of services, although out-of-pocket expenses incurred in performing the services can be deducted. The IRS requires a written statement from a charity acknowledging the taxpayer's out-of-pocket expenses if the taxpayer's expenses on behalf of that charity total more than $250 in a year. A gift of a future interest in tangible personal property is deductible only after all intervening interests in the use, possession, or enjoyment of the property either have expired or are held by someone other than the donor or his or her family. However, it is possible to transfer an undivided present interest in property and still be eligible for a charitable deduction. Treas. Reg. § 1.170A–5(a)(2) gives the specific example of a contribution of an undivided one-quarter interest in a painting to which the donee is entitled to possession during three months of each year. The contribution is treated as having been made upon the receipt by the donee of a formally executed and acknowledged

deed of gift; however, the period of initial possession by the donee may not be deferred in time for more than one year.

Under current law, a charitable deduction for income tax purposes generally is not allowed for the transfer of an original work of art to charity if the copyright is retained by the donor or transferred to a member of the donor's family. This is because when the donor transfers some specific rights and retains other rights, the transfer is not considered a contribution of an undivided interest. Yet, for the purposes of estate and gift tax charitable deductions, a work of art and its copyright are considered separate properties. Estates of decedents may take a charitable deduction for the transfer to charity of a work of art even if the copyright is retained by the estate or transferred to a noncharitable recipient.

Collectors must also be careful when imposing conditions and restrictions on charitable gifts or risk losing the charitable deduction. The restriction or condition must be placed on the gift at the time of the gift, and any restriction or condition that affects the marketability or use of the gift, such as deaccessioning restrictions, are likely to negatively impact the amount of the donor's charitable donation.

The amount of a particular charitable deduction is generally considered to be its fair market value but may have to be reduced depending on the character of the contributed property in the hands of the donor and its use by the donee. If the donated property would have produced short-term capital gains or ordinary income if sold, the deduction for its donation is limited to the property's adjusted basis. If the property is given to a private foundation or if it is tangible personal property and its use is unrelated to the purpose or function of the donee (such as a gift of livestock to a museum or a gift of a painting to Heifer International), then the amount of the deduction is reduced by the amount of any gain that would have been realized had the property been sold.

Donations valued in excess of $5,000 must be substantiated by a qualified appraisal document made within 60 days of the donation, which includes a description of the item, its physical condition, a statement that it was made for tax purposes, and the date of contribution, the terms of any agreement concerning the item made by the donor and donee, the appraiser's name, address and qualifications, the date of appraisal, the appraised value, the method of appraisal, and the basis used in determining value. Treas. Reg. § 1–1704–13. It is often the case with donations of art that experts disagree as to the fair market value of a particular piece. Fortunately, the taxpayer may deduct the cost of appraisal fees for a charitable contribution under IRC § 212(3), which allows a deduction for all ordinary and necessary expenses incurred in connection with the determination, collection, or refund of any tax. Rev. Rul. 67–461, 1967–2 C.B. 125 (1967), but as with any tax dispute, the taxpayer has the burden of proving that the amount claimed as a deduction is appropriate.

Moreover, if a work is substantially overvalued, the taxpayer may be assessed a penalty. IRC § 6662 provides a penalty in the form of an addition to tax, assessed against an individual, a closely-held corporation or a personal service corporation for underpayments of income taxes that are attributable to valuation overstatements. The penalty applies if the value of the property as claimed on the taxpayer's return is 200 percent or more of its correctly determined value and the underpayment of tax attributable to the total of all overvaluations made by the taxpayer for the taxable year amounts to $5,000 or more. The amount of the penalty is 20 percent of the underpayment if the claimed property value is 150% or more of its true value. A 40 percent penalty applies if the claimed property value is 200 percent or more of its true value. Thus, there are strong incentives for taxpayers to value works donated to charities as accurately as possible.

Valuation problems customarily fall into two general categories: Either the experts disagree with each other and the IRS on the value of the work, or the authenticity of the work is questioned. In order to resolve such problems, the IRS has established valuation guidelines, as well as special panels to review the deductions taken by the donor. These art advisory panels are often inconsistent, typically recommend lowering the value for works claimed by taxpayers as charitable donations and increasing the values for works contained within decedents' estates. When Alexander Calder died in 1976, the art advisory panel valued 1,292 gouache paintings in his estate at $897,230. Six weeks after Calder's death, his widow received 1,226 of the paintings and made gifts in trust of them for the couple's children and grandchildren. For gift tax, she valued them, as did the estate, at $897,230, but the IRS insisted that the art's value was $2.3 million and assessed Mrs. Calder for $459,419 more in gift tax.

After the death of art dealer Ileana Sonnabend, the IRS appraised "Canyon," by Robert Rauschenberg, at $65 million, although the artwork cannot legally be sold because it includes a taxidermied bald eagle. Sonnabend's heirs were able to work out an arrangement with the IRS whereby they avoided the $29.2 million tax bill (plus penalties) by donating the work to the Museum of Modern Art in New York and foregoing the tax deduction.

When the IRS art advisory panel determines that an overvaluation has resulted in an underpayment of tax, not only is the taxpayer liable for penalties, but the appraiser can, under certain circumstances, be liable for civil and criminal penalties.

D. ESTATE PLANNING

As the *Calder* and *Sonnabend* cases demonstrate, the importance of planning and providing for the disposition of art collections after the owner's death cannot be overemphasized. Collections present special problems not encountered with other kinds of personal property. A collection of a group of pieces may be more valuable if left intact rather than being split up among several beneficiaries. A given beneficiary may not desire to own works of art with their attendant maintenance costs and lack of liquidity. On the other hand, another beneficiary may

SEC. D ESTATE PLANNING 141

desire to keep a work of art, even though its monetary value is minimal.

The typical will disposes of tangible personal property by bequeathing it to the surviving spouse or, if the spouse does not survive the testator, to the testator's surviving descendants. If the property passes to the decedent's spouse, IRC § 2056 provides for an unlimited marital deduction for both estate and gift tax purposes. Income tax will be owed only if the spouse disposes of the property in his or her lifetime for more than its value at the time of death. If the property is not disposed of, it will be included in the spouse's estate at its fair market value at the date of the spouse's death, or, at the spouse's executor's election under IRC § 2032, within six months of the spouse's death.

If property is bequeathed to the testator's spouse, care must be taken that the transfer is not a terminable interest. Such an interest occurs under IRC § 2056 when the spouse's interest in property will terminate upon the occurrence or nonoccurrence of an event or upon the lapse of time, when another interest in the same property passes from the decedent to a third party for less than adequate consideration, and when the third party is able to possess or enjoy a part of the property upon termination of the spouse's interest. However, the IRC allows "qualified terminable interest" property to pass to the spouse tax free. Qualified terminable interest property is defined as property passing to a decedent's spouse in which the spouse has a qualifying income interest for life. If the spouse so elects and the conditions of a qualifying income interest are met, the entire value of the transferred property will qualify for the marital deduction.

There are a myriad of ways for a collector to reduce his or her estate tax liability other than relying solely on the marital deduction. In addition to being able to use the marital deduction, each individual is given a unified tax credit for gift tax liability during his or her lifetime, and any unused credit is applied to his or her estate tax liability. IRC § 2010. Currently up to $5.45 million worth of property may pass from a decedent without using the marital deduction. States with inheritance or estate taxes typically have lower exclusion amounts.

As noted in the preceding section of this chapter, charitable contributions enable the donor to take a deduction for all or part of the value of the property donated to charity. At the same time, such *inter vivos* transfers reduce the amount of property left in the collector's taxable estate. Noncharitable gifts also reduce the size of the collector's estate. In addition, under IRC § 2503, the first $14,000 of gifts to each person in each taxable year (other than gifts of future interests in property) made by an individual are excluded from gift taxes. A married individual whose spouse consents to the application of § 2513 is entitled to a $28,000 exclusion per person per year. Beyond this, there is no difference between the gift tax rates and the estate tax rates, so no real tax benefits to the collector or his or her estate will be realized by making an *inter vivos* gift unless the property is expected to appreciate substantially from

SEC. D   ESTATE PLANNING   143

the time of the gift to the time of the collector's death. If the tax consequences to the donee are also taken into account, however, it may be advantageous to leave appreciated property in the collector's estate and let the property pass to the donee upon the collector's death. The donee will then take the property with a fair market value basis (as of the date of death or six months thereafter) under IRC § 1014, thus reducing the donee's taxable gain if he or she later sells the property.

Care must be taken to avoid certain types of gift transactions occurring within the three years prior to the collector's death if his or her death can be anticipated. Under IRC § 2035(c), if the decedent or his or her spouse has made gifts that diminish the decedent's gross estate by the payment of gift taxes, the amount of each gift is includable in his or her gross estate. In addition, under IRC § 2035(d)(2), if a transfer of property made by a decedent within three years of his or her death is a transfer of property in which he or she has retained a life estate (§ 2036), a transfer taking effect at death (§ 2037), a revocable transfer during his or her life (§ 2038), or a transfer of the right to receive life insurance proceeds (§ 2042), then the value of the property transferred will be included in the decedent's gross estate.

Trusts also can be an attractive way of reducing estate tax liability. For estate tax purposes, property transferred into a properly structured trust will be excluded from the donor's gross estate so long as the donor does not die within three years of the transfer (IRC § 2035(a)) and so long as he or she does not retain a prohibited interest in or power over the trust (IRC §§ 2036–2038, 2041). For income tax purposes, the income produced by the trust if the property is sold will not be taxable to the donor but will be taxable to the trust or, if distributed, to the beneficiaries of the trust, assuming the trust is properly structured under the grantor trust rules in IRC §§ 671–677.

For very large estates, the practice of leaving property in trust for one's children, grandchildren, and great-grandchildren and thereby avoiding both estate and gift taxes as the property is enjoyed by successive generations is no longer possible. Since 1976, the IRC has imposed a tax on "generation skipping trusts," defined as a trust with beneficiaries in more than one generation below the generation of the grantor.

E. TAX SHELTERS

Tax shelters do not ordinarily relieve a taxpayer of the obligation of paying tax; rather, they are designed to postpone or defer tax liability. They generally accomplish this in two ways: (1) postponing current tax liability by accelerating deductions in the early years of the investment, rather than matching deductions with the income as it is generated, and (2) using leverage to increase the basis upon which the tax benefits are calculated without increasing the cash cost of the investment. These devices utilize loopholes in the tax law. Although shelters involving art can be very advantageous to the taxpayer, Congress and the IRS are extremely diligent in closing such loopholes as they are exploited. The reader should, therefore, be aware that this area is very dynamic, and should keep in regular contact with his or her attorney or CPA.

One of the major limitations of tax shelters is the at-risk provision of IRC § 465. Without detailing the section, it may be said that § 465 covers most taxpayers (including individuals, partners, S corporations and limited liability companies (LLCs) electing taxation as partnerships but excluding regular corporations) and a wide variety of activities (including activities that are part of a trade or business or activities that are engaged in for the production of income). The section limits a taxpayer's deduction of losses to the amount the taxpayer has at risk and could actually lose from the activity. The IRS applies different rules to different types of taxpayers, but, generally speaking, the amount considered to be at risk is the amount of cash the taxpayer contributes to the activity, the adjusted basis of property contributed to the activity, and the amount borrowed by the taxpayer for the activity on which he or she is personally liable.

The at-risk provision affects tax shelters in the following manner: In a typical example, for a stated purchase price the investor in art reproductions would receive the right to (1) an entire limited edition of prints, (2) the original master lithographic plate (although the artist may insist on the right to deface or "strike" the plate in order to make certain that the number of prints will be limited), and (3) the copyright in the master, including the exclusive right to use, manufacture, sell, distribute, promote, advertise, and license the master or the prints. If the purchase price were $100,000, it would normally be payable with a 10 percent cash investment, and the balance of $90,000 would be payable in the form of a note payable out of the profits derived from sale of the prints and the ancillary rights to market the image. The note used may be either a recourse note, which is one bearing the personal liability of the drawer, or a nonrecourse note, which is one not bearing the personal liability of the drawer but providing the holder security against the prints themselves.

If the note is a recourse note, the depreciation tax benefits would be calculated on the basis of the total $100,000 purchase price. If, on the other hand, the $90,000 note is nonrecourse, only $10,000 would be at risk. Under § 465, the losses stemming from the depreciation deduction (assuming the shelter produced no income) would be limited to the $10,000 at-risk amount. Those planning to be involved in these types of activities should consult with a tax advisor since there are additional limitations under the passive active rules.

In addition to the at-risk limitation, there are several other potential pitfalls to this type of tax shelter. For example, IRC § 168 specifies different depreciation rates for property in different useful life classes. The investor must be careful that the IRS does not conclude, as it did in Rev. Rul. 79–432, 1979–2 C.B. 289 (1979), that the property, there a lithographic plate master, is not at least eligible as three-year property. Similarly, IRC § 469 accords less attractive treatment to income produced from passive activity.

Certain property can also be subject to depreciation recapture. If depreciated tangible personal property is resold and the value of the property exceeds its adjusted basis, the depreciation is recaptured under IRC § 1245, which requires that the amount of gain attributable to the depreciation be characterized as ordinary income rather than as capital gain.

Another means by which a taxpayer can shelter income is to donate appreciated property. If, for example, an individual is lucky enough to purchase a valuable work of art for an amount less than its fair market value, he or she may hold the piece for one year and then donate it to a qualified charity. The tax deduction which may be taken for this donation is based on the fair market value of the work on the date of the donation. As discussed in Section C of this chapter, valuation is an important consideration, and a substantial penalty can be imposed if an underpayment of tax occurs as a result of overvaluation.

A taxpayer may take this donation concept one step further and set up a systematic plan of donations involving limited edition prints or books. In this situation, the investor purchases the prints, probably at a discount, or the books at cost, holds them for 12 months plus one day, and then donates them to museums or charities. He or she then may expect to take a charitable deduction in the amount of fair market value of the prints on the date of contribution and in the amount of retail list price of the books. However, two revenue rulings make it clear that the investor's activity with respect to these types of art shelters makes him or her substantially equivalent to a dealer who sells the objects in the ordinary course of a trade or business. Rev. Rul. 79–419, 1979–2 C.B. 107 (1979) and Rev. Rul. 79–256, 1979–2 C.B. 105 (1979). Therefore, the items contributed would be treated as ordinary income property held by the donor for sale to customers in the ordinary course of the donor's trade or business, regardless of whether the donor is actually engaged in such a trade or business.

Under IRC § 170, the taxpayer's charitable deduction would be reduced by the amount of gain that would not have been long-term capital gain had the objects been sold by the investor at their fair market value. Instead of taking a deduction in the amount of the fair market value on the date of contribution, under Treas. Reg. § 1.170A–1(e)(1), the taxpayer may take only a deduction in the amount of his or her cost. The IRS evidently will look at bulk acquisitions and subsequent disposal of substantial parts of, for instance, a limited edition of prints and probably will find that the activities are equivalent to those engaged in by an art dealer.

Another type of tax shelter involves an investment tax credit available under IRC § 46 for qualified rehabilitation expenditures. This is one of the few shelters which Congress appears to favor. It is a means by which the legislature can encourage rehabilitation activities that it deems beneficial. In these situations, the taxpayer deducts the tax credit directly from taxes owed. The amount of investment tax credit is 20 percent for certified historic structures and 10 percent for other qualifying structures. To qualify, most buildings must be nonresidential at the time rehabilitation begins; however, certified historic buildings can be either residential or nonresidential. The building also must have been placed in service before the beginning of the rehabilitation, and it must have been substantially rehabilitated, with 50 percent or more of the existing external walls retained as external walls. Also, the taxpayer must elect to use a straight-line method of depreciation rather than accelerated methods. For certified historic structures, approval of the rehabilitation must be obtained from the Secretary of the Interior.

Other tax shelters include freeports and temporary museum loans. Collectors can avoid paying taxes and duties on artwork during the time it is stored in a "freeport," which is a secure warehouse located in one of the free trade zones offered by many countries. In addition, in some cases, a collector can take advantage of a use-tax exemption in his or her home state simply by loaning newly purchased artwork to a museum in a state without a use tax (Alaska, Delaware, Montana, New Hampshire, Oregon) for a set period, usually three months. Unfortunately for collectors, not all states have a "first use" exemption.

Of course, collectors need to be sure that their plans to avoid or reduce taxes are legal. After Tyco

International's former chief executive L. Dennis Kozlowski was accused of failing to pay more than $1 million in state and city sales taxes on art purchases, the Manhattan District Attorney conducted a sales tax investigation beginning in 2002, resulting in numerous art dealers being charged with tax fraud and the collection of millions of dollars in unpaid sales taxes. The dealers were falsely stating that the purchases had been shipped out of state in order to avoid the payment of state sales tax.

There are many other ways to structure tax shelters and to reduce one's tax liability. New schemes are constantly being devised by creative lawyers and accountants. As indicated above, not all of these schemes produce the effects intended; when they do, the tax laws frequently are changed. Collectors, dealers, and investors in art, therefore, should plan their transactions carefully. With a proper awareness of the tax laws, significant amounts of money can be saved.

CHAPTER 9
TAX PROBLEMS: ARTISTS

A. PROPERLY CHARACTERIZING INCOME

Artists rarely think of themselves as being engaged in business. Many go to great lengths to avoid commercialism. The tax laws, however, treat the professional artist as a business person, and, as such, the artist is subject to many of the same tax provisions discussed in Chapter 8, *supra*, for collectors and dealers. Yet, artists may have erratic earning patterns and other income characteristics that other business people do not have. Many professional artists do not work for fixed wages, and their actual income can fluctuate radically in different tax years. Moreover, many of the tax provisions that are designed to facilitate investment are not available to artists. Artists, therefore, must utilize what provisions of the tax code they can to reduce their tax liability. There are two principal means of doing this. First, as discussed in Section B, *infra*, the artist may take certain deductions. Second, the artist can reduce or spread his or her taxable income using several provisions of the tax code designed to alleviate the tax burdens created by the receipt of income which is substantially higher than that earned in previous years.

Income tax is computed on the basis of seven tax rates ranging from 10% to 39.6%. Essentially, this means that the more income received in a given tax year, the greater the percentage of tax that must be paid. While the tiered income tax rates generally provide tax relief for the poor, the artist will be penalized when his or her income bunches in one tax year. This may occur when, for example, an artist who has not sold much work suddenly sells a very valuable piece, causing the past sales receipts to be taxed at higher rates.

One method of spreading income is the installment method of accounting. If an artist sells a work for a negotiable note or other deferred payment obligation that is essentially equivalent to cash, the artist theoretically may have to report the total proceeds of the sale as an amount realized when the note is received, not when the note is paid with cash. However, IRC § 453 enables artists, but not dealers, who sell property with payments being received in successive tax years to report the income on an installment basis.

Under this method, only a portion of each payment is recognized when received. For example, a sculpture that costs the artist $10,000 to make (expenses to the extent not already deducted) and which he or she then sells for $100,000 (the amount realized) will ordinarily create an immediate taxable gain to the artist of $90,000, but if the artist uses the installment method, with four payments of $25,000 plus interest received over four years, the artist must recognize only 90 percent of each payment ($90,000 gross profit divided by $100,000 total contract price), or $22,500 plus 100 percent of the interest in each year. In either case, the amount of gain that must be included in income is $90,000, but under the

SEC. A PROPERLY CHARACTERIZING INCOME 153

installment method, the amount is spread out over four years, thus taking advantage of lower marginal tax rates and deferral of tax. There are special rules for installment sales that the artist should discuss with a tax adviser. Note that pursuant to the Tax Relief Extension Act of 1999, taxpayers using the accrual method of accounting are no longer able to use the installment method of accounting.

The artist may also wish to spread his or her income among family members in order to reduce his or her total taxable income. In general, the overt assignment of income as a tax avoidance scheme is unsuccessful. The success of more subtle assignments frequently hinges on whether the item transferred is characterized as "income" or "property." When there is a transfer of property, there is an effective shift to the family member, although a gift tax may be imposed on the transfer. Another scheme to transfer income among members of a family is the creation of a family partnership. Such devices are allowed by the IRS but will be closely scrutinized to ensure that the partnership is not a sham.

Some families have even incorporated or created family-owned limited liability companies (LLCs). If the IRS questions the motivation for such an incorporation, the courts will examine the intent of the family members, and if the sole purpose of incorporation was tax avoidance, the scheme will not stand. If the IRS successfully contends that the corporation should be disregarded, the IRS can reallocate income from the corporation to the individual taxpayer. This will be done, for example, if the corporation does not engage in substantial business activity and does not observe corporate formalities, or if its separate status is not otherwise adhered to by the artist.

A bona fide, or genuine, C corporation or LLC, however, may provide some tax advantages for the artist. As an employee, the artist can control his or her individual taxable income with a limited salary, and part or all of the income the corporation receives from sales can be deferred at the personal level. In addition, certain fringe benefits, such as medical and dental expenses, may be purchased with pretax dollars. Although the corporation must recognize income whenever a sale is made, the corporation can deduct the artist's salary as well as other business expenses when they are paid.

Nevertheless, incorporation or creation of an LLC is seldom advantageous for tax purposes alone. Individual rates are now substantially in line with or lower than the corporate rates for most taxpayers. Additionally, there are some unavoidable legal and accounting expenses that will have to be paid by the corporation. If an artist's business operates on very small margins, a determination would have to be made as to whether the possible tax savings justify the additional cost of complying with the laws imposed on corporations or LLCs. The cost of payroll taxes, unemployment taxes, Workers' Compensation, and legal and accounting fees can be substantial. In addition, use of the corporate form is not necessary for setting up a retirement plan. A self-employed

SEC. A   PROPERLY CHARACTERIZING INCOME   155

person can set aside as much money for retirement as could be done through a corporate retirement plan.

Moreover, there are several potential corporate tax problems the artist should consider carefully before incorporating. In a C corporation, any distribution of profits to shareholders in the form of dividends will be taxed twice: once at the corporate level as corporate income, and again at the shareholder level as personal income when profits are distributed to the shareholders. Thus, although incorporation allows income to be shifted from the artist to other shareholders, such as family members, the shift occurs at the expense of double taxation. Obviously, it is important to consult with a CPA or tax advisor in order to determine whether the benefit of shifting income to a C corporation outweighs the effects of double taxation.

If an artist incorporates as a C corporation in order to postpone a significant portion of income, the IRS may impose an accumulated earnings tax. However, the IRC allows a maximum accumulation of $250,000 that is not subject to the accumulated earnings tax, although for "personal service corporations" (including those whose principal work is in the performing arts), the maximum is $150,000. Accumulated earnings beyond these maximums must be justified as reasonable for the needs of the business. Otherwise, they will be subject to a tax of 20 percent in addition to the regular corporate tax (currently 35% for personal service corporations, versus the regular corporate graduated rates, ranging from 15% to 35%).

The IRC also imposes an additional tax on most types of "passive investment income," that is, income retained by the corporation if the corporation is found to be a personal holding company. The rate is currently 20 percent. This may occur if a majority of the corporation's income consists of copyrights, royalties, dividends, or personal service contracts. If the owner sells his or her stock before the corporation has realized any income, the corporation could become a so-called "collapsible corporation," causing the gain realized on the sale of the stock to be taxed at ordinary income rates.

Another alternative for artists is to organize as an S corporation. S corporation classification allows the owners to elect to be taxed much like a partnership and thus avoid double taxation. LLCs can choose to be taxed as partnerships, as C corporations or as S corporations. These types of entities are often more suitable for small businesses than C corporations.

B. DEDUCTIONS

A professional artist may deduct his or her business expenses and thereby lower taxable income. The cost of rent or depreciation on a studio is a typical deduction. However, as with collectors and dealers, the artist must be able to establish that he or she is engaged in a trade or business and not merely a personal hobby. A dilettante is not entitled to trade or business deductions except to the extent of any income received. See Treas. Reg. § 1.183–2, discussed in Chapter 8, *supra*. While an artist is not presumed to be engaged in an activity for profit until he or she earns a profit for three of five years, artists have been allowed deductions even when they do not meet this test. In *Churchman v. Commissioner*, 68 T.C. 696 (U.S. Tax Ct. 1977), the tax court decided that even though the taxpayer artist had a history of losses, she did not depend on this activity for her livelihood and there was a significant recreational element in her activities, the taxpayer did, nevertheless, paint for profit. Churchman proved this by her training and teaching activities, her gallery exhibitions, and her meticulous and businesslike records. Her expenses were thus fully deductible. Had her activities not been characterized as engaged in for profit, her deductions could have been allowed only to the extent of the income derived from the artistic activities. Similarly, *Crile v. Comm'r*, T.C. Memo. 2014–202 (U.S. T.C. Oct. 2, 2014), found that a tenured art professor who had been a professional artist before becoming a professor and who devoted hundreds of hour a year to the administrative aspects of her art business, was trying to make a profit. She kept detailed and accurate records and consistently pursued a business plan that included marketing.

Note that, like any other business, artists must file 1099-MISC forms where required. The artist should carefully review IRS rules for such filings, since they are somewhat complex, but, generally speaking, an artist should file a 1099-MISC for anyone who is not an employee that the artist paid $600 or more in the tax year for services or rents. In addition, if the artist pays royalties for the use of someone else's intellectual property, a 1099-MISC should be filed for anyone the artist pays $10 or more. If the vendor or supplier is a corporation, in some, but not all, cases, filing is not required. An artist who makes direct sales of "consumer products" to a buyer for resale anywhere other than a permanent retail establishment must file a 1099-MISC on those receipts, as well. This includes sales made on a commission basis.

Even if an artist is entitled to trade or business deductions, some types of deductions still may present problems. For example, for some time the IRS disallowed deductions for studios in an artist's residence. This policy was challenged in a non-art case, *Curphey v. Commissioner,* 73 T.C. 766 (U.S. Tax Ct. 1980), in which a physician managed rental properties as a sideline. The doctor's rental business was run out of an office in his house, and the space was used only for this particular business. When the physician deducted the expenses attributable to this home office, the IRS disallowed the deduction, but the tax court reversed and reinstated the home office deduction. The court was apparently convinced by the physical set up of the room that the doctor used it exclusively and regularly as an office in connection with his rental business. The court noted the room had no television, sofa, or bed.

This holding is codified in IRC § 280A. As a general rule, a business deduction is not allowed with respect to the use of a dwelling which is used by the taxpayer during the taxable year as a residence. Use as a residence is defined as the use of the unit for personal purposes for more than 14 days of the taxable year, but IRC § 280A(c)(1)(A) reverses this general rule in limited circumstances, allowing the taxpayer to take a deduction for a portion of a dwelling unit "exclusively used on a regular basis ... as the principal place of business for any trade or business of the taxpayer," even if that business is not the taxpayer's primary source of income.

The requirement of exclusivity means that the artist may not mix personal use and business use. Essentially, this means that artists will have to partition large loft studios into separate working and living areas to claim a deduction. The requirement of regularity means that the use of the room must not be merely incidental or occasional.

The Taxpayer Relief Act of 1997 expanded the definition of a taxpayer's principal place of business to include the place where administrative and management activities are conducted if there is no other fixed location for the accomplishment of such tasks. Thus, an artist who creates work in a rented studio space could take the deduction for an office at home if the administrative aspects of the business, such as contacting galleries regarding sales, ordering supplies, and the like, were conducted from the home office.

The amount of the deduction is limited to the excess of the gross income derived during the taxable year from the use of the studio over any deductions for property tax and mortgage interest attributable to that use. Thus, if the artist is operating the studio at a loss, even if he or she otherwise complies with the requirements of the statute, the deduction will be disallowed, though the losses may be carried forward indefinitely and can be used in subsequent years when there is sufficient income.

Unfortunately, the nonrecognition of gain treatment otherwise allowed when a personal residence is sold is partially disallowed if the home office deduction has been taken. Ordinarily, a taxpayer can exclude up to $250,000 of the gain ($500,000 for joint filers) from income, with some restrictions. This deferral of gain, however, is not allowed to the extent that the home was used in the business; that is, if 20 percent of expenses were deducted, 20 percent of the gain would be recognized. Tax must be paid only on the amount actually deducted for depreciation, however, if the artist has both (1) owned the home for two of the last five years, and (2) used the home exclusively for personal use for two of the last five years. Note that if the home office is located in the same dwelling unit as the principal residence, the taxpayer is treated as having used the entire home as a principal residence and thus may exclude the entire gain from sale, except for depreciation recapture, subject to the $250,000/$500,000 limitation noted above.

C. CHARITABLE DEDUCTIONS

Unlike the deduction for charitable contributions by collectors and dealers, the law of charitable deductions for artists is not very advantageous. Individuals who donate items they have created may deduct only the cost of materials used to create the items. This provision has had unfortunate effects on libraries and museums which, since the law's passage in 1969, have experienced enormous decreases in charitable contributions from authors and artists. The Museum of Modern Art, for example, received 52 paintings and sculptures from artists from 1967 to 1969; between 1972 and 1975, only one work was donated.

Even a painter, Alex Katz, who bought his own work *American Soldier* on the secondary market years after he had given away the sculpture, was held to be subject to the rule that only what he paid for the work (in this case, the amount paid at an auction) could be deducted rather than the sculpture's fair market value.

Although several modifications of the law have been proposed, Congress continues to resist change in the area of tax treatment of artists' donations of their own work. However, the states have been more responsive. A few states, such as Oregon (O.R.S. 316.838), Maryland (Md. Code, Tax-Gen., §§ 10–208(f)) and Arkansas (Ark. Code Ann. § 26–51–422), now allow artists to deduct the fair market value of their creations donated to certain charities.

In the past, an artist who donated intellectual property could receive a deduction equal to the fair market value of that intellectual property, so long as it had been held for more than one year. In 2004, however, President Bush signed the American Jobs Creation Act of 2004, which limits the deduction to the lesser of the fair market value or the taxpayer's basis. The taxpayer may deduct additional amounts based on a specified percentage of the income earned by the recipient that is directly attributable to the intellectual property.

D. ESTATE PLANNING

There are several unique problems confronted by the artist's estate planner. One of these is the impact of the estate tax laws that tax the estate at its fair market value on the date of the artist's death or, at his or her executor's election under IRC § 2032, within six months of his or her death. Since artists' estates may contain large amounts of appreciated artwork, federal estate and state inheritance taxes can be substantial. Even when an artist sells the majority of his or her marketable works before death, previously worthless artwork in the artist's possession can suddenly become quite valuable when the artist dies. In anticipation of these problems, some artists have taken drastic measures. It is rumored that Thomas Hart Benton destroyed a million dollars' worth of his art because his wife could not afford to pay the estate taxes. The late Ted de Grazia also decided to resolve his estate problems by destroying his creations during his lifetime, beginning by burning 100 paintings which he valued at $1.5 million in 1976.

Fortunately, with proper planning, there are other less destructive means available to manage an artist's estate. The burden of paying estate taxes for an incorporated artist can be lessened by taking advantage of IRC § 6166, which applies when more than 35 percent of the value of an estate consists of the decedent's interest in a closely-held corporation.

This provision enables the estate to defer a portion of the estate tax payments for five years and to spread out the payments for 10 additional years. If artwork is sold to pay estate taxes, sales expenses, and commissions can be deducted. However, under *Estate of David Smith v. Commissioner*, 57 T.C. 650 (U.S. Tax Ct. 1972), only those expenses incurred to generate monies for taxes are deductible under IRC § 2053(a), not the expenses for liquidating the entire estate. In several states, and in some foreign countries (for example, France and the United Kingdom), estate taxes can also be paid directly with works of art. See Conn. Gen. Stat. Ann. § 12–376d; 27 Me. Rev. Stat. Ann. §§ 92–93; and N.M. Stat. chapter Ann. §§ 7–7–18.

Of course, the best way of managing payment of one's estate taxes is to owe a smaller amount of tax or no tax at all. This can be done by reducing the size of the estate. One fairly obvious way of doing this is by making *inter vivos* gifts of property. However, several provisions of the tax laws make this a less attractive solution for artists. As noted in Section C to this chapter, *supra*, artists do not get the tax advantages that collectors do when they donate works of art to charity.

Gifting art will remove subsequent appreciation of the gifted property from the donor's estate, and gifts may not be subject to either estate or gift taxation if the value of the gift is less than the $14,000 per donee annual gift tax exclusion ($28,000 for husband and wife), as noted in Section D of Chapter 8, *supra*. Yet an artist may find *inter vivos* gifts of his or her artwork an unattractive solution if he or she is concerned about the subsequent tax consequences to beneficiaries. This is because the artist's basis in his or her work is so low. When property is acquired from a decedent, IRC § 1014 provides that the recipient's basis will be the fair market value. This is very advantageous, since if the property appreciates and is later sold, the high basis will cause the recipient's taxable gain to be lower. When property is acquired by gift, on the other hand, the donee's basis for the purposes of calculating gains will be the same basis as the donor's, which for an artist's work will be only the cost of materials. This low basis will create a larger taxable gain to the donee when the work of art is later sold. Thus, the effect of a gift is not to reduce overall taxes but, rather, simply to shift taxes from the artist's estate to the donee. Depending on the artist's particular circumstances and the tax brackets of the estate and the donee, reducing the artist's estate by *inter vivos* gifts, therefore, may not be as advantageous as one might think, since income tax rates are significantly lower than estate tax rates; a lifetime sale by the donor may actually result in a smaller tax payment. In addition, even if an *inter vivos* gift does appear to have tax advantages for a particular artist, certain types of gift transactions can cause those benefits to vanish if the gift is made within the three years prior to the artist's death. See Chapter 8, § D, *supra*.

Tax advantages upon the artist's death can be realized if the artist incorporated during his or her lifetime in order to avoid an "income in respect of a decedent" problem which arises only in lifetime installment sales. However, it is necessary that all income from sales and personal service contracts be paid to the corporation. Otherwise, under IRC § 691, the income in respect of the decedent must be included in the gross income of the artist's estate or, if the right to receive the income is not acquired by the estate, the beneficiary who acquires the right to receive it. Absent this potential problem, the artist's estate is taxed only on the artist's share of the corporation. The estate and the beneficiaries receive the artist's stock with a fair market value basis, creating little, if any, gain on sale, when the stock will be taxed at capital gain rates.

Unless the corporation is liquidated by other shareholders, the corporation will continue in existence after the artist's death. While the continuation of the corporate form may aid the beneficiaries in continuing to exploit the artist's work, it may create tax problems. In C corporations, continuing income from royalties and post-death sales will be taxed as corporate income, without the corresponding deduction for salary paid to the artist. Distributions to the shareholders or the estate will also be taxable to them. This means that the income will be taxed twice, both at the corporate and shareholder levels. If, on the other hand, the corporation withholds the income, it may become subject to the accumulated earnings tax, even if it successfully avoided the accumulated earnings tax during the artist's lifetime. The solution, therefore, may be to liquidate the corporation. If a corporate liquidation is properly structured, the shareholders will take corporation's assets with a fair market value basis (§ 334).

Incorporation with subsequent liquidation upon the artist's death is not the solution to every artist's tax problem, however. In electing a corporate form, the artist becomes subject to many state laws governing the creation, operation, and dissolution of a corporation or LLC. Most states require a corporation to have a board of directors, and since state laws customarily charge the board with responsibility for the management of the corporation, the artist must be able to choose trustworthy directors. In addition, if the artist wishes to minimize his or her taxable estate by making his or her beneficiaries owners of the corporation or LLC, he or she may have to retain at least 51 percent of the stock or LLC interests to maintain control, although there may be some tax advantages in not retaining control. Depending on his or her particular circumstances, therefore, an artist may find that these and other corporate characteristics make remaining unincorporated the best alternative. If so, the artist should concentrate on other methods of spreading his or her taxable income, claiming deductions and planning his or her estate to reduce his or her tax liability.

CHAPTER 10
AID TO THE ARTS

A. DIRECT AID

1. HISTORICAL DEVELOPMENT

The framers of the Constitution apparently recognized the importance of the "useful arts" (see U.S. Const. Art. I, § 8), yet, little was done to aid art directly until the Great Depression of the 1930s. Perhaps it was felt that the struggling new nation should devote its limited resources to more practical endeavors. Today, while appropriations to the arts vary in different political and economic climates, governmental aid is among the most important sources of funding for the professional artist and for nonprofit art institutions. Artists and art organizations should thus be aware of these funding sources and the qualifications required for obtaining aid.

The first federal effort to become involved with the arts was initiated in the 1850s when President Buchanan attempted to establish the National Commission of Fine Arts. This project was aborted within a year because Congress failed to appropriate funds. The same fate befell the Council of Fine Arts proposed in 1909 by Theodore Roosevelt. In 1910, President Taft was successful in enacting the National Commission for Fine Arts Act of May 17, 1910, c. 243 § 1, 36 Stat. 371 (codified at 40 U.S.C. § 104). This organization funneled private donations to the government and determined the appropriate location for each donation. These early half-hearted efforts suggest that the United States government apparently desired an active art program, though it was unwilling to make any meaningful sacrifice for such projects. Several municipal programs attempted to fill the void created by federal inaction, most notably the Civil Works Administration (CWA) of New York City. The CWA sponsored paintings, murals, and art education, but its primary goal was to create employment. Most individuals were chosen from the relief rolls, and the only requirement for employment was the assertion that the applicant was an artist. Thus, the art produced tended to be the work of unskilled amateurs.

Several federal programs developed during the Depression prior to the emergence of the Federal Art Project, a branch of the Works Progress Administration (WPA), but none lasted as long or produced so much artwork. Over its life, the WPA spent $35 million on the Federal Art Project and produced approximately 1,500 murals, 18,800 sculptures and 108,000 paintings, as well as other works of art. The Federal Art Project was patterned after some of the early municipal efforts but tried to avoid some of the problems of the CWA by emphasizing production of works of high technical competence, utilizing defined hiring guidelines, and encouraging creativity and experimentation. It still required personnel to be on the relief rolls, thus disqualifying many of the better artists, although notables such as Beniamino Bufano, Jackson Pollock, Mark Rothko, and David Smith did work for the

WPA. See page 399 for a photograph of a Bufano sculpture. The Federal Art Project paid a "security wage," an amount calculated to fall between the prevailing wage and the relief grants of the region involved, which was graduated according to skill level. During its later years, funding was uncertain and labor disputes arose over classifications and rates of pay. The WPA effectively ended with the advent of World War II, and sadly, many of the records and file sources, as well as the works themselves, disappeared. For examples of murals created under the WPA, see pages 400–402.

During the war, the graphic section of the War Services Program employed some artists, principally focusing on camouflage, posters, and other activities necessary to the war effort. For the most part, however, the United States government reverted to its pre-Depression attitude toward art. Appropriations were cut. Even a purchase of paintings by the government came under such severe criticism that the government was forced to sell the works, receiving only 10 percent of their value. With the development of the Cold War, the federal government realized that cultural exchange can promote diplomatic ends. By 1956, the United States allocated over $2 million dollars annually to send artists abroad for cultural presentations. In addition, by 1960, 176 American cultural centers were established in 80 foreign countries. However, there was no domestic funding during this time.

2. THE NATIONAL ENDOWMENT FOR THE ARTS

In 1965, the first statute supporting the arts since the Depression was passed and signed into law. The National Foundation on the Arts and the Humanities Act of 1965, Pub. L. No. 89–209, 79 Stat. 845 (1965) (codified as amended at 20 U.S.C. §§ 951–960), established the National Foundation for the Arts and the Humanities. The legislation was unique. For the first time in the history of the United States, an agency was created that was devoted to the arts and humanities. The legislation established the National Endowment for the Arts (NEA) and the National Endowment for the Humanities. In addition, a Federal Council on the Arts and Humanities was created to consist of agency heads in the federal government whose work related, or could relate, to cultural development and to prevent duplication of effort in a new area of governmental activity. Unlike the WPA's goal, the NEA's goal is not to provide employment but, rather, to make the arts more widely available to Americans, to preserve our rich cultural heritage, and to encourage the creative development of our nation's finest artistic talent.

Activities supported by the NEA generally fall into two categories: block grants and specific project grants. Block grants are made through national initiatives and to art councils in all 50 states, the District of Columbia, and United States territories. Each council must adhere to the high standards contained in the legislation, and each has its own program guidelines to dispense the federal money it receives. Allotments to the state art councils are made annually. Once the funds are allotted, prospective grant applicants apply for funds directly from the state.

Block grants are the only NEA category of funding mandated by the federal statute, but the preponderance of NEA appropriations is used for direct project grants to private groups in all the arts. To be eligible, the group must be a nonprofit organization, and it must be tax-exempt under Section 170 of the Internal Revenue Code of 1954. As a general rule, the total amount of NEA grants may not exceed 50 percent of the project's cost. The applicant's matching funds may be in cash or, in certain situations, in-kind contributions calculated at the fair market value of the property or services donated by the grantee or other public or private institutions or individuals. Fellowships (individual support) also are granted to individuals of exceptional talent engaged in certain types of projects; no matching funds are required of fellowship applicants.

The specific programs within these categories may vary. To apply for a grant, the applicant should ascertain which type of assistance among a wide variety of programs and categories corresponds to its specific needs by contacting the NEA or the appropriate state art organization. Applicants must strictly comply with the federal or state grant application guidelines. Application procedures for state councils vary in accordance with state statutes and regulations which should be consulted before applying. Applications to the NEA are reviewed by the NEA's professional panelists and outside consultants. All applications are then referred to the National Council on the Arts, comprised of presidential appointees and the NEA Chairperson. The Chairperson reviews the Council's recommendations and makes the final decision on all grant awards.

One factor underlying the government's role in the arts is its potential control of the direction of artistic growth. Critics of the NEA claim that there is a tendency to reward those artists who have already received recognition and thus discourage experimentation. However, the NEA has funded numerous *avant garde* projects and has taken initiatives along the frontiers of artistic expression. Controversy surrounded NEA funding when it was discovered that the NEA had given $30,000 to Robert Mapplethorpe and $15,000 to Andres Serrano, two artists whose works were deemed obscene. In response, Congress mandated that the NEA no longer fund obscene art. All artists would be required to sign a pledge that their works were not obscene. Numerous artists turned down substantial grants rather than sign. Others filed suit, contending that the pledge requirement was unconstitutional. See *Bella Lewitzky Dance Foundation v. John Frohnmayer; Newport Harbor Art Museum v. NEA*, 754 F. Supp. 774 (C.D. Cal. 1991).

In 1991, Congress deleted the obscenity language and replaced it with a watered-down version. The Act directed the NEA Chairperson to ensure that "artistic excellence and artistic merit are the criteria by which applications are judged, taking into consideration general standards and respect for the diverse beliefs of the American public." The artist no longer had to sign a nonobscenity pledge, and while the artist still had to comport with standards of decency, these standards were to be judged by the courts, not the NEA.

The "decency" clause was held void for vagueness in *Finley v. National Endowment for the Arts,* 795 F. Supp. 1457 (C.D. Cal. 1992), a suit brought by four artists whose grant applications were denied. The court held that, because the decency clause reached a substantial amount of protected speech, confining NEA funding only to what was decent, it was overbroad as well as vague.

This decision was overturned by the U.S. Supreme Court in 1998. The court held that the government has the right to withhold funding from art it considers obscene. "If the NEA were to leverage its power to award subsidies on the basis of subjective criteria into a penalty on disfavored new points, then we would confront a different case." *National Endowment for the Arts v. Finley,* 524 U.S. 569 (1998).

Another criticism of NEA funding is that, with increased governmental appropriations, other patrons might feel that art is already adequately funded and thus withhold their support. In difficult economic times, this argument has been used to support proposals to reduce government appropriations, as in 1981 when the Reagan administration proposed a 50 percent cut in the budget for the National Foundation on the Arts and the Humanities. The administration claimed that its reduction of the arts budget would encourage individuals and corporations to make up the difference. Many have labeled this view as unrealistic. The Congress resisted all such reductions, convinced that NEA funding has greatly increased private and nonfederal assistance, rather than tending to replace it. As Edward M. Block, an AT & T vice president, stated before the House Appropriations Subcommittee on the Interior, "If the Federal Government gives authority to the notion that the arts are merely frivolous diversions to be indulged in good times but abandoned in bad times, I strongly suspect that the private sector will not be disposed toward heroic efforts to pick up the shortfall." N.Y. Times, Mar. 26, 1981, § C, at 15, col. 1.

The NEA's legislation clearly recognizes the essential nature of private support for the arts. In fact, in 2014, only four percent of US arts funding came from public sources. About 40 percent came from earned income, such as sales of tickets and gift shop items. The remainder came from individuals, corporations and foundations.

3. OTHER DIRECT AID

Direct government aid to the arts is by no means confined to NEA funds. All state commissions receive state appropriations, which are used for administrative purposes or for direct grants. A few of the larger states permit local subdivisions to establish their own commissions, which also grant funds. Employment programs have also provided artists with funding for various projects.

The arts have come to be one of the first casualties in the budget-slashing process, however, and some states have tried innovative solutions to this problem. For example, Oregon raised funds for its Arts Commission through the use of a taxpayer "check-off." The Oregon Revised Statutes, 316.485 (1981) (repealed by 1995 c. 79, s. 166), provided that taxpayers receiving a state income tax refund could contribute a portion of their refund to an art commission fund by marking the appropriate space provided on their tax returns. Some have feared that the legislature may not feel compelled to continue its financial support of the arts but, rather, leave the burden on the taxpayers to donate through this check-off system.

City and state arts funding is not immune from the types of political issues that have arisen with NEA funding. For example, the City of San Antonio disqualified the Esperanza Peace and Justice Center, a non-profit cultural arts and education center, from arts funding in 1997. Apparently, some believed that the City should not fund any group that was "advocating a gay and lesbian lifestyle." The court determined that plaintiffs' constitutionally protected conduct was a substantial or motivating factor in the decision of a majority of council members. *Esperanza Peace and Justice Center v. City of San Antonio*, 316 F. Supp. 2d 433 (W.D. Tex. 2001). After the ruling, the City agreed to pay Esperanza $550,000.

B. INDIRECT AID

Indirect aid is also an important form of governmental support for the arts. While this type of legislation does not provide direct funding for professional artists and art institutions, it creates heightened public awareness of art and provides artists with new outlets for their work. There are several methods that are used. Governmental entities may require a percentage allocation for art in new construction projects, or they may enact regulations concerning the public display of art or the preservation of historic landmarks, thus providing outright support or tax incentives.

1. PERCENTAGE ALLOCATION FOR ART

One of the most effective means of indirect governmental aid to the arts is the percentage allocation regulation, which has been adopted by 26 states, Washington, D.C. and Guam, as well as numerous municipalities. These regulations require a percentage of the building cost of new governmental structures, usually one percent, to be spent on art. The implementation of such legislation does not merely enhance the specific buildings involved; the entire art community is benefited. Supporters are relieved from the task of lobbying and applying for grants in each instance, and artists commissioned to work on public art projects may also teach and exhibit their works locally. Disputes can arise, however, as to how the percentage allocations should be spent. For example, when the Metropolitan Arts Commission in Portland, Oregon, approved the purchase of a cedar hawk sculpted by 19th-century Pacific Northwest Indians for a new building under construction, the purpose of the art acquisition was called into question. If the reason for the art allocation is to stimulate the public's awareness of art, the antique cedar hawk appeared to be a justifiable purchase. On the other hand, if, as the local artists claimed, the expenditure was to stimulate work in the art community, a commissioned work would have been a more appropriate acquisition.

Many states also require their state art commissions to approve building design and location plans when state buildings are being constructed, when state money is being used to construct any building, or when a building is constructed on public land. While no appropriations are involved, this type of regulation seeks to improve the appearance of localities and to broaden the public's exposure to artistic works and values. Such efforts were held constitutional in *Walnut & Quince Streets Corp. v. Mills*, 303 Pa. 25, 154 A. 29 (1931), *app. dismissed*, 284 U.S. 573 (1931), where a municipal art jury refused to permit a theater owner to construct a large marquee extending over the sidewalk. The owner claimed that the statute permitted the jury to act in an arbitrary fashion, which deprived him of due process of law. He further contended that the legislature did not possess the power to regulate aesthetics and thus could not delegate it to a jury. The court rejected these arguments, holding that the statute was a legitimate part of the legislative regulation of public property.

2. LANDMARK PRESERVATION

Landmark preservation laws are also an important means of indirect aid. While this type of regulation does not directly benefit contemporary artists, historic preservation increases the public's awareness of the need for beautification and preserves the works of past generations. Historic preservation is encouraged not only by means of regulations that prohibit the destruction and alteration of historic landmarks, but also by means of funding for preservation, although the latter is quite limited. The Internal Revenue Code also provides some tax incentives for conservation and restoration of old buildings. See 26 U.S.C. § 47.

At first glance, efforts to restore, and subsequently keep intact as restored, buildings and structures of historic importance seem laudatory and uncontroversial. The private individuals and groups who own these properties, however, often view such protection as overly restrictive and an undue burden tantamount to a taking of private property without compensation. It is for this reason that, in Oregon, if a property owner objects to the historic property designation made by a local government, the local government must remove the designation. O.R.S. 197.772.

The application of landmark preservation laws to limit a property owner's rights to his or her property has been held to be constitutional. In *Penn Central Transportation Co. v. New York City*, 438 U.S. 104 (1978), the U.S. Supreme Court held that the New York City Landmarks Preservation Commission's failure to approve plans for construction of a 50-story office building over Grand Central Terminal, which had been designated a landmark, was not an unconstitutional taking. The interference with the plaintiffs' use of its property was not of such a magnitude that there was an exercise of eminent domain with the attendant requirement of compensation, the court stated, because the plaintiffs had not shown that they had been deprived of all uses of their property.

First, the plaintiffs' use of the existing building itself was not compromised. Second, there was no evidence presented that the commission, in denying the plaintiffs' application, had prohibited any construction over the terminal; the plaintiffs could have modified their plans to build a smaller structure more in harmony with the existing structure. Third, under New York City's transferable development rights program, owners of real property who have not developed their property to the full extent permitted by the applicable zoning laws are allowed to transfer development rights to contiguous parcels on the same city block and to other approved parcels.

In the case of the proposed construction over the Grand Central Terminal, the development rights could have been transferred to at least eight parcels in the vicinity, one or two of which were suitable for the construction of new office buildings. While the court stated that these rights might not have constituted adequate compensation if a taking had occurred, they did mitigate the financial burdens the law had imposed on the plaintiffs and were thus to be taken into account in estimating the magnitude of the regulation's impact for the purposes of determining whether a taking had occurred at all. See page 403 for a photograph of Grand Central Terminal.

However, in 1991 the Pennsylvania Supreme Court ruled that designating a piece of property as an historic landmark constituted a taking of property if done without the consent of the owner and, therefore, violated the state constitution. *United Artists Theater Circuit, Inc. v. City of Philadelphia*, 528 Pa. 12, 595 A.2d 6 (1991). The state Supreme Court granted a rehearing and held that the designation of a privately owned building as historic without the consent of its owners is not a taking.

In *Lucas v. South Carolina Coastal Council*, 505 U.S. 1003 (1992), the Supreme Court held that any regulation prohibiting all economically beneficial use of land cannot be newly legislated without compensation, unless the law does no more than duplicate the result that could have been achieved in the courts. The Supreme Court confirmed that *Penn Central* is the controlling case for analyzing takings claims in *Palazzolo v. Rhode Island*, 533 U.S. 606 (2001), and clarified that the *Lucas* ruling applies only in extreme situations where there has been a "total wipeout" of economic value.

Another constitutional issue is free exercise of religion. *First Covenant Church of Seattle, Wash. v. City of Seattle*, 114 Wash. 2d 392, 787 P.2d 1352 (1990), *cert. granted and judgment vacated sub nom. City of Seattle v. First Covenant Church of Seattle,*

Wash., 499 U.S. 901 (1991), *on remand, First Covenant Church v. City of Seattle*, 120 Wash. 2d 203, 840 P.2d 174 (1992), the state supreme court held that application of the city's landmark preservation ordinances to the church violated the free exercise of religion clause of the First Amendment. Seattle's laws prohibited the alteration of the exterior of designated sites without prior authorization from the Landmarks board. To the court, the authorization mandated secular control over matters directly related to the practice of religion.

Other states have had their landmark preservation laws upheld at least to the exterior of houses of worship. When Trinity Evangelical Lutheran Church applied for a permit to demolish a building, the city refused and Trinity filed suit. In *Trinity Evangelical Lutheran Church v. City of Peoria*, 07–cv–1029 (C.D. Ill. Mar. 31, 2009), the court ruled that the applicable ordinance did not prevent the Church from continuing its religious ministries or place a substantial burden on the Church's activities.

The designation of church interiors as historic landmarks has been found to violate at least one state constitution. In *Society of Jesus of New England v. Boston Landmarks Com'n*, 409 Mass. 38, 564 N.E.2d 571 (1990), the court concluded that a landmark designation for portions of a church's interior violated the Massachusetts constitutional guarantee of freedom of religion.

These types of indirect and direct aid are important to the professional artist. Through indirect governmental aid, the public's perception and awareness of art is heightened, and new markets for art are created. In addition, through direct aid, funding over and above revenues from sales and royalties are made available to artists to pursue their work. While such funding—both public and private—is extremely sensitive to changes in economic conditions, it provides an important resource for artists and contributes to the arts in America.

CHAPTER 11
THE WORKING ARTIST

A. PLACES TO WORK AND SELL

Achieving economic stability as an artist is an uphill climb. Many artists are forced to take "day jobs" for sustenance until their skill is recognized. Some take shelter in the academic realm or in arts administration work, where, notwithstanding the security and contact with other artists afforded by such positions, many artists find they no longer have the time or creative energy to produce their own work. A few artists support themselves by leading double lives, creating what is referred to as "schlock art" under a *nom de plume* while simultaneously pursuing their own creative style. These schizophrenic working conditions can take a great emotional toll.

Gaining economic success and recognition as an artist is thus not only a matter of achieving artistic skill, but of effective marketing as well. The first step is finding places in which to sell one's work. The depressing experience of having a portfolio rejected by one gallery after another has caused some artists to postpone gallery contacts until they have had their work acknowledged in contests or juried shows. Some artists have been successful in using what is known as "alternative space," such as banks, restaurants, subways, hospitals, hotels, and even taxicabs. The work is frequently displayed with the artist's name and the price. If the item is sold, the institution typically retains a small commission. Some alternative spaces are former public buildings or warehouses renovated to provide studio and display space to unknown artists at minimal costs. This form of marketing enables many artists to get public exposure before they are acknowledged by galleries. State and federal aid to arts programs also may provide artists with employment and outlets for their work. See Chapter 10, *supra*.

The Internet is another venue for art sales, whether an artist sells his or her work directly or through an online gallery or auction house, such as eBay. While online sales still make up less than 10 percent of the art market, many lower priced works are sold through Amazon, art.com, Artsy, 1stDibs and other online venues.

Other artists rent booths at fairs or craft exhibits and try to market their own work. However, this too can be an awkward experience for many artists, and some, therefore, find they prefer to have an associate attend to the retail booth. A similar arrangement is to pool works with others and rotate the sales responsibility. Occasionally this may evolve into the formation of a cooperative gallery. Several cooperative galleries around the country have achieved a good deal of success. Before forming a cooperative, however, it is necessary for the members to devote some attention to the inevitable internal conflicts and resolve them at the outset. Members of an effective cooperative must cultivate the temperament and business acumen necessary to achieve effective merchandising. These traits are not possessed by all artists. Another potential problem is that when a cooperative provides for equal apportionment of earnings among the members, it is often necessary to prevent a drain on the cooperative by providing incentives to retain members who become successful and who might otherwise move on.

Some art galleries and cooperatives have attempted to function as tax-exempt entities to reduce overhead costs. In order to qualify as a tax-exempt organization under the Internal Revenue Code, an organization must be created and operated exclusively for charitable, educational, or scientific purposes. Income Tax Regulations §§ 1.501(c)(3)–1(d)(3)(ii) state that museums and similar organizations are examples of exempt educational organizations. However, in Rev. Rul. 71–395, 1971–2 C.B. 228, the Internal Revenue Service took the position that a cooperative gallery that did not charge admission but sold the works of its members and remitted a portion of the proceeds of sale to the artist who created the work was not entitled to tax-exempt status. The IRS apparently felt that the economic benefit to the artist members was sufficient to deprive the organization of its exempt status.

Subsequently, in Rev. Rul. 76–152, 1976–1 C.B. 152, the IRS affirmed and clarified its position. Here a group of patrons formed an organization to promote community understanding of art trends by displaying contemporary art in its gallery. Works selected for display were consigned by the artist for sale. The organization retained only a 10 percent commission on sales of the works. The remaining operating expenses were obtained by the organization's solicitation of contributions. The IRS took the position that the organization was not entitled to tax-exempt status as an educational organization. It was felt that the organization was serving the private interests of the artists who consigned the works, since they received 90 percent of the proceeds of sale. The IRS distinguished the facts in Rev. Rul. 66–178, 1966–1 C.B. 138, where an organization fostered and developed the arts by holding an art exhibit at which the works of unknown but promising artists were gratuitously displayed. None of the works were sold or offered for sale.

Later, in *Goldsboro Art League, Inc. v. Commissioner of Internal Revenue,* 75 T.C. 337 (U.S. Tax Ct. 1980), the tax court held that two galleries that displayed works for sale were tax exempt under IRC § 501(c)(3). The galleries selected works through art juries. Eighty percent of the proceeds of sale were remitted to the artist whose work was sold, while the remaining 20 percent was retained by the organization to defray its expenses. The court stated that the primary function of those galleries was educational, whereas their sales activities were merely secondary. The tax court appears to have ignored the fact that galleries that are exempt from federal income tax are given an economic advantage over their tax-paying competitors. Since a tax-exempt gallery does not have to pay taxes, it could, therefore, reduce the retail price of the work it sells by the tax savings and undersell its business competitors. In *Cleveland Creative Arts Guild v. Commissioner,* T.C. Memo. 1985–316 (U.S. Tax Ct.

1985), the tax court examined the activities of another nonprofit art organization located in a rural area. The guild was formed to "enhance the cultural life of the community," primarily through the operation and maintenance of art studios and classrooms. However, the guild also sponsored art festivals and craft shows. The court, after considering the holding in *Goldsboro*, found the sales activity secondary and incidental to the organization's exempt purposes.

In Private Letter Ruling 8634001 (Aug. 31, 1986), another art organization dedicated to education and community awareness obtained a favorable ruling on rental and sales activity that it conducted on a consignment basis. The service found that the sales and rental activity made up only a small part of the organization's art-related activities, which included sponsoring rotating exhibits, organizing trips to museums, assisting in musical and theatrical productions, and conducting seminars, lectures, workshops, and competitions.

More recently, in Private Letter Ruling 201516066 (Jan. 21, 2015), an artist co-operative that operated an art gallery was found not to qualify as a tax exempt organization, though the gallery also engaged in educational and charitable activities, including providing one-day art workshops, hosting an annual 5K and fun run, awarding scholarships and providing community art/artist talks and school/youth tours of the gallery.

B. GALLERIES AND COMMISSIONS

Galleries are the most important outlets available for an artist to sell his or her work. Unfortunately, few artists are aware of the legal bases of their relationships with galleries and the rights upon which they should insist. Frequently, artists and dealers give little attention to details, with the result that misunderstandings and disappointed expectations are disturbingly common.

There are two basic types of legal arrangements between an artist and a gallery. The first, most commonly used in Europe, is an outright purchase agreement, where the dealer purchases the work from the artist and resells it. He or she may be under no contractual obligation to the artist beyond payment of the purchase price. The agreement may apply to an artist's entire output or only a portion of it. It may consist wholly or in part of a right of first refusal, which consists of the artist's duty to offer his or her work to the dealer first and the dealer's option to buy.

The second type of legal arrangement, consignment, is the norm in the United States. In fact, more than 30 states and the District of Columbia have passed legislation creating automatic consignments upon delivery of artworks by an artist to a dealer. A consignment agreement creates an agency relationship in which the gallery or dealer (the consignee) acts as the selling agent for the artist (the consignor). This fiduciary relationship requires the dealer to act only in the interest of the artist and to forego all personal advantage from the transaction (except, of course, the agreed commission). The dealer is under a duty to respect the confidential nature of the relationship as well. Sixteen states provide protection to artists by requiring the artist and dealer to sign a contract assuring many of the protections provided in other states directly by statute. Required contract terms typically include a specified commission rate or fee amount, a statement of the value of the work and minimum sales price, as well as allocation to the dealer of responsibility for loss or damage. In all the other states with consignment statutes, except New Jersey and Texas, consigned art and subsequent sale proceeds are designated trust property, although in Connecticut the sale proceeds but not the works themselves are trust property. Any property designated as trust or bailment property is neither subject nor subordinate to claims of the dealer's creditors. Most states not requiring contracts also hold the dealer liable for loss or damage to consigned works.

In addition, the Uniform Commercial Code is available to fill some of the gaps in artist-dealer contracts where the parties have failed to provide for certain contingencies. Section 2–509 of the U.C.C., *Risk of Loss in the Absence of Breach*, states that the risk of loss is generally on the party possessing the goods; Section 2–309, *Absence of Specific Time Provisions*, provides that the time for shipment or delivery or other action, if not agreed upon, shall be a reasonable time; Section 2–308 provides that unless otherwise agreed, the place of the seller's business ordinarily is the place for delivery; and

Section 2–305 indicates that if the price is not settled, it shall be a reasonable price.

The U.C.C. provisions, however, may not be what the parties actually desire, and many of its sections have been given strained interpretations by the courts. Moreover, there are many areas important to the artist-gallery relationships that the U.C.C. and state consignment laws do not cover. Reducing an agreement to writing can have the effect of clarifying the parties' needs and expectations and thereby avoiding many potential misunderstandings.

There are several items that should be specifically covered in artist-gallery contracts. The contract should define the extent of the gallery's authority, such as the types of work covered, the geographic limits of the gallery's authority, the duration of the agreement (including options to extend or procedures to terminate), and whether the gallery has exclusive authority to sell or whether other galleries also may sell the artist's work. The contract should state the amount of commissions that will be paid to the gallery and should spell out who will bear costs such as storage, insurance, promotion, exhibitions, catalogs, framing, transportation, and the like. If the gallery will sponsor a show of the artist's work, a separate clause should state who bears the costs of the show and when the show will occur.

Insurance usually warrants a separate clause stating who pays the premiums and what the extent of coverage is. Artists should note that even if a gallery picks up the insurance, few galleries insure for the full value of the works. Thus, the artist may want to obtain his or her own floater policy for complete coverage. Other contract provisions which should be included in an artist-gallery contract are: (a) an accounting clause, which gives the artist a right of access to records of sales and expenses and requires the gallery to periodically send the artist an itemized statement of works sold, prices, money received, gallery commissions, and amounts due the artist, and (b) a death clause, which determines the disposition of the artist's works upon the death of either the artist or gallery key personnel, such as the owner.

It is especially important that the artist and the gallery agree on the extent of the gallery's duties for promotion and marketing. If shows will be arranged, will they be solo shows or group shows? Will the gallery campaign to have the artist included in museums and appropriate traveling exhibits? Will the gallery arrange for the artist's work to be sold at other galleries outside the local area or entered in juried shows and competitions? Does the gallery have a rental program designed to attract new business from old clients, as well as individuals not previously interested in acquiring art? Many galleries can be quite aggressive in marketing the work of artists who contract with them, so the artist should choose the gallery carefully and negotiate the most active marketing and publicity program possible.

Artists must use caution when dealing with galleries, which have often been accused of undervaluing artists' paintings, buying them outright for a low price and immediately reselling them for substantially higher prices. For instance, the estate of Francis Bacon contended that Marlborough Galleries had done just that. The lawsuit was settled in 2002, but the terms of the settlement have not been made public, other than that each side would pay its own costs, and the gallery would supply the estate with a complete accounting. Al Hirschfeld, the caricaturist, filed suit against his long-time dealer Margo Feiden, asking for more control over the sale and exhibition of his drawings and a more rigorous accounting of sales. The suit was dropped in October 2002 when the parties reached agreement on a revised contract that gave Hirschfeld more control over museum exhibition of his work.

Many galleries will actively seek out special commissions for artists by contracting with architects and interior designers who need artwork, book publishers who need illustrations, and publishers of limited editions and reproductions. If the artist receives a commission through the gallery, the artist-gallery contract should specify the gallery's fee, if any. Whether or not the gallery is involved, however, the artist should realize that commissions can raise special problems of their own.

Since a work of art exists in the mind's eye of the creator until it is actually completed, it is difficult for a purchaser to anticipate what the prospective art object will look like. If the purchaser is dissatisfied with the final product, he or she may attempt to refuse it. This was the case in *Wolff v. Smith*, 303 Ill. App. 413, 25 N.E.2d 399 (2d Dist. 1940), in which the artist agreed to paint a portrait of the defendant's father "to your entire satisfaction." The court held that this language, combined with the artist's express promise to paint a portrait that was as "outstanding and exact a likeness" as another portrait he had previously done for the defendant, created an arrangement by which the defendant would be deemed the sole judge of whether he would accept the portrait. Since the defendant had rejected the portrait, the artist could not recover his fee.

Some courts will imply a personal satisfaction guarantee even where none was expressly made by the artist. In *McCrady v. Roy*, 85 So. 2d 527 (La. App. Orleans 1956), the artist argued that a likeness is an interpretation and that his portrait of the defendant's wife was his interpretation of her appearance. The court disagreed, establishing a "reasonable likeness" standard and stating that the portrait simply did not accurately portray the subject's features, coloring or figure. Apparently the problem could have been avoided if the artist had discussed with his client the difference between a portrait, that is, a slightly flattering, accurate likeness, and an interpretive creation.

Where the artist cannot complete a portrait due to a lack of cooperation from the subject, the artist may be able to recover for a breach of contract. In *Brockhurst v. Ryan*, 2 Misc. 2d 747, 146 N.Y.S.2d 386 (Sup. Ct. N.Y. Cnty. 1955), the plaintiff artist contracted to paint five separate portraits of the defendant and each of the members of his family. Two pictures were completed and paid for, but the remainder of the commission was not fulfilled because the defendant refrained from arranging any further sittings. The artist sued for breach of contract and was allowed to recover the $11,000 contract price less the $24 cost of completing the portraits.

C. WORKING CONDITIONS

Artists rarely operate on a standard nine-to-five day; rather, they tend to work in their own studios or on location under varying conditions. During the early years, artists are rarely able to own separate studios and, therefore, may convert portions of their living quarters into workshops. Whereas the Internal Revenue Code now makes it possible for many artists to deduct the cost of a home studio from their taxes (see Chapter 9, § B, *supra*), municipal zoning regulations may prohibit these types of arrangements. In many commercially zoned areas where artists can rent low-cost lofts and studios, local codes may preclude maintaining a residence. In residential areas, the artist may have to comply with regulations that require permits and licenses and restrict the size and use of the studio.

Some governments have responded to the hardships these zoning ordinances create for artists. In New York City, a municipal dwelling law was enacted exempting artists and their families from restrictions against living and working in the same apartment unit. The State of California also enacted enabling legislation that grants local municipalities the right to adopt zoning ordinances that would accommodate artists who live in industrially or commercially zoned areas. While these laws solved the immediate problem of artists living and working in the same location, new problems were created. Once it became possible for artists to live and work in Soho in New York City, the area became a magnet for galleries, boutiques, restaurants, and tourists. The Soho lofts that once housed small businesses and textile factories became lavish apartments. "Soho Syndrome" has hit other areas artists have moved into, including the Chelsea, Greenpoint, and Bushwick neighborhoods in New York.

Before Soho became fashionable, no new industry could be enticed into the area, so landlords were pleased to have artists leasing their commercial property. Once development caught on, though, buildings changed hands more often, and artists who had invested substantial sums in their lofts found that their commercial leases afforded little protection. However, *Mandel v. Pitkowsky,* 102 Misc. 2d 478, 425 N.Y.S.2d 926 (Sup. Ct. App. Term 1979), *aff'd*, 76 A.D.2d 807, 429 N.Y.S.2d 550 (1st Dep't 1980), may provide residential loft tenants with some degree of comfort. Pitkowsky and sculptor Ulrich Niemeyer rented commercial quarters for 10 years. The lease limited their occupancy to an artist's studio. Nevertheless, their landlord encouraged them to convert the studio into their residence. Both sides were happy to abide by this illegal arrangement, apparently secure in the knowledge that the city was not diligently inspecting these properties. When the lease expired, the landlord demanded a threefold increase in the rent. The landlord claimed that because the property was commercial rather than residential, it was not subject to the city's rent stabilization laws. The court did not agree: The landlord's express approval of the tenants' 10-year residency converted the studio into a *de facto* residential multiple dwelling.

Another type of regulation that can adversely affect artists are federal laws that inhibit cottage industries. For 40 years, the Department of Labor actively enforced a 1943 regulation that forbid individuals from producing certain craft categories in their homes for profit: knitted outerwear, embroidery, women's apparel, gloves and mittens, buttons and buckles, jewelry, and handkerchiefs. In 1984, the Department of Labor repealed the prohibition on knitted outerwear. Several years later, the prohibitions on the remaining categories, except for women's apparel, were lifted, although in the case of jewelry, the prohibition was lifted only for nonhazardous jewelry work. This greatly decreases the difficulties that have faced home craftworkers in the past, but the Department of Labor continues to regulate homework in these industries, including requiring certification.

When artists work for others under adverse conditions, they may be able to obtain compensation if they are injured. In *Gates v. Central City Opera House Association,* 107 Colo. 93, 108 P.2d 880 (1940), the plaintiff artist was employed to paint murals on an outside wall of an arcade. The employer refused to allow him to postpone the job, notwithstanding the subfreezing temperatures, and the artist suffered frostbite of the fingers. Because the artist stayed on the job for the convenience of his employer, the court allowed him to recover for his injuries.

Artists also may be exposed to disease and injury because of the materials with which they work. Solvent fumes, chemical-based paints, torches and bacteria-laced clay may be quite toxic. The Labeling of Hazardous Art Materials Act (LHAMA) (15 U.S.C. § 1277) was passed in 1988 to require manufacturers to post warning labels on their products based on voluntarily adopted standards. The law requires art supplies to be labeled if they could cause chronic health problems.

Unfortunately, these mandates are often ignored by art supply manufacturers, and many feel that the law's criteria for toxicity are not stringent enough. In addition, art supply manufacturers can avoid these requirements simply by selling their products through hardware stores rather than art supply stores, as only materials marketed as art supplies are required to be labeled under LHAMA. Many products regularly used by artists, such as ammonia, are not classified as art supplies and thus do not carry labels warning against hazardous uses in a studio setting. Even warnings on those supplies which do carry the mandated labels may be inadequate. While most government health warnings are based on exposure to a substance on an occasional basis or, at most, during an eight-hour workday, artists often live and work in the same place and thus have a potential exposure of up to 24 hours.

Not only are artists exposed to hazardous materials when using certain supplies, but the environment surrounding the studio or factory may also be at risk. In 2016, art-glass facilities, which use metal oxides to create different colors of glass, came under fire after the discovery that Bullseye Glass in Portland, Oregon, was emitting heavy metals, including cadmium and arsenic, into the air. Residents near Bullseye Glass have filed a class action law suit seeking a billion dollars in damages, and the EPA is reevaluating requirements for these types of businesses. Faced with the expense of complying with new regulations, Spectrum Glass, one of the leading makers of art glass in the Pacific Northwest, chose to shut down.

As these and other issues demonstrate, much of the activity necessary to improve the working conditions of artists is focused on seeking legislative solutions and on increasing public awareness. Many support organizations exist to help in this effort, including New York Artists Equity Association, Philadelphia/Tri State Artists Equity Association and Volunteer Lawyers for the Arts. These organizations pursue legislative action, educate the public about artists' rights, and assist artists and art organizations with their legal problems. Beyond this assistance, however, the working artist is largely on his or her own. His or her awareness of the practical problems he or she can encounter in creating and selling his or her work, as well as potential solutions to those problems, is, therefore, an important part of achieving success.

CHAPTER 12
COPYRIGHT

A. HISTORICAL: COMMON LAW, COPYRIGHT AND PREEMPTION

All property has been described as conceptually consisting of a "bundle of rights." *Standard Oil Co. v. Clark*, 163 F.2d 917, 930 (1947). For the artist or author, perhaps one of the most important parts of that bundle is the copyright. The ownership of any tangible or intangible property gives the owner the right to use, possess, and enjoy it. Yet, these rights may be inadequate for one who creates the property. Economically, in order to provide an incentive to create, the law gives creators the additional right to profit economically from their investment of time, skill, and energy. Perhaps the most important element of profit for creators is the income derived from the reproduction, adaptation, distribution, performance, and display of their own work. These rights are secured by giving qualifying creators a limited monopoly in their creative work, in the expectation that the public ultimately will benefit from enhanced creative activity.

These basic considerations are embodied in Article I, § 8, cl. 8 of the United States Constitution, which provides that Congress shall have the power "to promote the progress of science and the useful arts, by securing for limited times to authors and inventors the exclusive right to their respective writings and discoveries." Pursuant to this power, the first Congress enacted the Copyright Law of 1790, which was periodically revised until 1909 when Title 17 of the United States Code was enacted. There were no subsequent major revisions of the law until Congress passed the Copyright Revision Act of 1976 (17 U.S.C. § 101 *et seq.*), which became effective January 1, 1978.

Concurrent with the development of federal statutory copyright protection, state courts recognized the existence of common law rights known as common law copyright. These state rights provided an individual numerous rights, including the right to be the first to publish the work and the right to prevent its unauthorized copying. These rights automatically attached when the work was created and existed even if the proprietor was ignorant of them. No formalities were required.

Traditionally, common law copyright protection was available until publication of the work, at which time the work generally became eligible for federal statutory copyright protection under the 1909 Act. By 1976, it was recognized that there was friction between the concurrent state and federal copyright systems. Section 301 of the 1976 Act thus declares that on and after January 1, 1978, federal copyright law preempts the entire field for works and rights within its scope. 17 U.S.C. § 301. It might, therefore, be assumed that common law copyright has been totally abrogated; however, some residue remains. Section 301(b)(1) recognizes that state law may (but is not required to) protect those categories of works that fall outside the scope of the federal statute. For example, choreography which has never been "fixed in a tangible medium of expression" by being filmed or notated and extemporaneous, unrecorded conversations, and speeches fall outside the protected categories of 17 U.S.C. § 102, and, therefore, whatever state protection exists for such works is not preempted. Section 301(b)(2) also provides that federal preemption is not retroactive so that any cause of action arising before January 1, 1978, is preserved.

Finally, Section 301(b)(3) leaves perhaps the greatest residue of common law rights. This section leaves intact state rights that are not equivalent to any of the rights specified in 17 U.S.C. § 106.

Section 301(b)(4) leaves intact state rights with respect to state and local landmarks, historic preservation, zoning, or building codes relating to architectural works protected under Section 102(a)(8).

The above reference to Section 106 is by way of identification and not limitation. Section 106 may be said to identify the general nature of the rights that fall within the general scope of copyright. Copyright protection subsists in an original work of authorship and consists of the right to prohibit reproduction, performance, distribution, or display of such a work. If the act of reproduction, performance, distribution, or display will in itself infringe a right created under state law, then the state right is preempted, but if the state law cause of action requires other elements in addition to or instead of the acts of reproduction, performance, distribution, or display, then the right does not lie within the general scope of copyright, and there is no preemption. 17 U.S.C. § 301. See *Ryan v. Editions Ltd. West, Inc.*, 786 F.3d 754 (9th Cir. 2015); *Rosciszewski v. Arete Associates, Inc.*, 1 F.3d 225 (4th Cir. 1993).

For example, crucial to liability under a deceptive trade practices cause of action is the element of misrepresentation or deception, which is not a part of the copyright infringement cause of action. Similarly, defamation and invasion of privacy may sometimes occur by acts of reproduction, distribution, performance, or display, but the essence of those torts does not lie in such acts. State defamation and invasion of privacy laws will not generally be preempted.

Similarly, state law against "blind bidding" of motion pictures, although it compelled a trade screening of the film as a condition to marketing the film, was held not to be subject to preemption despite the plaintiff's contention that such a screening constituted a public performance within the meaning of the Copyright Act and that the state law, therefore, violated its right to control publication of its work. *Allied Artists Pictures Corp. v. Rhodes*, 496 F. Supp. 408 (S.D. Ohio 1980), *aff'd in part, remanded in part*, 679 F.2d 656 (6th Cir. 1982). The circuit court judge specifically approved of the lower court's analysis of the preemption issue and agreed with its decision that Ohio's state trade regulation, aimed at preventing fraud and misleading trade practices in the bidding process, was not preempted by the Copyright Act because the provision did not deprive the plaintiffs of their right to decide whether or not to perform their work publicly, and because the rights involved were clearly not equivalent.

In *Sturdza v. United Arab Emirates*, 281 F.3d 1287, 1307 (D.C. Cir. 2002), the court found that claims including tortious interference, intentional infliction of emotional distress, and conspiracy to commit fraud rested on more than the defendant's alleged unauthorized copying and thus were not preempted by the copyright law. Similarly, the federal circuit court held that the Copyright Act did not preempt a shrink wrap license agreement that prohibited reverse engineering of the software. *Bowers v. Baystate Technologies, Inc.*, 320 F.3d 1317 (Fed. Cir. 2003). In *Rodrigue v. Rodrigue*, 55 F. Supp. 2d 534 (E.D. La. 1999), *rev'd*, 218 F.3d 432 (5th Cir. 2000), however, the Eastern District of Louisiana ruled that the Copyright Act does preempt Louisiana community property law regarding ownership of paintings the husband created during the marriage, though on appeal the Fifth Circuit found that while the author-spouse retains exclusive control of the copyright pursuant to federal law, the economic benefits of the copyrighted work are community property. *Id.* at 441.

B. SCOPE OF PROTECTION

Statutory copyright does not confer an absolute monopoly. If two original works, similar in all respects, are independently created, each may enjoy protection under the copyright law. Statutory copyright also does not provide, in itself, economic benefits. It merely gives the owner of the copyright specified intangible rights so that he or she may bargain with potential purchasers or users of his or her work for future economic benefits such as royalties.

The rights that are protected by statutory copyright are limited to those specified in the statute. Section 106 of the 1976 Act defines the five exclusive rights granted to the copyright owner. They are the rights to (1) reproduce the copyrighted work by any means, (2) prepare derivative works based on the copyrighted work, (3) distribute copies or phonorecords of the copyrighted work to the public by sale or other transfer of ownership or by rental, lease, or lending, (4) in the case of literary, musical, dramatic, and choreographic works, pantomimes, motion pictures, and other audiovisual works, to perform the work publicly, and (5) in the case of literary, musical, dramatic, and choreographic works, pantomimes and pictorial, graphic, or sculptural works, including the individual images of a motion picture or other audiovisual work, to display the copyrighted work publicly.

These rights may be exercised by the copyright owner or by his or her authorized agent. They are cumulative and may overlap in some cases. A copyright owner may assign, transfer, license, or convey any one or more of the so-called bundle of rights contained in Section 106 and retain the rest. The transferee, assignee, exclusive licensee, or owner of any one of these rights is expressly given the right to maintain any action to protect that right by

Section 201. In addition, the owner of any of these rights may record his or her interest pursuant to Section 205.

Prior to the effective date of the 1976 Act, protection of a work before its publication was governed by common law copyright. With regard to one-of-a-kind works like a painting or a sculpture, some state courts held that all rights in the work passed automatically to the purchaser unless those rights were explicitly retained by the creator in a written agreement. *Pushman v. New York Graphic Society, Inc.*, 39 N.E.2d 249 (N.Y. 1942). The 1976 Act federalized prepublication protection for such works and, in a reversal of the *Pushman* rule, provides that unless there is a written agreement that specifically transfers rights to the purchaser, the creator retains all rights in the work sold. Ownership of the tangible embodiment of the work in the art form is now recognized under federal law as separate and distinct from ownership of the intangible rights in the work.

An important exception to the general rule that the creator of a work owns the copyright in the work is found in the "work made for hire" doctrine. Section 101 of the 1976 Act establishes two categories of work made for hire. The first of these focuses on the employment situation and provides that works created by employees within the scope of their employment are works made for hire and that the copyright in these works belongs to the employer. The second category embraces a number of situations where the creator is an independent contractor rather than an employee. The statute assumes as a starting point that the independent contractor is the copyright owner of any work he or she creates, but Section 101 provides that for works in this second category, the parties may alter their relationship in writing and designate the person for whom the work was made as the copyright owner. Thus, a work specially ordered or commissioned for use as a contribution to a collective work, as part of a motion picture or other audiovisual work, as a translation, as a supplementary work, as a compilation, as an instructional text, as a test, as answer material for a test, or as an atlas will be considered a work made for hire with the copyright ownership residing with the one commissioning or ordering the work—only if this is expressly agreed to in writing prior to creation of the work.

In *Community for Creative Non Violence v. Reid*, 490 U.S. 730 (1989), the court made it clear that the determination of the status of the person creating the work as either an employee or independent contractor must be made in accordance with the rules set forth in the Restatement (Second) of the Law of Agency. The court also pointed out that if the copyrightable work is created by an independent contractor and the parties do not comply with 17 U.S.C. § 101 (definition of "Work made for hire") by having a written agreement on works within the nine categories enumerated in that section, then the independent contractor will retain the copyright in the work unless the contributions of each party are for the purpose of creating a unitary work. In this latter situation, the parties will be considered joint authors.

SEC. B SCOPE OF PROTECTION

The work made for hire test uses the common law agency test of who is an employee vs. who is an independent contractor, but some factors matter more in the analysis, as shown in the following chart is based on the following cases: *Reid*, 490 U.S. 730; *Gary Friedrich Enterprises, LLC v. Marvel Characters, Inc.*, 716 F.3d 302 (2d Cir. 2015); *Lewis v. Activision Blizzard, Inc.*, No. 13–17391, 2015 WL 9258962 (9th Cir. Dec. 18, 2015); *Marvel Characters, Inc. v. Kirby*, 726 F.3d 119 (2d Cir. 2013), *cert. dismissed sub nom. Kirby v. Marvel Characters, Inc.*, 135 S. Ct. 42 (2014); *Carter v. Helmsley-Spear, Inc.*, 71 F.3d 77 (2d Cir. 1995); *Aymes v. Bonelli*, 980 F.2d 857 (2d Cir. 1992); *Lewin v. Richard Avedon Found.*, No. 11–CV–8767 (KMW) (FM), 2015 WL 3948824 (S.D.N.Y. Jun. 26, 2015); *Foster v. Lee*, 93 F. Supp. 3d 223 (S.D.N.Y. 2015); *Urbont v. Sony Music Entertainment*, 100 F. Supp. 3d 342 (S.D.N.Y. 2015); *Vaad L'Hafotzas Sichos, Inc. v. Krinsky*, No. 11–CV–5658 FB JO, 2015 WL 5719826 (E.D.N.Y. Sept. 30, 2015); *Carol Wilson Fine Arts, Inc. v. Qian*, 71 F. Supp. 3d 1151 (D. Or. 2014):

If the situation involves ...	Then the situation leans toward a finding that the relationship is ...
Employer has the right to control the manner and means of production—hours of work, time for completion, order and nature of work	Employer-Employee
Artist sets hours of work, time for completion, order and nature of work	Employer-Independent Contractor
Work must be done at employer's site	Employer-Employee
Work is done at artist's studio or home	Employer-Independent Contractor
Employer supplies tools, materials, equipment	Employer-Employee
Artist supplies tools, materials, equipment	Employer-Independent Contractor
Artist paid a salary	Employer-Employee
Artist paid a one-time fee	Employer-Independent Contractor
Artist paid on commission	Inconclusive. Could go either way

If the situation involves . . .	Then the situation leans toward a finding that the relationship is . . .
Employer has right to assign more work to artist	Employer-Employee (unless contract terms explain this another way)
Employer pays employee benefits or takes care of Social Security, FICA, and payroll tax withholding	Employer-Employee. This is a hugely important factor, the mother of all factors. If the employer is doing this, there is an excellent chance that the court will find an employer-employee relationship no matter what the above factors might argue for or against. See *Aymes*, 980 F.2d at 863; *Carter*, 71 F.3d at 85–88.

C. STATUTORY SUBJECT MATTER

The Copyright Revision Act of 1976 establishes several conditions required for the existence of a copyright. These requirements are found in 17 U.S.C. § 102, which provides that "copyright subsists . . . in original works of authorship fixed in any tangible medium of expression" and then lists eight categories of works of authorship that qualify for copyright protection. The list is not intended to be exhaustive but, rather, is meant to leave the door open for the protection of new types of works that emerge from evolving technologies. Regardless of the form of the work, however, in order to be copyrightable, the work must be an original work of authorship and must be fixed in a tangible medium of expression.

1. ORIGINAL WORK OF AUTHORSHIP

"Originality" in a copyright sense is not synonymous with the "novelty" requirement for patent protection. *Compare Feist Publications, Inc. v. Rural Tel. Serv. Co.*, 499 U.S. 340, 345–51 (1991) (copyright originality requirement), *with* 35 U.S.C. § 103, *and KSR Int'l Co. v. Teleflex Inc.*, 550 U.S. 398, 399 (2007), *and Graham v. John Deere Co. of Kansas City*, 383 U.S. 1, 12–13 (1966) (patent requirements for invention, not anticipated by the prior art). It merely means that the work must be independently created, that is, not copied from another work. *Feist*, 499 U.S. at 345–51. It does not require the work to be unique. *Id*. A work will not be denied copyright protection simply because it is substantially or even completely identical to a work previously created, so long as the later work was not copied from the earlier version. Learned Hand's oft-quoted statement expresses this concept well: "If by some magic a man who had never known of it were to compose a new Keats' 'Ode on a Grecian Urn,' he would be an 'author,' and, if he copyrighted it, others might not copy that poem, though they might of course copy Keats." *Sheldon v. Metro-Goldwyn Pictures Corp.*, 81 F.2d 49, 54 (2d Cir. 1936). Thus, if two artists

SEC. C STATUTORY SUBJECT MATTER 211

independently create identical works, each will be entitled to his or her own copyright and neither will infringe the other's copyright. It is for this reason that many cartographers intentionally include minor errors in their maps: If the identical error appears on another later map, the error will be strong evidence that the later map was copied from the earlier one.

There also is a requirement that the work involve some minimal creativity. In copyright law, the words "creative" or "creativity" have little to do with words such as inventive, inspired, and ingenious, and are almost completely tied to the words "created" and "creator." What creativity means in copyright, therefore, is "created by the author," and little else.

The remaining part of creativity beyond the terms "created" and "creator" is that the work must be conceived of in the mind of the author and then rendered into existence in an act of creation. In *Feist*, 499 U.S. at 345–51, the Supreme Court held that a purely mechanical activity, such as collecting and alphabetizing names and addresses in a telephone directory, will not support a copyright. Sweat of the brow alone is not sufficient to give rise to copyright protection.

Creation means that the artist must render the expression for which copyright protection is sought. If the expression preexists the act of creation, it will not be part of the author's copyright. It is only the artist's particular original and creative expressions of the common attributes of a natural subject (such as an animal) or common theme (such as Santa Claus) that may be protected in copyright. See *id.* at

361. A good example of this is the case of *Satava v. Lowry*, 323 F.3d 805, 812–13 (9th Cir. 2003), which held that the artist's copyright did not prevent others from depicting jellyfish within a clear outer layer of glass. *Satava* implicated the doctrines of copyright law that preclude the complete copyright monopolization of the appearance of real, natural, preexisting objects, or the standard features of stock scenes and themes in art and literature, which are referred to as the "merger" and "scènes à faire" doctrines. See *id.* at 812–13; *Nola Spice Designs, L.L.C. v. Haydel Enterprises, Inc.*, 783 F.3d 527, 549 (5th Cir. 2015); *Oracle Am., Inc. v. Google Inc.*, 750 F.3d 1339, 1363 (Fed. Cir. 2014), *cert. denied*, 135 S. Ct. 2887 (2015); *Zalewski v. Cicero Builder Dev., Inc.*, 754 F.3d 95, 102 (2d Cir. 2014); *Harney v. Sony Pictures Television, Inc.*, 704 F.3d 173, 181 (1st Cir. 2013); *Seng-Tiong Ho v. Taflove*, 648 F.3d 489, 497 (7th Cir. 2011); *Leigh v. Warner Bros.*, 212 F.3d 1210, 1215–16 (11th Cir. 2000); *Ets-Hokin v. Skyy Spirits, Inc.*, 323 F.3d 763, 765–66 (9th Cir. 2003).

2. FIXED IN A TANGIBLE MEDIUM OF EXPRESSION

In order to be copyrightable, a work also must be fixed in a tangible medium of expression. 17 U.S.C. § 101 (definition of "fixed"). This requirement reflects the basic rule that copyright protects the expression of ideas, not the ideas themselves. See 17 U.S.C. § 102. In *Musto v. Meyer*, 434 F. Supp. 32 (S.D.N.Y. 1977), *aff'd*, 598 F.2d 609 (2d Cir. 1979), for example, it was alleged that the book *The Seven Percent Solution* infringed on an article published in a medical journal speculating that Sherlock Holmes had been addicted to cocaine. The works had several similarities in the details of the story, but the court held that the similarities were limited to the idea that Holmes had been tricked by Watson into traveling to Europe to be treated for his cocaine addiction by Sigmund Freud and that the copying of this idea was not an infringement. Similarly, in *Miller v. Columbia Broadcasting System, Inc.*, CV 78–4291–RMT(SX), 209 U.S.P.Q. 502, 1980 WL 1179, at *1 (C.D. Cal. June 5, 1980), a television series about an ex-convict who obtained a law degree in prison was held not to infringe on a copyrighted biography with the same plot. The court noted that if an author could prevent others from using ideas and conceptions, science, poetry, and fiction would be hindered by copyright instead of being promoted.

Section 102 of the 1976 Act reflects this rationale. In order to obtain a copyright, works must be "fixed in a tangible medium of expression, now known or later developed, from which they can be perceived, reproduced, or otherwise communicated, either directly or with the aid of a machine." Section 102(b) further specifically prohibits the copyrighting of ideas. "In no case does copyright protection . . . extend to any idea, procedure, process, system, method of operation, concept, principle, or discovery, regardless of the form in which it is described, explained, illustrated or embodied."

"Fixed in a tangible medium" also means that only certain types of works qualify for copyright protection. The definition in Section 101 of the Act provides that a work is fixed when its tangible embodiment is "sufficiently permanent or stable to permit it to be perceived, reproduced, or otherwise communicated for a period of more than transitory duration." 17 U.S.C. § 101 (definition of "fixed"). Thus, for example, a particular live performance of a play is not independently copyrightable, but a script of the play or a film or videotape of a performance of the play is.

3. OTHER REQUIREMENTS

Within these broad limits, the medium in which a work is executed does not affect its copyrightability. Section 102 contains a list of copyrightable subject matter, which includes: (1) literary works, (2) musical works, including any accompanying words, (3) dramatic works, including any accompanying music, (4) pantomimes and choreographic works, (5) pictorial, graphic, and sculptural works, (6) motion pictures and other audiovisual works, (7) sound recordings, and (8) architectural works. Yet, this list is not intended to be exhaustive, and courts are free to recognize as protectable types of works not expressly included in the list.

Most of these eight categories are undefined. A few definitions in Section 101, however, contain important limitations as to the type of subject matter that may be copyrighted. "Pictorial, graphic and sculptural works," which include works of art, are defined as including:

> ... works of artistic craftsmanship insofar as their form but not their mechanical or utilitarian aspects are concerned; the design of a "useful article," as defined in this section, shall be considered a pictorial, graphic or sculptural work only if, and only to the extent that, such design incorporates ... features that can be identified separately from and are capable of existing independently of, the utilitarian aspects of the article.

Much confusion and litigation have arisen concerning objects with both utilitarian and non-utilitarian aspects and concerning the overall design of utilitarian items. In *Mazer v. Stein*, 347 U.S. 201 (1954), the Supreme Court upheld the copyrightability of a statue used as a lamp base because the statue was capable of existing as a copyrightable work of art separate from the lamp. The language of the 1976 Act expressly endorses the holding of the *Mazer* decision.

Following the *Mazer* ruling, the Copyright Office adopted a regulation that provided:

> If the "sole" intrinsic function of an article is its utility, the fact that it is unique and attractively shaped will not qualify it as a work of art [for copyright purposes]. However, if the shape of a utilitarian object incorporates features ... which can be identified separately and are capable of independent existence as a work of art, such features will be eligible for [copyright] protection.

The "sole intrinsic function" language of the regulation caused some problems, however. In *Esquire, Inc. v. Ringer*, 591 F.2d 796 (D.C. Cir. 1978), the circuit court of appeals reversed a lower court's ruling that had permitted the modern design of an outdoor light fixture to be copyrighted because, as plaintiffs argued, the street light was not solely utilitarian in function but, rather, served both to decorate and to illuminate. The appeals court disagreed and endorsed the view of the Copyright Office that no one could validly claim ownership of the overall shape or configuration of a utilitarian object, no matter how aesthetically pleasing that shape or configuration might be. See page 405 for a picture of the Esquire lamp. In a later case, *Kieselstein-Cord v. Accessories by Pearl, Inc.*, 632 F.2d 989 (2d Cir. 1980), the court upheld the copyrightability of certain belt buckles described as sculptured designs cast in precious metals. This is because they were conceptually if not physically separate from the buckle's utilitarian features, as evidenced by the fact that some people used the buckles as necklaces.

In adopting the language of the new Act, Congress changed "sole intrinsic function" to "an intrinsic function" in order to draw as clear a line as possible between copyrightable works of applied art and uncopyrightable works of industrial design. Thus, under the present law, although the shape of an industrial product may be aesthetically satisfying, copyright protection will be denied unless that shape is physically or conceptually separable from the product. When the copyrightable aspects are separable, copyright protection extends only to those aspects and not the article itself. Recent cases on conceptual and physical separability include: *Varsity Brands, Inc. v. Star Athletica, LLC*, 799 F.3d 468 (6th Cir. 2015); *Home Legend, LLC v. Mannington Mills, Inc.*, 784 F.3d 1404 (11th Cir. 2015); *Inhale, Inc. v. Starbuzz Tobacco, Inc.*, 755 F.3d 1038 (9th Cir. 2014); *Klauber Bros., Inc. v. Target Corp.*, 2015 Copr. L. Dec. P 30, 795, 116 U.S.P.Q.2d 1165 (S.D.N.Y. Jul. 16, 2015).

Courts have recognized that copyright protection extends not only to an original work as a whole, but also to "sufficiently distinctive" elements, such as characters contained within the work that are "especially distinctive." *DC Comics v. Towle*, 802 F.3d 1012, 1019 (9th Cir. 2015), *cert. denied*, 136 S. Ct. 1390 (2016); *Halicki Films, LLC v. Sanderson Sales & Mktg.*, 547 F.3d 1213, 1224 (9th Cir. 2008); *Olson v. National Broadcasting Co.*, 855 F.2d 1446 (9th Cir. 1988). To meet this standard, a character must be "sufficiently delineated" and display "consistent, widely identifiable traits." *Towle*, 802 F.3d at 1019; *Halicki*, 547 F.3d at 1224; *Rice v. Fox Broadcasting Co.*, 330 F.3d 1170 (9th Cir. 2003) (citing *Toho Co., Ltd. v. William Morrow & Co., Inc.*, 33 F. Supp. 2d 1206, 1215 (C.D. Cal. 1998) (Godzilla)). Superman and Mickey Mouse, for example, have both been successfully protected from being copied in several cases. See *Detective Comics, Inc. v. Bruns Publications*, 111 F.2d 432, 433–34 (2d Cir. 1940); *Walt Disney Productions v. Air Pirates*, 581 F.2d 751 (9th Cir. 1978). Characters that exist in nongraphic media, like novels and stories, however, remain in a sort of copyright limbo. The more developed the character, the more likely it is to be copyrightable.

D. FORMALITIES

Under the 1976 Act, unpublished works are protected by the federal copyright law, provided that the works fall within the subject matter of the Act. See generally 17 U.S.C. § 102(a). Failure to comply with the formal requirements of notice, registration, or deposit for published works was no longer automatically fatal to the existence of a copyright, as it generally was under the old law. Yet, even today, compliance with the statutory formalities is necessary to maintain an action for infringement, and compliance creates certain presumptions and procedural advantages under the Act that are important if a suit becomes necessary. Compliance with the formalities, therefore, is always prudent.

Although registration is not required to create a copyright, the 1976 Act provides several incentives for registration:

> First, if the registration is made within five years after the first publication of the work, there is a presumption of the validity of the copyright and of the facts stated in the Certificate of Registration. 17 U.S.C. § 410. This presumption applies in "any judicial proceedings."

> Second, registration is a prerequisite to certain remedies for infringement. Statutory damages and attorneys' fees may be available

for the infringement of an unpublished work if the work was registered prior to the commencement of the infringement. 17 U.S.C. § 412(1). In the case of an infringement occurring after a work is first published, statutory damages and attorneys' fees are available only if the work is registered prior to the infringement.

Third, if the work is registered within three months after the first publication, registration is deemed to have been made as of the date of first publication. 17 U.S.C. § 412(2).

Under the 1909 Act, all published copies of a copyrighted work had to contain the proper notice. With few exceptions, any omission, misplacement, or imperfection in the notice on any copy distributed by authority of the copyright owner placed the work forever in the public domain. Since publication marked the beginning of statutory copyright protection and the termination of common law copyright, the question of whether the work was "published" frequently became the central issue in many notice cases.

Determining when publication had occurred was not easy. Cases involving art that was exhibited for display purposes and not in contemplation of a sale were particularly troublesome. In *Letter Edged in Black Press, Inc. v. Public Building Commission of Chicago*, 320 F. Supp. 1303 (N.D. Ill. 1970), for example, Pablo Picasso contracted to design a large sculpture for the plaza in front of the proposed Chicago Civic Center. He first created a maquette (model) of the sculpture which was placed on public exhibit at the art institute. Pictures of the maquette and of a larger aluminum working model of the sculpture were published in Chicago newspapers and national and international magazines, and picture postcards of the models were sold to the public. Neither the pictures nor the models bore any copyright notices, but when the sculpture itself was ultimately erected, it bore a copyright notice in the name of Chicago's Public Building Commission.

Five months later, the commission applied for and was granted a certificate of copyright registration. Plaintiffs challenged the validity of the copyright, claiming that the public exhibition of the models, the wide distribution of photographs of them, and the sale of postcards to the public without notice of copyright had placed the work into the public domain so that copyright protection was irretrievably lost. The defendant commission argued that the full-sized sculpture, the only work for which copyright protection was being claimed, had been exhibited with the required copyright notice and that the registration was, therefore, valid. The court agreed with the plaintiffs, holding that publication of the models without notice of copyright caused the work to pass into the public domain. At the time the models were created, the court said, the full-size sculpture was only an uncopyrightable idea not yet embodied in a tangible form. The court characterized the full-size sculpture as merely a copy, albeit on a grand scale, of the models that were indisputably in the public domain and, therefore, held the commission's claim of copyright in the sculpture invalid. See page 404 for a photograph of the *Chicago Picasso*.

Publication of a work is still of some importance for works published after January 1, 1976, and prior to March 1, 1989. Publication during this period determines whether a work must bear notice of copyright. "Publication" is defined by Section 101 of the Act as "the distribution of copies of phonorecords of a work to the public by sale or other transfer of ownership, or by rental, lease, or lending." The definition further provides that a "public performance or display of a work does not of itself constitute publication."

Cases prior to the 1976 Act drew a distinction, accepted under the new Act, between general and limited publication, holding that the statutory consequences of publication did not apply when a work was distributed only to a "definitely selected group and for a limited purpose, without the right of diffusion, reproduction, distribution or sale." *White v. Kimmel*, 193 F.2d 744 (9th Cir. 1952). Thus, when an artist distributes prints or copies of his or her work to close associates for comment with the understanding that these copies are not to be further reproduced and distributed, the work is not considered to have been published. Similarly, the distribution of copies of the artist's work to magazines or newspapers for purposes of review and criticism does not constitute general publication. Rather, such activities merely involve limited publication without statutory significance.

For works published between January 1, 1978, and March 1, 1989, Section 401 of the 1976 Act requires that a proper copyright notice "be placed on all publicly distributed copies from which the work can be visually perceived, either directly or with the aid of a machine or device." The form of this notice is the symbol "©," the word "copyright," or its abbreviation "copr." plus the full name of the copyright owner and the year of first publication. A short form of notice omitting the year of first publication could be used only when copyrighted artwork is reproduced "in or on greeting cards, postcards, stationery, jewelry, toys, or any useful articles." An abbreviation of the name of the copyright owner or an alternative designation may be used if the name can be recognized or the designation is generally known.

The notice itself need not be placed on the front of the copy, but it must be situated so "as to give reasonable notice of the claim of copyright." The Copyright Office's regulations, 37 C.F.R. § 201.20 (1999), state that where a work is reproduced in two-dimensional copies, a notice must be affixed so as to withstand normal use on the front or back of the copies or attached to any backing, mounting, matting, framing, or any other material to which the copy is attached. Where the work is reproduced in three-dimensional copies, a notice must be affixed to any visible portion of the work or to any base, mounting, framing, or any other material on which the copy is durably attached. Where it is not possible or practical to affix the notice because of the size or material of the work, notice is acceptable if it appears on a tag attached to the work.

The copyright proprietor may have to modify the copyright notice if he or she wishes to secure international protection. Under the Universal Copyright Convention, signed at Geneva on Sept. 6, 1952 (see Paul J. Sherman, *The Universal Copyright Convention: Its Effect on United States Law*, 55 COLUM. L. REV. 1137, 1167, 1175 (1955)), protection exists only if the long form of notice is used with the international copyright symbol ©. The short form notice, without the date, is inadequate. This provision is largely academic, however, because the Uniform Copyright convention has almost entirely been superseded by the Berne Convention, mentioned below, and thus state parties such as the United States will be governed by Berne's more relaxed notice standards.

Copyright protection in the Western Hemisphere also is available under the Buenos Aires Convention if the legend "All Rights Reserved" is added to the copyright notice and if the proprietor has complied with his or her own nation's copyright laws. See Buenos Aires Convention, signed at Buenos Aires, Aug. 11, 1910; ratified by the United States, March 12, 1911; proclaimed July 13, 1914. Mexico is the most recent country to ratify this convention. Decree signed by President Ruiz Cortinas of Mexico on Jan. 5, 1953. Diario Oficial 6–7, Feb. 21, 1953; Copyright Office Bibliographical Bulletin, Vol. 2, No. 2, p. 1, Feb. 1953.

If notice of copyright was not properly affixed prior to March 1, 1989, the work fell into the public domain. However, Section 405(a) of the 1976 Act provides for limited circumstances in which publication without notice did not invalidate a statutory copyright. If notice was omitted from "a relatively small number of copies or phonorecords distributed to the public," the copyright was not lost. Similarly, the copyright was not lost if the work was registered within five years after the publication without notice and if a reasonable effort was made to add notice to all copies or phonorecords distributed in the United States after the omission was discovered. Finally, the copyright was not lost if the omission of notice was "in violation of an express requirement in writing" that the copies or phonorecords bear the prescribed notice.

Although statutorily unexcused omissions of notice prior to March 1, 1989, placed a work in the public domain, noncompliance with the statutory requirements of deposit and registration did not. The copyright owner must, however, register his or her work within five years of publication in order to take advantage of the excuse for omission of notice provided for by Section 405(a)(2) when the notice was required.

The United States became a party to the Berne Convention on March 1, 1989. See Berne Convention Implementation Act. As a result of U.S. participation in this treaty, U.S. copyright proprietors enjoy protection in 170 other countries. See http://www.wipo.int/treaties/en/ShowResults.jsp?treaty_id=15.

In order to join the Berne Union, however, it was necessary for the United States to relax some of the formalities. On or after March 1, 1989, it is no longer necessary to utilize the copyright notice after publication of a work in order to retain a copyright. This relaxation of the notice requirement does give rise to a dilemma since it is now difficult to determine whether a published work without a copyright notice is protected or not. In order to defeat a possible defense of "innocent infringement," copyright proprietors should continue to use the copyright notice.

If registration takes place within three months after first publication of the work, the plaintiff is entitled to the full range of remedies provided by the Act against infringers, but if the copyright owner waits longer than three months after publication to register, Section 412 provides that remedies are limited to injunctive relief and actual damages, and the copyright owner is not entitled to statutory damages or attorneys' fees for infringements occurring prior to registration. Even if the copyright owner misses the three-month deadline, it is still in his or her interest to register promptly, for under Section 410(c), if registration takes place within five years of first publication, the registration certificate constitutes "*prima facie* evidence of the validity of the copyright and of the facts stated in the certificate." The evidentiary weight of a certificate when a work is registered more than five years after publication is completely within the discretion of the court.

In order to register a claim to copyright, the copyright proprietor must comply with the provisions of Section 408 by completing an online or paper application form, paying a registration fee, and depositing copies of the work with the Copyright Office, Library of Congress, Washington, D.C. 20559. The fees vary according to the type of application:

Registrations online:

Single Application (single author, same claimant, one work, not for hire) $35

Standard Application (all other filings) $55

Registrations on paper:

Paper filing on Form TX, Form VA, Form PA, Form SE, and Form SR $85

See Copyright.gov—Fees, http://www.copyright.gov/docs/fees.html. For purposes of Section 408, one complete copy must be deposited if the work is unpublished and two complete copies of the best edition if the work is published. Copies deposited at the Library of Congress under Section 407, which is discussed in the next paragraph, may be used to satisfy the deposit requirements of Section 408 only if they are accompanied by the prescribed application and fee. The Register of Copyright is given considerable flexibility by Section 408(c)(1) with respect to administrative classifications, aggregations of collective works and alternative forms of deposit.

Unlike the 1909 Act, the 1976 Act separates the registration and deposit requirements and allows a person to satisfy the deposit requirements without ever having to register the work. Under Section 407 of the 1976 Act, within three months of a work's first publication, the copyright owner must deposit in the

Copyright Office two complete copies of the best edition of the work. The Register of Copyrights is given discretion under Section 407(c) to issue regulations varying this deposit requirement or exempting certain categories of work completely, and it has done so. If copies are not submitted within three months of publication, the Register of Copyrights may demand the required deposit. If copies are not submitted within three months after demand has been made, the person upon whom demand was made may be liable under Section 407(d) for a fine for each work not submitted. In addition, he or she may be required to pay the Library of Congress an amount equal to the retail cost of the work or, if no retail cost has been established, the reasonable costs incurred by the Library in acquiring copies on its own. Finally, if the copyright owner willfully or repeatedly refuses to comply with a demand, he or she may be liable for a substantial additional fine. While the deposit of copies pursuant to Section 407 is not a condition of copyright protection, in light of the penalty provisions, it would indeed be foolish not to comply.

E. DURATION

The duration of copyright depends upon when and how the work was created. In general, if the author is an individual, works created on or after the effective date of the 1976 Act, January 1, 1978, will have copyright protection from the instant of creation until 70 years after the author's death. For works created jointly, the period is measured by the life of the last surviving author plus 70 years. The copyright in works made for hire, corporate-owned works, and for anonymous or pseudonymous works lasts 95 years from the year of first publication, or 120 years from the year of the work's creation, whichever period expires first.

Unlike the 1909 Act, the 1976 Act requires no renewal. Renewal of copyrights in works first published prior to January 1, 1978, however, was required in the 28th year after first publication (codified at 17 U.S.C. § 104A).

A law providing for the automatic renewal of such works was enacted in June 1992. Pub. L. 102–307.

A provision of the General Agreement on Tariffs and Trade (GATT), effective in 1996, automatically restored copyright protection to certain foreign works that were in the public domain. Congress enacted this provision to bring the United States into closer harmony with the Berne Convention. To have its copyright restored pursuant to this provision, a work:

(1) Must have a "source country" that is not the United States and that is a member of Berne Convention, World Trade Organization, or that is a country as to which the President has issued a proclamation;

(2) If the work is published, have been first published in a country that is not the United States, is a member of Berne or the World Trade Organization, or is a country as to which the President has issued a proclamation, and not have been published

in the United States within 30 days of its first publication;

(3) Must still be protected by copyright in its source country; and

(4) Must be in the public domain in the United States for one of three designated reasons:

    (a) Because the copyright owner failed to comply with formalities once imposed by U.S. copyright law, including a failure to renew, a lack of proper notice, or failure to comply with domestic manufacturing requirements;

    (b) Because the work is a pre-February 15, 1972, sound recording; or

    (c) Because the work was first published in a country with which the United States did not then have a copyright treaty or reciprocal proclamations.

A work's source country is the country of the author's or rightholder's nationality or domicile, and the rightholder is the person who first fixes a sound recording with authorization or who acquires the rights to a sound recording from such a person. The duration of a copyright restored pursuant to this provision is the same as it would have been had the work never entered the public domain in the United States. That is, the duration of restored copyrights will depend on whether the work in question was first published or registered before 1978.

Persons who copied or created derivative works of now-protected works which were previously in the public domain ("reliance parties") are granted some rights to continue to do so. The length of time depends on whether and when the copyright owner makes certain filings with the Copyright Office or serves certain notices on reliance parties.

Copyright owners often assign or license the right to exploit a work at a time when the work's true value is unknown. Congress dealt with potential problems by giving individuals who created the work, other than when the work is a work made for hire, an opportunity to renegotiate earlier agreements. Under Section 203, the grant of a transfer or license may be irrevocable for 35 years, but after that period, the grantor, or his or her successor, has five years within which to terminate the grant or license. This termination is not automatic, and Section 203(a)(4) requires that notice be given within a proscribed period of time prior to the termination. Termination divests the transferee or licensee of the right to exploit the copyrighted work, although termination of a grant of a transfer or license of copyright does not affect rights arising under any other federal, state, or foreign law.

In *Eldred v. Ashcroft*, 537 U.S. 186 (2003), the U.S. Supreme Court upheld the constitutionality of the Sonny Bono Copyright Term Extension Act of 1998, which extended copyright duration by an additional 20 years.

F. INFRINGEMENT

1. ELEMENTS OF INFRINGEMENT

Section 501 of the 1976 Act provides that "[a]nyone who violates any of the exclusive rights of the copyright owner . . . is an infringer of the copyright." Reduced to fundamental terms, the plaintiff in an infringement action needs to establish only two facts: that he or she is the copyright owner of the work and that the defendant's use of the work violated one of the plaintiff's exclusive rights. See *Feist*, 499 U.S. at 361; *Range Road Music, Inc. v. East Coast Foods, Inc.*, 668 F.3d 1148, 1153 (9th Cir. 2012). Where the work has been registered within five years of the plaintiff's action, as pointed out above, the registration certificate constitutes *prima facie* evidence of all the facts stated therein.

In infringement cases, direct evidence of copying by the defendant is frequently difficult to obtain. The case, *Rogers v. Koons*, 960 F.2d 301 (2d Cir. 1992), is an exception, because the artist and alleged infringer, Jeffrey Koons, actually wrote to his ceramic sculptors telling them to make their work look more like the original postcard they were supposed to be copying, thus leaving a paper trail of his copying. *Id.* at 305. See page 406 for photographs of the two works at issue in *Rogers v. Koons*. Copying is ordinarily established indirectly by proof of the defendant's access to the plaintiff's work and by showing substantial similarity between the plaintiff's and the defendant's works. See *Bouchat v. Baltimore Ravens, Inc.*, 241 F.3d 350, 353 (4th Cir.

2001); *Ty, Inc. v. GMA Accessories, Inc.*, 132 F.3d 1167, 1170 (7th Cir. 1997). Once a plaintiff has established "access" and "substantial similarity," a defendant claiming that the work was independently created has the burden of establishing that fact.

Some courts have defined access as the actual viewing or knowledge of the plaintiff's work, but since direct evidence of access is often as difficult to establish as direct evidence of copying, most courts analyze access in terms of whether the defendant had a reasonable opportunity to copy the plaintiff's work, for example, where the plaintiff's work had been widely disseminated before the defendant's work was published. In a recent music copyright infringement case, Michael Skidmore, the representative of the estate of a member of the rock group Spirit, accused Led Zeppelin greats Jimmy Page and Robert Plant of lifting a guitar passage from Spirit's song, *Taurus*, and using it for the opening guitar passage in the iconic hit, *Stairway to Heaven*. *Skidmore v. Led Zeppelin*, No. 2:15–CV–03462–RGK–AGR (C.D. Cal. 2016). The trial judge allowed the infringement case to be submitted to the jury in part because the two bands had toured together in the late 1960's, creating the inference that Page or Plant of Led Zeppelin would have had opportunities to hear Spirit play the song, *Taurus*. See Kory Grow, *Led Zeppelin Win in 'Stairway to Heaven' Trial*, Rollingstone.com (June 23, 2016), available at http://www.rollingstone.com/music/news/led-zeppelin-prevail-in-stairway-to-heaven-lawsuit-20160623. The jury ultimately determined that Led Zeppelin's *Stairway to Heaven* and *Taurus* were not substantially similar, and that

Page and Plant had not infringed on the work. In contrast, Robin Thicke and Pharrell Williams were ordered to pay $5.3 million to the estate of Marvin Gaye because a jury determined that Thicke and Williams' song, *Blurred Lines*, infringed on Gaye's song, *Got to Give it Up*. See Kory Grow, *Robin Thicke, Pharrell Lose Multi-Million Dollar 'Blurred Lines' Lawsuit*, Rollingstone.com (Mar. 10, 2015), available at http://www.rollingstone.com/music/news/robin-thicke-and-pharrell-lose-blurred-lines-lawsuit-2015 0310; Ashley Cullins, *Judge Denies Marvin Gaye Family's Request for Pharrell and Robin Thicke to Pay Their Legal Fees*, Hollywood Reporter (Apr. 12, 2016 at 12:21pm PT), available at http://www.hollywoodreporter.com/thr-esq/judge-denies-marvin-gaye-familys-883093.

If the similarity between the plaintiff's and the defendant's works is striking and substantial, copying may be inferred even in the absence of proof of access. See, e.g., *Singleton v. Dean*, 611 Fed. Appx. 671, 672 (11th Cir. 2015); *Repp v. Webber*, 132 F.3d 882, 889 (2d Cir. 1997); *Corwin v. Walt Disney Co.*, 475 F.3d 1239, 1253 (11th Cir. 2007); *Selle v. Gibb*, 741 F.2d 896, 901 (7th Cir. 1984). This is done in two steps. The first step involves a comparison of the work's extrinsic similarities: subject matter, setting, materials used, and the like. Expert testimony is admissible as to these elements. The second step involves a more subjective measurement of the two works' intrinsic similarity. The test here is whether an average lay observer would recognize that the defendant's work has been copied from the plaintiff's work. No expert testimony is customarily allowed in making this determination.

2. REMEDIES

Even before trial, the copyright owner can obtain some relief. See 17 U.S.C. § 501 *et seq.* For example, the court has discretion to order the impoundment of all the existing copies of the allegedly infringing work and of the mechanical means to produce further copies. If this is done, the court will generally require the plaintiff to file an affidavit and post a bond.

If the defendant's work is held to be an infringement, the court may grant an injunction under Section 502 against all future infringements and may, under Section 503(b), order the destruction of all infringing copies and the means of making them. The infringer also may be held liable for money damages under Section 504, either for the copyright owner's actual damages plus any additional profits the infringer made or for statutory damages. The choice between these two remedies is up to the copyright owner. Under Section 504(b), the copyright owner is entitled to recover "the actual damages suffered . . . as a result of the infringement, and any profits of the infringer that are attributable to the infringement and are not taken into account in computing the actual damages." In proving profits, the copyright owner need only establish the gross revenues the infringer received. The infringer then must prove deductible expenses and any elements of profit not attributable to the infringement.

At any time before final judgment is rendered, the copyright owner of a work that was registered prior to the infringement or within three months of first publication may waive the claim for actual damages and elect instead to recover statutory damages under Section 504(c). The amount of statutory damages is at the discretion of the court, within certain guidelines. The court can award no less than $750 and no more than $30,000 per work infringed. The maximum possible recovery is increased to $150,000 if the copyright owner proves that the infringement was committed willfully. On the other hand, the minimum possible recovery may be reduced to not less than $200 if the defendant proves that he or she was unaware and had no reason to be aware that the infringing acts constituted an infringement. In addition, the court shall not award statutory damages if the infringer believed and had reasonable grounds for believing that the use of the copyrighted work was a fair use under Section 107 and the infringer was an employee of any of several organizations listed in Section 504(c)(2).

In addition to injunctive relief and actual and statutory damages, Section 505 gives the court discretion to award the full costs of litigation to the prevailing party in appropriate cases where the work was registered prior to the date of infringement or within three months of publication. The costs of litigation may include reasonable attorneys' fees to the prevailing party, whether it be a plaintiff or a defendant. *Kirtsaeng v. John Wiley & Sons, Inc.*, No. 15–375, 2016 WL 3317564 (U.S. June 16, 2016).

The United States Justice Department is empowered by Section 506 to bring a criminal action against a copyright infringer. The prosecution must prove beyond a reasonable doubt that the infringement was committed willfully and for the purpose of commercial gain. If convicted, the infringer can be fined and sentenced to jail for up to one year, with even higher penalties for film or record piracy. There is also a fine that may be imposed for fraudulently placing a false copyright notice on a work, for fraudulently removing or altering a copyright notice, or for knowingly making a false representation of a material fact in an application for copyright registration.

3. FAIR USE

Not all situations that involve copying of a copyrighted work necessarily constitute an infringement. While most of the exceptions and exclusions of Sections 107–118 of the 1976 Act are beyond the scope of this book, one is particularly relevant to artists. This is the fair use doctrine, originally a judicially created doctrine and now codified in Section 107, which provides:

> Notwithstanding the provisions of sections 106 and 106A, the fair use of a copyrighted work, including such use ... as criticism, comment, news reporting, teaching (including multiple copies for classroom use), scholarship, or research, is not an infringement of copyright. In determining whether the use made of a work ...

is a fair use the factors to be considered shall include:

(1) the purpose and character of the use, including whether such use is of a commercial nature or is for nonprofit educational purposes;

(2) the nature of the copyrighted work;

(3) the amount and substantiality of the portion used in relation to the copyrighted work as a whole; and

(4) the effect of the use upon the potential market for or value of the copyrighted work.

The Act does not rank these four criteria; nor does it exclude other factors in determining fair use. The Supreme Court once held that the economic factor was the most important. *Stewart v. Abend*, 495 U.S. 207, 237 (1990); *Sony Corp. of Am. v. Universal City Studios, Inc.*, 464 U.S. 417, 448 (1984). However, in *Campbell v. Acuff-Rose Music, Inc.*, 510 U.S. 569, 579 (1994), the Supreme Court softened its emphasis on the profitability of copying alleged to be fair use. Justice Souter, writing the decision of the court, noted that "the mere fact that a use is educational and not for profit does not insulate it from a finding of infringement, any more than the commercial character of a use bars a finding of fairness." *Id.* at 584. *Campbell* held that the copyright statute, section 107, like the First Amendment-driven law and public-policy it codifies, "calls for case-by-case analysis. . . . Nor may the four statutory factors be treated in isolation, one from another. All are to be explored, and the results weighed together, in light of the purposes of copyright." *Id.* at 577–78. The court emphasized that no one factor was a decisive factor, and opined that a good score on one or more factors could overcome a bad score on other factors. See *id.* at 577–93.

Artists who use a tangible object, such as book pages, postcards, and the like, as part of their art, have argued that they have the right to do so under the "first sale doctrine," 17 U.S.C. § 109(a) (that is, the right of an owner of a particular copy to use and resell the copy regardless of the original creator's copyrights), in conjunction with the fair use doctrine, which allows use of copyrighted art for certain expressive or educational uses (discussed in more detail below). Two United States Court of Appeals cases dealing with repurposed art have been decided on this issue, but the results of the cases conflict. In *Mirage Editions, Inc. v. Albuquerque A.R.T. Co.*, 856 F.2d 1341 (9th Cir. 1988), *cert. denied*, 489 U.S. 1018 (1989), the Ninth Circuit held that A.R.T., which removed selected pages from a book of Patrick Nagel it had purchased and mounted them on ceramic tiles, had infringed the rights of the copyright owner. The Seventh Circuit, however, held in *Lee v. A.R.T. Co.*, 125 F.3d 580, 582 (7th Cir. 1997), that the mounting of Annie Lee's note cards and lithographs on ceramic tiles was not infringing, analogizing the process to the framing an artwork. The *Lee* case seems to have the better of the argument, particularly after the Supreme Court has re-endorsed and strengthened the "first sale doctrine" in *Kirtsaeng v. John Wiley & Sons, Inc.*, 133 S. Ct. 1351 (2013).

4. PARODY

Parody is an unauthorized use of copyrighted material that can fall into the category of fair use. Courts must apply the four factors cited in the Act in order to determine whether a particular parody is a fair use.

In *Fisher v. Dees*, 794 F.2d 432 (9th Cir. 1986), Marvin Fisher and Jack Segal, the composers of the 1950s standard *When Sunny Gets Blue*, refused the request of comic Rick Dees and his recording company to use the music in a comic rendition. A parody of the song was recorded nevertheless and released as part of a record album. The parody runs for 29 seconds and is entitled *When Sonny Sniffs Glue*. The composers sued for copyright infringement and defamation.

As to the copyright infringement action, Dees argued that use of the song for parody constituted a fair use. The court agreed and affirmed the lower court ruling in favor of the defendants. Four facts were analyzed in the court's decision:

- The subject of the parody was the song itself and singer Johnny Mathis's distinctive rendition of it. It was held that if the song was used as a vehicle for comedic effect unrelated to the song, then fair use protection would not be available since use of the song would not have been necessary.

- Dees' conduct did not constitute bad faith according to the court. Parodists are rarely able to acquire permission from composers,

- even for royalties or fees. The parody defense exists in part for that very reason. Dees should not be penalized because he showed some consideration.

- The court held that the use was of a commercial nature, which is usually an unfair exploitation, but a defendant can rebut that presumption by showing that the parody does not diminish the economic value of the original work, which is the fourth factor considered.

- This court felt that the economic factor, that is, the effect on the potential market value of the work, was the most important one. In this case, the parody was not intended as a substitute for the original. Consumers wanting to listen to a romantic ballad would not purchase the parody instead. Thus, the parody had no economic impact.

For those reasons, plus the fact that Dees used only a brief portion of the original in the parody, the use was found to be a fair use, and the copyright infringement claim was dismissed.

In a case combining both parody and fair use, the United States Court of Appeals for the Ninth Circuit in a divided opinion held that Jerry Falwell's use of a parody of him that appeared in *Hustler Magazine* was fair use despite the fact that Mr. Falwell used the work in its entirety and for fundraising purposes. The majority pointed out that "an individual in rebutting a copyrighted work containing derogatory information about himself may copy such parts of the work as are necessary to permit understandable comment." *Hustler Magazine, Inc. v. Moral Majority, Inc.*, 796 F.2d 1148 (9th Cir. 1986).

In a related case filed by Mr. Falwell against *Hustler Magazine*, the United States Supreme Court held that public figures and public officials may not recover damages for the intentional infliction of emotional distress by reason of the publication of parody without showing in addition that the publication contains a false statement of fact which was made with actual malice. *Hustler Magazine v. Falwell*, 485 U.S. 46 (1988).

As described in *Campbell*, 510 U.S. at 580–81, and other parody fair use cases, such as *Leibovitz v. Paramount Pictures Corp.*, 137 F.3d 109, 110 (2d Cir. 1998), and *Suntrust Bank v. Houghton Mifflin Co.*, 268 F.3d 1257 (11th Cir. 2001), if the defendant asserting a fair use defense achieves a purpose and character of parody, the other fair use factors fall neatly into line:

- Defendant is allowed to make commercial uses of the original material (factor 1);

- Defendant can use famous, extremely valuable, copyrighted works, and produce the parody in the same medium as the original— e.g., a sound recording parody of another sound recording; a motion picture parody of another motion picture (factor 2);

- Defendant gets to take vast amounts of the work in order to "conjure up" the original—

meaning, identify the target of the criticism (factor 3); and

- Defendant has a fair chance to convince the court that its parody will not dilute or undercut the market for the original because people who like and pay for the original are unlikely to want to pay for a spoof of the original (element 4).

The defendant must convince the court that one of the purposes for creating the work is to make fun of, spoof, or criticize the original work; after that, it will not hurt that defendant also wanted to accomplish other objectives with the work. Parody does not have to be the sole purpose or even the primary purpose, as long as one purpose for the work was parody. *Campbell*, 510 U.S. at 580–81; *Leibovitz*, 137 F.3d at 110.

5. THE TRANSFORMATIVE TEST

The transformative test has become the consummate test for fair use in United States copyright cases. The transformative test looks to whether a fair use merely supersedes the objects and intentions of the original work—meaning, does it simply take the whole or part of the original and repeat it for its original expressive purpose—or does the new work add something new, creating new content, meaning and expression, because of some transformative treatment of the original material. *Campbell*, 510 U.S. at 579. The transformation can be by adding an overwhelming amount of new content, so that the original work no longer shines through in the final work. *Cariou v. Prince*, 714 F.3d 694, 699–700 (2d. Cir. 2013); *Seltzer v. Green Day, Inc.*, 725 F.3d 1170, 1176 (9th Cir. 2013). It can also be by "recontextualizing" the original work—placing it in a new context so that it no longer serves the same function and purpose for which it originally was created. See *A.V. ex rel. Vanderhye v. iParadigms, LLC*, 562 F.3d 630, 639 (4th Cir. 2009); *Perfect 10, Inc. v. Amazon.com, Inc.*, 508 F.3d 1146, 1165 (9th Cir. 2007); *Blanch v. Koons*, 467 F.3d 244, 252 (2d Cir. 2006); *Bill Graham Archives v. Dorling Kindersley Ltd.*, 448 F.3d 605, 608–09 (2d Cir. 2006). But see *Salinger v. Colting*, 607 F.3d 68 (2d Cir. 2010) (although Colting added new characters and situations, a new plot, and a completely different take on the "Catcher in the Rye" motif, the court found the work "60 Years Later-Coming Through the Rye" was not transformative of Salinger's original work, and not a fair use); *Gaylord v. United States*, 595 F.3d 1364 (Fed. Cir. 2010) (although Gaylord changed many aspects of the appearance of the Korean War Memorial, affecting the meaning, tone, and "mood" of the work, the court found his image was not transformative of the memorial, and not a fair use); *Dr. Seuss Enters., LP v. Penguin Books USA*, 109 F.3d 1394 (9th Cir. 1997) (although the second work, "The Cat Not in the Hat" contained a completely new plot and new characters commenting on the O.J. Simpson trial, the court found the work did not comment on or criticize the original "Cat in the Hat" by Geisel, and it was not a transformative fair use). The new function and purpose should be something beneficial to the public (although it usually benefits the new user, too).

The formula that led the Supreme Court to adopt the overarching fair use concept of transformation in *Campbell*, 510 U.S. at 579, is deceptively simple: Transformation of existing material creates new material—new expression that communicates new ideas and new meaning through new content or a new context. E.g., *The Authors Guild v. Google, Inc.*, 804 F.3d 202 (2d Cir. 2015); *Katz v. Google Inc.*, 802 F.3d 1178 (11th Cir. 2015); *Neri v. Monroe*, No. 11–CV–429–SLC, 2014 Copr. L. Dec. ¶ 30, 571, 110 U.S.P.Q.2d 1506 (W.D. Wis. 2014); *Morris v. Young*, 925 F. Supp. 2d 1078 (C.D. Cal. 2013); *Morris v. Guetta*, No. LA CV12–00684 JAK, 2013 WL 440127 (C.D. Cal. Feb. 4, 2013); *North Jersey Media Group Inc. v. Pirro and Fox News Network, LLC*, 74 F. Supp. 3d 605 (S.D.N.Y. 2015). But see *Kienitz v. Sconnie National LLC*, 766 F.3d 756 (7th Cir. 2014) (discounting the use of the transformative test in fair use determinations). And the promotion of new expression to benefit the public was the reason we have copyright protection in the first place.

CHAPTER 13
TRADEMARK

A. INTRODUCTION

In addition to copyright protection, discussed in the preceding chapter, another form of intellectual property important to the arts community is trademark law. On the federal level, the following laws define the trademark law of the United States, codified in the United States Code at 15 U.S.C. § 1051 *et seq.*:

- Lanham Act of 1946
- Trademark Law Revision Act of 1988
- Federal Trademark Dilution Act of 1995
- Anticybersquatting Consumer Protection Act (1999)
- Madrid Protocol Implementation Act (2002), (15 U.S.C. §§ 1141–1141n)
- Trademark Dilution Revision Act of 2006

Together, these laws govern the regulation of trade and service marks and provide for their registration with the U.S. Patent and Trademark Office.

Artists from time to time may want to use a trademark as a symbolic communicative device. They want to use the mark as a shorthand symbol to represent the business or industry or individual company for which it stands, and the theme, or message, or values that the mark communicates.

Many museums and historical societies manufacture and market products that they wish to have identified with their institutions. This may be accomplished through the use of trademarks. Additionally, a service mark is a common way for a museum to protect its name. For example, *The Museum of Modern Art* has been a registered service mark since 1962. Artists and dealers may also desire to protect their trademarks.

B. BACKGROUND

The federal trademark laws were enacted by Congress pursuant to its power under the Commerce Clause of the United States Constitution. *In re Trade-Mark Cases*, 100 U.S. 82, 87–88 (1879). The primary purpose of trademark law is the protection of consumers, *Merck Eprova AG v. Gnosis S.p.A.*, 760 F.3d 247, 262 (2d Cir. 2014); *Mattel, Inc. v. Walking Mountain Productions*, 353 F.3d 792, 806–08 (9th Cir. 2003), so that they can identify the source of a particular product or service, although consumers do not have standing to enforce the statute. *Island Insteel Systems, Inc. v. Waters*, 296 F.3d 200 (3rd Cir. 2002). Rather, enforcement is vested in the proprietor of the mark. *Scotch Whiskey Ass'n v. Majestic Distilling Co., Inc.*, 958 F.2d 594 (4th Cir. 1992), *cert. denied*, 506 U.S. 862 (1992).

C. FEDERAL COMMON LAW TRADEMARK

A trademark is "any word, name, symbol, or device, or any combination thereof used . . . to identify and distinguish . . . goods, including a unique product, from those manufactured or sold by others and to indicate the source of the goods, even if that source is unknown." A service mark distinguishes the services of one person from the services of others. 15 U.S.C. § 1127. Both trademarks and service marks are commonly referred to as "marks."

The key concept is that the mark must be distinguishable. (See 15 U.S.C. § 1052.) The most distinctive marks are those that are fanciful, that is, those that have no particular meaning or connotation other than to identify the source of a particular product or service. For example, the mark *Coloratura* to identify wearable art is fanciful. Less distinctive are arbitrary marks that have another meaning. They are afforded substantial protection since the other meaning bears no resemblance to the product or service identified, such as *Uroboros* (the image of the serpent swallowing its own tail) to identify art glass. Other marks that merely suggest attributes without being directly descriptive are called suggestive and are also protected. For example, *Kroma* is a suggestive mark for decorative dichroic glass since it sounds like "chroma," the Greek word for color.

Generic and descriptive trademarks are not considered distinctive. A generic mark merely identifies the product for what it is and is never afforded trademark protection. See *Park 'N Fly, Inc. v. Dollar Park & Fly, Inc.*, 469 U.S. 189, 194 (1985); *Pom Wonderful LLC v. Hubbard*, 775 F.3d 1118, 1126 (9th Cir. 2014); *Miller's Ale House, Inc. v. Boynton Carolina Ale House, LLC*, 702 F.3d 1312, 1317 (11th

Cir. 2012). A descriptive mark, which characterizes the attributes or qualities of the product, however, may be protected in limited circumstances. A descriptive mark may be protected if the trademark proprietor can prove that it has acquired a secondary meaning. *KP Permanent Make-Up, Inc. v. Lasting Impression I, Inc.*, 543 U.S. 111, 122 (2004); *Vail Associates, Inc. v. Vend-Tel-Co.*, 516 F.3d 853, 866 (10th Cir. 2008). "Secondary meaning" is an association in the public mind between a product and its source. Such meaning may be shown through direct consumer testimony, consumer surveys, advertising and sales, the length and manner of use, the exclusivity of the use, and whether the mark was intentionally copied. See *Jysk Bed'N Linen v. Dutta-Roy*, 810 F.3d 767, 778–79 (11th Cir. 2015); *Welding Servs. Inc. v. Forman*, 509 F.3d 1351, 1357 (11th Cir. 2007); *Echo Travel, Inc. v. Travel Associates, Inc.*, 870 F.2d 1264 (7th Cir. 1989).

Trademarks may be used to protect distinctive words, letters, numbers, abbreviations, nicknames, slogans, symbols and designs, colors in certain contexts, product and container shapes, building appearances, clothing, sounds, and scents. See, e.g., *Gund, Inc. v. Fortunoff, Inc.*, 3 U.S.P.Q.2d 1556 (S.D.N.Y. 1986) (teddy bears); *Calvin Klein Cosmetics Corp. v. Parfums de Coeur, Ltd.*, 824 F.2d 665 (8th Cir. 1987) (*Obsessions* cologne); *In re Owens-Corning Fiberglas Corp.*, 774 F.2d 1116 (Fed. Cir. 1985) (pink insulation); *Coca-Cola Co. v. Alma-Leo U.S.A., Inc.*, 719 F.Supp. 725 (N.D.Ill.1989) (Coke bottle). Protection may be available for distinctive artists' styles as well.

An unregistered mark is protectable, although greater protection is secured through federal or state registration. Common law protection will allow the trademark proprietor to recover monetary damages and injunctions in the event of infringement.

Merely adopting a distinctive mark is insufficient to secure trademark protection; the mark must actually be used in commerce. Use is necessary for federal and state registration as well as common law protection. A trademark is considered used when it has been placed on the product in any manner or on its containers or the displays associated with it or on any of the tags or labels affixed to the product. Thus, it is not always necessary that the trademark actually be physically affixed to the goods. The trademark must be associated with the product at the point of sale, however, and in such a way that the product can be readily identified as coming from a particular manufacturer or source. Thus, to ensure trademark protection, the trademark proprietor would be well advised to physically affix the trademark to the product. In this way, the product is certain to bear the trademark when it is sold.

Common law protects the trademark proprietor against someone else who subsequently uses a trademark that is confusingly similar. Generally, trademarks will be deemed to be confusing if they are similar in sound or appearance, *In re Spirits Int'l, N.V.*, 563 F.3d 1347, 1351 (Fed. Cir. 2009); *Enrique Bernat F., S.A. v. Guadalajara, Inc.*, 210 F.3d 439, 443 (5th Cir. 2000); *Dreamwerks Prod. Grp., Inc. v. SKG Studio*, 142 F.3d 1127, 1131 (9th Cir. 1998), particularly if the trademarks are affixed to similar products or if the products are marketed throughout similar channels of commerce. See *Tillamook Country Smoker, Inc. v. Tillamook County Creamery Ass'n*, 465 F.3d 1102 (9th Cir. 2006). *Gallo* cheese and *Gallo* wine, for example, were held to be confusingly similar because cheese and wine are often served together. See *E. & J. Gallo Winery v. Gallo Cattle Co.*, 12 U.S.P.Q.2d 1657 (E.D.Cal. 1989). If, on the other hand, two products bearing similar trademarks are unrelated or marketed in different areas, there may be no infringement. Compare *Brookfield Commc'ns, Inc. v. W. Coast Entm't Corp.*, 174 F.3d 1036, 1054 (9th Cir. 1999), with *Weiner King, Inc. v. Wiener King Corp.*, 615 F.2d 512, 520 (C.C.P.A. 1980), and *Pinocchio's Pizza Inc.*, 11 U.S.P.Q.2d 1227 (P.T.O. Apr. 25, 1989). For instance, *Gold Circle* department stores and *Gold Circle* insurance were held not to be confusingly similar in *Federated Department Stores, Inc. v. Gold Circle Ins. Co.*, 226 U.S.P.Q. 262 (Trademark Tr. & App. Bd. 1985).

Section 43(a) of the Lanham Act prohibits the use of "a false description of origin, or any false description or representation" in connection with any goods or services which are introduced into commerce. 15 U.S.C. § 1125(a). This prohibition includes any false express or implied representation that a particular person has authorized or approved use of a product. A plaintiff who brings a Section 43(a) action is not required to prove the defendant's intent to deceive; demonstrating the likelihood of customer confusion with respect to the source of the goods is sufficient.

SEC. C FEDERAL COMMON LAW TRADEMARK

A personal name is not inherently distinctive; therefore, it is not protectable as an unregistered mark under Section 43(a) of the Lanham Act. No person has an absolute right to use his or her own name to identify a product or service. Surnames are subject to the same rules of priority as any other mark. However, if there is an established customer association between the name and the artist's work, the artist's name will be said to have developed secondary meaning.

The name *Picasso*, for example, has been held to be a trademark and was afforded protection under Section 43(a) in *Visual Arts and Galleries Ass'n v. Various John Does*, 80 Civ. 4487 (1980). Picasso and his heirs licensed various goods, such as carpeting, eyewear, clocks, art reproductions, posters, and scarves, which were distributed throughout the United States. In addition to systematically using the mark, its owner must exercise control over the nature and quality of the goods or services for which the mark is used. In the *Picasso* case, the licenses were subject to periodic inspection and prior approval of the goods before any merchandise could be sold. The court recognized that the name *Picasso* and the famous signature had acquired a secondary meaning and that his heirs had a right to advertise and profit from the use of his name and reputation. The court also enjoined the unauthorized use of a facsimile of Picasso's signature on T-shirts. This requirement of secondary meaning, however, would be difficult, if not impossible, for a relatively unknown artist to meet.

Some forms of use may result in the loss of trademark rights. A number of well-known trademarks, such as *Aspirin*, *Thermos*, and *Escalator*, have been lost as a result of improper usage. Generally, trademark protection is lost because the mark is used in some capacity other than as an adjective modifying a noun. When the trademark is used as a noun or verb, it no longer functions to identify the source of the product but, rather, becomes the name of the product or service. At that point, the mark becomes generic and no longer protectable. See *Abercrombie & Fitch Co. v. Hunting World, Inc.*, 537 F.2d 4, 4–15 (2d Cir. 1976) (safari hat); *King-Seeley Thermos Co. v. Aladdin Industries, Inc.*, 321 F.2d 577 (2d Cir. 1963) (thermos); *Bayer Co. v. United Drug Co.*, 272 F. 505 (S.D.N.Y. 1921) (aspirin); *Haughton Elevator Company v. Seeberger (Otis Elevator Company Substituted)*, 85 U.S.P.Q. (BNA) 80, 1950 WL 4178 (Comm'r Pat. & Trademarks 1950) (escalator).

D. FEDERAL REGISTRATION

Although trademark rights are secured by common law, the federal Lanham Act provides a central clearinghouse for existing trademarks via registrations. In 1989, the Trademark Law Revision Act became effective, adding needed details to make the Lanham Act a more complete body of law.

A trademark registration remains in effect for a period of 10 years and may be renewed in additional 10-year increments by filing an application for renewal during the last year of registration or within a six-month grace period. Federal registration enables the owner to use the symbol "®" in conjunction with the mark. Proprietors of unregistered marks or marks registered only by a state are prohibited from using ® with their marks but may use "TM" for trademarks or "SM" for service marks. While these designations have no official status, they provide notice to others that the user is claiming a property right in the mark.

It should be noted that there are two official registers for trademarks: the Principal Register and the Supplemental Register.

1. PRINCIPAL REGISTER

Both trademarks and service marks are eligible for registration on the Principal Register. To qualify for registration, the mark must function to identify and distinguish goods or services, and the mark must have been affixed to the goods or to displays associated with the goods at the point of sale or have been used in connection with the sale, performance or advertising of services and have been used in commerce. The benefits of a Principal Register registration are numerous. First, such a registration is *prima facie* evidence of the registrant's ownership and exclusive right to use the mark. Second, such a registration is constructive notice of a claim of ownership so as to eliminate any defense of good faith adoption by subsequent users. Finally, a registered mark that has been in continuous use for five years may become incontestable upon a filing of the appropriate form and payment of a filing fee. Thus, the owner of a registered mark may secure rights superior to those of a prior but unregistered user if the original user does not object to the registrant's use within five years of registration.

Under the TLRA, actual use of the mark is still required in order for a mark to be registered, although a mark may receive limited protection for a limited period of time based on the bona fide intent to use that mark in the future.

Once actual use in commerce has been established, the mark can be registered. All marks must be classified according to the goods or services to which they relate. At present, there are 34 international classifications for goods; 11 classes for services; two classes for certification marks, which are marks used to certify products or services, such as the *Good Housekeeping Seal of Approval* or *Rated PG*; and one class for collective marks, which are marks used for membership organizations, such as fraternities and sororities. A trademark proprietor may register a mark in all applicable categories with a single application. The Patent and Trademark Office classification is, however, irrelevant to the issue of likelihood of confusion; the sole purpose of the classification is administrative convenience. If the examining officer at the Patent and Trademark Office accepts the application for registration on the Principal Register, the mark will be published for opposition in the *Official Gazette*. Anyone believing that they would be injured by the issuance of the registration has 30 days within which to file an opposition to registration. If no one objects, or if the objections are found to be without merit, a certificate of registration will be issued; or, in the case of an Intent to Use application, a Notice of Allowance will be sent.

2. SUPPLEMENTAL REGISTER

Registration on the Supplemental Register provides protection for individuals and businesses capable of distinguishing their marks from those of others but whose marks do not comply with the requirements for registration on the Principal Register. A Supplemental Register registration confers no substantive trademark rights beyond those under common law, as it does not serve as *prima facie* evidence of exclusive ownership, serve as constructive notice of the claim of ownership, or become incontestable. Also, applications filed on the Supplemental Register cannot be based on intent-to-use: The applicant's mark must be in lawful use in commerce, meaning a bona fide use in the ordinary course of trade. Marks for the Supplemental Register are not published for or subject to opposition; they are, however, published as registered in the *Official Gazette*. If a person believes that he or she will be damaged by the registration of another's mark on the Supplemental Register, that person may at any time petition for cancellation of the registration.

E. INFRINGEMENT

The basic test of trademark infringement is likelihood of confusion by a reasonably prudent buyer. *Arrowpoint Capital Corp. v. Arrowpoint Asset*

Mgmt., LLC, 793 F.3d 313, 319 (3d Cir. 2015); *Rearden LLC v. Rearden Commerce, Inc.*, 683 F.3d 1190, 1214 (9th Cir. 2012); *Brennan's, Inc. v. Brennan's Restaurant, LLC*, 360 F.3d 125 (2nd Cir. 2004). Confusion arises when consumers mistakenly think the junior user's goods or services are from the same source as or are connected with the senior user's goods or services. See 15 U.S.C. § 1125(a); *Boston Duck Tours, LP v. Super Duck Tours, LLC*, 531 F.3d 1, 12 (1st Cir. 2008); *Custom Mfg. & Eng'g, Inc. v. Midway Servs., Inc.*, 508 F.3d 641, 647 (11th Cir. 2007). Reverse confusion, where customers purchase the senior user's goods or services under the mistaken impression that they are getting the junior user's goods or services is also actionable. *Dastar Corp. v. Twentieth Century Fox Film Corp.*, 539 U.S. 23, 27 (2003); *Kehoe Component Sales Inc. v. Best Lighting Products, Inc.*, 796 F.3d 576, 586–87 (6th Cir. 2015), *reh'g denied* (Sept. 14, 2015).

When an artist painted a montage of images related to the Masters Golf Tournament, including Tiger Woods' image, Woods brought suit for, among other claims, trademark infringement. The Sixth Circuit held that as a general rule, a person's image or likeness cannot function as a trademark. The court noted that no single image of Woods had been used on specific goods. *ETW Corp. v. Jireh Publishing*, 332 F.3d 915 (6th Cir. 2003).

A trademark proprietor can sue an infringing party for monetary damages, an injunction prohibiting the infringing use, or both. *Abercrombie and Fitch Co. v. Moose Creek, Inc.*, 486 F.3d 629 (9th

Cir. 2007); *JCW Investments, Inc. v. Novelty, Inc.*, 482 F.3d 910 (7th Cir. 2007). Monetary damages can be measured by the defendant's profits, the plaintiff's actual business damages, or the plaintiff's lost profits. See 15 U.S.C. § 1117(a); *Kelley Blue Book v. Car-Smarts, Inc.*, 802 F. Supp. 278, 292 (C.D. Cal. 1992). The courts have discretion to increase the damages to treble damages or to decrease damages in an award of profits if excessive. In exceptional circumstances, where a defendant's conduct is willful and flagrant, the plaintiff may be awarded punitive damages and attorneys' fees.

Other facts and circumstances can also establish that the infringement was willful. In *Images International of Hawaii, Inc. v. Hang Ups Art Enterprises, Inc.*, CV 90 4106 R (1991), the court permanently enjoined Hang Ups Art from using the plaintiff art gallery's marks *Images* and *Images International* and awarded the plaintiff the profits earned by the defendant while using the infringing marks to conduct art sales. The court also awarded the plaintiff interest and attorneys' fees. In this case, the plaintiff notified the defendant to cease the infringements, and the defendants agreed. Subsequently, though, the defendants violated their agreement and conducted several art shows using the plaintiff's marks. The court felt that these latter infringements were indicative of the defendant's willful conduct.

A willful trademark infringement is not dischargeable in bankruptcy. In *In re Klayminc*, 37 B.R. 728 (Bkrtcy. S.D. Fla. 1984), the court held that the debtor's continued infringement of the plaintiff's trademark after entry of a federal injunction constituted a "willful and malicious injury" that rendered the trademark infringement claim nondischargeable.

Several defenses may be available to a defendant in a trademark infringement suit, even when the plaintiff's mark has become incontestable, including abandonment, fraud in obtaining the registration or its incontestability status, misrepresenting the source of the goods or services, fair use of an individual's name, a descriptive term or geographic term other than in a trademark sense, preregistrations in local use without knowledge of the registrant's prior use, violation of the antitrust laws, and equitable defenses, such as laches and unclean hands. See 15 U.S.C. § 1115(b); *Pennzoil-Quaker State Co. v. Miller Oil & Gas Operations*, 779 F.3d 290, 294 (5th Cir. 2015); *Oriental Fin. Grp., Inc. v. Cooperativa de Ahorro y Credito Oriental*, 698 F.3d 9, 21 (1st Cir. 2012); *Univ. of Alabama Bd. of Trustees v. New Life Art, Inc.*, 683 F.3d 1266, 1281–82 (11th Cir. 2012); *Kellogg Co. v. Exxon Corp.*, 209 F.3d 562, 568 (6th Cir. 2000).

Trademark law provides remedies for infringements of marks that are in actual use in commerce, therefore, precluding intent-to-use applicants from suing for infringement. Under the TLRA, all remedies available for infringement actions are also available for actions of unfair competition.

The Anticybersquatting Consumer Protection Act makes it illegal for a person to register, traffic in, or use a domain name that is identical or confusingly similar to another's distinctive or famous trademark if such person has a bad faith intent to profit from that trademark.

F. DILUTION

The Federal Trademark Dilution Act of 1995 created antidilution protection for "famous" marks, amending Section 43 of the Trademark Act (15 U.S.C. § 1125) by adding a provision entitling the owner of a famous mark to an injunction against another person's commercial use in commerce of a mark where such use begins after the mark has become famous and causes dilution of the distinctive quality of the mark. See *Rosetta Stone Ltd. v. Google, Inc.*, 676 F.3d 144, 167–73 (4th Cir. 2012); *Starbucks Corp. v. Wolfe's Borough Coffee, Inc.*, 588 F.3d 97, 105–11 (2d Cir. 2009). Willful intent to trade on the owner's reputation or to cause dilution of the mark may also entitle the owner of the mark to the same remedies as those set forth for trademark infringement, including damages, costs, and attorneys' fees.

Dilution is defined in 15 U.S.C. § 1127 as "the lessening of the capacity of a famous mark to identify and distinguish goods or services, regardless of the presence or absence of (1) competition between the owner of the famous mark and other parties, or (2) likelihood of confusion, mistake or deception."

Although "famous" is not defined by the statute, a list of factors to be considered in determining whether a mark is famous is set forth in Section 43. These factors are:

(1) The degree of inherent or acquired distinctiveness of the mark;

(2) The duration and extent of the use of the mark in connection with the goods or services with which the mark is used;

(3) The duration and extent of advertising and publicity of the mark;

(4) The geographical extent of the trading area in which the mark is used;

(5) The channels of trade for the goods or services with which the mark is used;

(6) The degree of recognition of the mark in the trading areas and channels of trade used by the mark's owner and the person against whom the injunction is sought;

(7) The nature and extent of use of the same or similar marks by third parties; and

(8) Whether the mark was registered under the Act of March 3, 1881, or February 20, 1905, or on the Principal Register.

Ownership of a valid registration under the Act of March 3, 1881, or February 20, 1905, or on the Principal Register is a complete bar to a state or common law antidilution action against an owner with respect to that mark. In addition, the following nonactionable uses of a mark are set forth in Section 43: fair use of a famous mark by another person in comparative commercial advertising or promotion to identify the competing goods or services of the owner of the famous mark; noncommercial use of a mark; and all forms of news reporting and news commentary.

The U.S. Supreme Court held in *Moseley v. V Secret Catalogue, Inc.*, 537 U.S. 418 (2003), that an "actual" (rather than "likely") lessening of the capacity of the famous mark to identify and distinguish goods or services must be proven, whether through circumstantial evidence or consumer surveys. 15 U.S.C. § 1125(c). After *Moseley*, Congress responded by amending section 1125(c) to remove the requirement of proof of actual dilution. Section 1125(c) now provides that recovery for dilution is possible "regardless of the presence or absence of actual or likely confusion, of competition, or of actual economic injury."

G. STATE TRADEMARK LAWS

A trademark may be registered under state law, as well as under federal law. State trademark statutes generally grant rights similar to those of the Lanham Act, except that those rights do not extend protection beyond the borders of the state. In order to obtain trademark protection under state law, the trademark proprietor must file a trademark application with the appropriate state officer, along with documentation similar to that required by the Lanham Act.

As with federal protection, state registration affords no rights to a mark that has not actually been used. State trademark law and registrations cannot override rights provided by federal law for federal registrations. Thus, a state registration will not necessarily block a later federal registration.

Prior to the enactment of the federal Dilution Act, many states adopted antidilution laws that grant protection to strong, well-recognized marks, even in the absence of a likelihood of confusion, if the defendant's use is such as to tarnish, degrade, or dilute the distinctive quality of the mark. Such laws may afford more protection to trademark owners; unfortunately for some trademark owners, the federal law provides that if a diluting mark is federally registered, any state dilution remedies are preempted.

The dilution theory generally has been successful when the defendant used the plaintiff's mark in an unwholesome or degrading context. Several cases have found dilution where the defendant used the plaintiff's mark in the context of X-rated movies and cartoons, drug culture music, and topless bars. See, e.g., *Dallas Cowboys Cheerleaders, Inc. v. Pussycat Cinema, Ltd.*, 467 F. Supp. 366 (S.D.N.Y. 1979), *aff'd*, 604 F.2d 200 (2nd Cir.1979); *Pillsbury Co. v. Milky Way Productions, Inc.*, Civil No. C78–679A, 1981 WL 1402 (N.D. Ga. Dec. 24, 1981); *General Foods Corp. v. Mellis*, 203 U.S.P.Q. 261 (S.D.N.Y. 1979); *Community Federal Sav. and Loan Ass'n v. Orondorff*, 678 F.2d 1034 (11th Cir. 1982). Other cases indicate that tarnishment may include use in a context which is merely out-of-keeping with the plaintiff's high quality image. See, e.g., *Steinway & Sons v. Robert Demars & Friends*, 210 U.S.P.Q. 954 (C.D. Cal. 1981); *General Elec. Co. v. Alumpa Coal Co., Inc.*, 205 U.S.P.Q. 1036 (D. Mass. 1979).

H. INTERNATIONAL TRADEMARK PROTECTION

In November 2002, President Bush signed the Madrid Protocol Implementation Act of 2002, which allows U.S. trademark owners to register marks in all participating countries through the U.S. Patent and Trademark Office. Nearly 100 countries are parties to the Madrid Protocol. See http://www.wipo.int/treaties/en/ShowResults.jsp?treaty_id=8. The Implementation legislation was made effective November 2, 2003.

In order to file an International Registration application, a U.S. trademark owner must first have a trademark application or registered trademark in the United States. The International Bureau of the World Intellectual Property Organization (WIPO), which oversees the Protocol system, reviews the application to ensure that it complies with the Protocol rules, then forwards the application to every country designated in the application. Each such country's trademark office examines the mark, using the same criteria as it would for a domestic registration within that country.

I. TRADE DRESS

Artists have attempted to use the trade dress law to protect their styles. "Trade dress" is the overall appearance or "look" of a product or service. While normally not federally registered as a trademark on either the Principal Register or the Supplemental Register, it can be if it meets the requirements for trademark registration.

A successful claim for trade dress infringement under Section 43(a) of the Lanham Act requires proof that the trade dress is nonfunctional and that the competitor's trade dress is so similar to that of the plaintiff that confusion as to the source of the goods or service is likely. *Qualitex Co. v. Jacobson Products Co.*, 514 U.S. 159 (1995); *Fair Wind Sailing, Inc. v. Dempster*, 764 F.3d 303, 309 (3d Cir. 2014); *Christian Louboutin S.A. v. Yves Saint Laurent Am. Holdings, Inc.*, 696 F.3d 206 (2d Cir. 2012). The third element had varied depending on the jurisdiction. A number of courts required that the trade dress have acquired secondary meaning (see, e.g., *First Brands Corp. v. Fred Meyer, Inc.*, 809 F.2d 1378 (9th Cir. 1987)), while other courts required that the trade dress either have secondary meaning or be inherently distinctive. See, e.g., *Chevron Chemical Co. v. Voluntary Purchasing Groups, Inc.*, 659 F.2d 695 (5th Cir. 1981). In *Two Pesos, Inc. v. Taco Cabana, Inc.*, 505 U.S. 763 (1992), the Supreme Court held that trade dress that is inherently distinctive is protectable without a showing that it has acquired secondary meaning. More recently, however, the Supreme Court held that product configuration trade dress is protectable only if it has acquired secondary meaning. *Wal-Mart Stores, Inc. v. Samara Brothers, Inc.*, 529 U.S. 205 (2000).

An artist's style was held to be a protectable trade dress in *Romm Art Creations Ltd. v. Simcha International, Inc.*, 786 F. Supp. 1126 (E.D.N.Y. 1992). Romm Art, licensed to be the exclusive worldwide distributor of posters and limited editions by Israeli artist Itzchak Tarkay, sued Simcha, the distributor of Patricia Govezensky posters and limited editions, for trade dress infringement. The court found that the plaintiff's trade dress was nonfunctional, as, other than aesthetic gratification, the images serve no purpose other than to identify their source; that Tarkay's posters and limited editions were inherently distinctive; and that a likelihood of confusion existed since the *Patricia* line of posters and limited editions was strikingly similar to the *Tarkay* line.

Other courts have, however, found that trade dress does not protect the artist's style. *Leigh v. Warner Bros.*, 10 F. Supp. 2d 1371 (S.D. Ga. 1998), distinguished use of the work to identify the artist and use of the work to identify the artist as a source of goods or services. The court held that to allow trade dress protection of an artist's style where that style merely identifies the artist would undermine the copyright law by granting a monopoly over ideas and themes. See also, for example, *Hughes v. Design Look, Inc.*, 693 F. Supp. 1500 (S.D.N.Y. 1988), which held that none of the Andy Warhol paintings at issue were ever used to identify the source of any particular goods or services, and *Galerie Furstenberg v. Coffaro*, 697 F. Supp. 1282 (S.D.N.Y. 1988), which held that Salvador Dali's style is not a trademark and that the claim could be brought only under the copyright laws.

J. CONCLUSION

The trademark law is an important item in the art lawyer's arsenal. Knowledge of this form of intellectual property is essential when working with artists, galleries, collectors, and museums.

CHAPTER 14
MORAL AND ECONOMIC RIGHTS

A. MORAL RIGHTS

Art is a form of property requiring unique consideration. The intimate bond between the creator and the thing created gives rise to a need for nonpecuniary rights in the artist that do not arise in connection with other chattels. Artists have an interest in deciding whether to disclose their work, seeing that their creations retain the forms they gave them and ensuring that they are credited with their creations. While these rights indirectly affect artists' economic interests, they more basically affect artists' character, reputation, dignity, and persona, and, therefore, generally are referred to as moral rights, or *droit moral*.

The artist's moral rights are recognized in most countries throughout the world, including the United States, and have been codified in the 1928 Berne Convention, discussed in Chapter 12, *supra*, which has been ratified by 171 nations. See *Contracting Parties—Berne Convention*, http://www.wipo.int/treaties/en/ShowResults.jsp?treaty_id=15 (last accessed June 26, 2016). This Convention covers international copyright protection in addition to many other elements of the *droit moral*.

While moral rights principles are often considered antagonistic to the property rights of owners in the United States, protection of certain minimal moral rights became mandatory when the United States became a signatory to Berne in 1988. Prior to that time, the United States had become a signatory to the Universal Copyright Convention.

In 1990, Congress passed the Visual Artists Rights Act (VARA) (17 U.S.C. § 106A), which amends the Copyright Act by providing to "authors" of certain singular or limited edition artworks the rights of attribution and integrity. Leonard DuBoff, coauthor of this book, was involved in drafting this law at the request of the late Ted Kennedy, senator of Massachusetts. Under VARA, moral rights were codified within the Copyright Code, 17 U.S.C. § 106A, and thus, they may be enforced by any applicable remedy, other than criminal penalties, otherwise available for infringement under the Copyright Code. These rights belong solely to the artist and are not transferable.

The protection of VARA is limited to a genus of work referred to as a "Work of Visual Art," which is defined in the statute as "a painting, drawing, print, or sculpture, existing in a single copy, in a limited edition of 200 copies or fewer that are signed and consecutively numbered by the author," and "a still photographic image produced for exhibition purposes only, existing in a single copy that is signed by the author, or in a limited edition of 200 copies or fewer that are signed and consecutively numbered by the author." 17 U.S.C. § 101 (definition of "Work of Visual Art").

However, VARA by itself does not meet the minimal protections called for by the Berne Convention. Not only does VARA fail to encompass all creative acts within its scope of explicit moral rights protection, but certain specific omissions, such as the right to anonymity or pseudonymity, are conspicuous departures from a growing worldwide compliance with Berne.

Droit moral was originally conceived in France where it evolved and developed. Codified in the Law of March 11, 1957, #57–296 (1957), J.O. 2723 (1957), B.L.D. 197, the *droit moral* includes many rights. By virtue of its longevity, this law has generated more litigation than any other body of moral rights law; it thus forms a useful basis for comparison of the different rights.

1. THE RIGHT TO CREATE

One of the rights included in the *droit moral* is the right to create—or to refrain from creating. The right of artists to be the sole judge of whether their work is worthy and ready to be placed before the public is their protection of the right to create. This would seem axiomatic, but conflicts do arise, for instance, when an artist has agreed under contract to produce a specific product and fails to deliver the commissioned work. Can the court require its completion?

French courts have long held that completion of a creation cannot be judicially mandated. See *Eden v. Whistler*, [1898] Recueil Dalloz [D.P. II] 465 (Cour d'appel, Paris), *aff'd*, [1900] Cass. civ. lre 489 (Cour de cassation). Lack of inspiration is held to be a normal risk of a contract for creation which is reasonably foreseen by both parties, and no damages may be had for nonperformance of the contract on this ground. French law also provides that an artist may not be required to produce a specific quantity of paintings for a requirements contract. Conversely, a patron cannot get an injunction prohibiting an artist from creating a work of art. However, when a patron who commissions a work is to take part in the completion of that work, the artist may be able to mandate its completion, even when the contract includes a liquidated damages clause.

In America, the artist's right to create is protected through the well-established principle that contracts for personal services are not specifically enforceable. There are several rationales for this rule. One is the difficulty of enforcing the decree and gauging the quality of the service rendered. Artists do not work well under compulsion, and few courts relish the idea of having to determine whether an artistic performance is adequate. In addition, it is rarely desirable to enforce the continuance of a close relationship between the parties after disputes have arisen and confidence and loyalty have been destroyed. Finally, specific enforcement of a personal service contract is inconsistent with the constitutional prohibition against involuntary servitude. American law insists on liberty, even at the expense of broken promises.

Yet, even artists must bow to the law of contracts, and a breaching party in a contract for personal services still may be held liable for damages. Moreover, some courts impose a negative covenant so that the breaching artist is prohibited from working for others in the same general field during the term of the contract. Thus, for example, in *Paramount Pictures Corp. v. Davis*, 228 Cal. App. 2d 827, 39 Cal. Rptr. 791 (2d Dist. 1964), Bette Davis was enjoined from performing under a later contract until she completed the production of the movie *Hush, Hush Sweet Charlotte*. Decades later, actress Kim Basinger learned the same lesson under U.S. law when she backed out of the main role in *Boxing Helena*, and was charged $8.1 million for breaching her contract, causing the actress to file for bankruptcy.

A question related to the right to create is whether the artist may create a work that infringes on the copyright the artist no longer owns in an earlier work. In *Franklin Mint Corp. v. National Wildlife Art Exchange, Inc.*, 575 F.2d 62 (3rd Cir. 1978), the court concluded that dissimilarities in color and composition established that the second painting constituted "a diversity of expression rather than only an echo." However, in *Gross v. Seligman*, 212 F. 930 (2nd Cir. 1914), the court held that in spite of small differences, the photographer had copied his earlier photograph and was thus liable for copyright infringement.

2. THE RIGHT OF DISCLOSURE

Related to the right to create or not create is the right to decide whether or not to disclose a work. This right allows an artist to enjoin another from publishing a work that the artist has discarded. In *Carco v. Camoin*, D.P.II 88, Cour d'Appel, Paris (1931), the artist Camoin had cut up and discarded some painted canvasses. Carco found the pieces, reconstructed the works, and sold them at an auction. The Paris Court of Appeals held that the artist was within his rights to oppose any restoring of the canvasses and to demand, if necessary, that they be destroyed, despite the inherent conflict with the rights of a finder of abandoned property.

In the United States, the right of disclosure may be protected by the constitutional right of privacy. In their seminal article *The Right of Privacy*, 4 HARV. L. REV. 193, 198–200 (1890), Justice Louis Brandeis and his law partner, Samuel Warren, described this right as including "the right of determining, ordinarily, to what extent [an individual's] thoughts, sentiments, and emotions shall be communicated to others. . . . It is immaterial whether [the mode of expression] is by word or by signs, in painting, by sculpture, or in music. The right is lost only when the author . . . publishes it."

The right of disclosure may also be protected both before and after publication under the Copyright Act of 1976, 17 U.S.C. §§ 101–810. The exclusive rights given to the copyright owner include Section 106(1), the right to reproduce the copyrighted work; Section 106(3), the right to distribute copies (including the original work by virtue of Section 101) by sale or other transfer of ownership or by rental, lease or lending; and Section 106(5), the right to display the copyrighted work publicly. Since statutory copyright protection under the 1976 Act begins when the work is embodied in a tangible form, most cases involving a violation of the right of disclosure by an individual who reproduces, sells, or displays a work without authorization will fall within this penumbra of protected rights.

3. THE RIGHT TO WITHDRAW

By contrast to the right to prevent disclosure of a work, the right to withdraw a work after it has been disclosed is not recognized in the United States. Even in France, its scope is limited, because its statutory codification applies only to publishing contracts and requires authors to pay for all sold copies that are withdrawn and, in some circumstances, to pay the publisher damages. In American jurisprudence, it has been held that an actor may not withdraw a film, even though the film injured the actor's reputation due to its inferior quality. *Autry v. Republic Productions, Inc.*, 213 F.2d 667 (9th Cir. 1954). Furthermore, under Section 109 of the 1976 Copyright Act, the owner of a particular copy lawfully made has the unqualified right to display that copy publicly or to sell or otherwise dispose of that copy. Only if the copy has been altered or mutilated in some way could the artist have a cause of action for a violation of the integrity of the work, discussed in Section 5, *infra*.

4. NAME ATTRIBUTION

After an artist has made a decision to communicate a creation to the public, the artist obviously has an interest in seeing that it is properly attributed. This right of paternity is not intended to protect reputation so much as it is intended to protect the creative act itself. In France, the right to create includes the right to be acclaimed as the creator, and any contract which negates this right may be declared void. Thus, in *Guille v. Colmant*, D.S.Jur. 284, Gaz.Pal. I. 17, Cour d'Appel, Paris (1967), the court voided a contract in which the artist was to sign a certain pseudonym to some of his work and to place no signature on the rest. Conversely, an artist also has a right in France not to have his or her name attached to a work which he or she does not acknowledge as his or her own.

In the United States, VARA allows an artist to claim authorship of a work he or she created. The author also has the right "to prevent the use of his or her name as the author of the work of visual art in the event of a distortion, mutilation, or other modification of the work which would be prejudicial to his or her honor or reputation." 17 U.S.C. § 106A(a)(2); *Massachusetts Museum of Contemporary Art Found., Inc. v. Büchel*, 593 F.3d 38 (1st Cir. 2010). While Massachusetts and New Mexico, in their moral rights statutes (Massachusetts Art Preservation Act, Mass. Gen. Laws ch. 231, § 85S (1985); N.M. Stat. Ann. § 13–4B–3B (1991)), additionally provide the right to pseudonymity, VARA does not. The rights guaranteed by VARA may be waived if the author expressly agrees to such waiver in a signed written instrument which applies to specifically identified works. 17 U.S.C. § 106A(e).

Artists not protected by VARA fare better when there has been a false imputation of paternity rather than a mere omission of attribution. The constitutional right of privacy may prevent another from imputing to an artist that which the artist has not acknowledged as his or her work, but a lack of imputation cannot be said to invade privacy. Similarly, under the common law doctrine of unfair competition, a person may be enjoined from falsely placing an artist's name on a product that is in competition with the artist's own product. The common law doctrine of defamation is also used where the work falsely attributed to the author is of an inferior quality and consequently damages his or her reputation. If falsity, malice, and damages can be proven, the artist may have grounds to restrain the false imputation of paternity.

False attribution also has been found to constitute a violation of Section 43(a) of the Lanham Act, 15 U.S.C. § 1125(a), which prohibits false designations of origin and false descriptions. State statutes governing deceptive trade practices have also been used. See Chapter 13, *supra.* In *Sanchez v. Stein,* No. 80CV1208 (1980), the plaintiff, an elderly artist, alleged that Mrs. Stein commissioned him to create several pieces, which she then sold as her own creations. After a great deal of public name calling, the plaintiff filed suit for defamation and deceptive trade practices. The case was settled in December 1982, and the plaintiff was acknowledged as the artist. See page 407 for a photograph of *Winged Wolves*, the sculpture involved in this case.

By contrast, an artist ordinarily may not object to the use of his or her name in a truthful statement that the artist created the work or that the work is based on or derived from the artist's work, in the absence of contractual provisions to the contrary. Similarly, the omission of an artist's name from a work ordinarily is not actionable unless the omission amounts to a breach of contract or the work is covered by VARA or a state law. California provides that an artist who creates an original painting, sculpture, or drawing retains "the right to claim authorship," even after the work is sold (West's Ann. Cal. Civ. Code § 987). Similarly, New York law provides that "the artist shall retain at all times the right to claim authorship or, for just and valid reason, to disclaim authorship of" a work of fine art. N.Y. Arts & Cult. Aff. Law § 14.03.

The omission of an artist's or creator's name is not actionable where a purchaser or licensee acquires the rights to the name. In *Dastar Corp. v. Twentieth Century Fox Film Corp.*, 539 U.S. 23, 28 (2003), the Supreme Court held that the trademark "false designation of origin" claim could not be used as an end run around copyright or patent rights acquired over material that originally was created by the artist or inventor. In *Vargas v. Esquire, Inc.*, 164 F.2d 522 (7th Cir. 1947), *cert. denied*, 335 U.S. 813 (1948), the plaintiff, who was to furnish drawings for the defendant's magazine, agreed to a fairly typical contract clause, giving the defendant the right to use, lease, sell, or otherwise dispose of the names *Varga*, "*Varga Girl, Varga, Esq.*, and any and all other names designs or material used in connection therewith." This grant of rights was held to include the right not to use the plaintiff's name in connection with his drawings. Such a contract would constitute

5. INTEGRITY

Artists also have some rights to prevent their works from being altered, distorted, or destroyed. This right of integrity is unquestioned in France. When a work of art is communicated to the public and is acknowledged to be the work of a particular artist, he or she has a protected interest in seeing that it retains its original form. When an artist painted the exterior of a refrigerator as "an indivisible artistic unit," and the refrigerator was later disassembled, the artist was able to enjoin the sale of the separated individual panels. *Buffet v. Fersig,* [1962] Recueil Dalloz (D.Jur.) 570 (Cour d'Appel, Paris) (Note Desbois). For example, France has recognized colorization as an alteration of a film which can be prevented by an artist who otherwise holds no copyright in the film. A civil court in Barcelona convicted a former secretary of Salvador Dali of having violated the artist's moral rights by cutting up and reconfiguring a Dali painting and displaying it as an original work.

In the United States, VARA affords artists the right "to prevent any intentional distortion, mutilation, or other modification of that work which would be prejudicial to his or her honor or reputation...." 17 U.S.C. § 106A(a)(3)(A). Any intentional distortion, mutilation, or modification of the work is a violation of that right. Unlike VARA, the French law does not distinguish between intentional or negligent alterations. VARA is careful to exclude from prohibition any "modification resulting from passage of time or the inherent nature of the materials" (§ 106A(c)(1)) and "any modification which is the result of conservation, or of the public presentation, including lighting and placement of the work, is not a destruction, distortion or other modification unless caused by gross negligence." Section 106A(c)(2). Unlike VARA, the French law contains no requirement for a showing of damage to honor or reputation. However, this requirement is likely to be of little consequence.

Site-specific, conceptual art is unlikely to receive full protection under VARA's right of integrity provision when the lawful owner of the work moves the art or parts of the art. See *Kelley v. Chicago Park Dist.*, 635 F.3d 290 (7th Cir. 2011); *Phillips v. Pembroke Real Estate, Inc.*, 288 F. Supp. 2d 89 (D. Mass. 2003), *aff'd*, 459 F.3d 128 (1st Cir. 2006). The courts in these cases found independent grounds to deny the relief—the *Kelley* court found that the "Wildflower Works" installation involved in the case was uncopyrightable because it was not creative (i.e., not created by the artist), and not fixed, thus it could not be protected under VARA, which only applies to works eligible for copyright protection; the *Phillips* court refused protection because it found that VARA afforded the owner of an artwork the right to move the artwork for display, thus it could not be the case that moving parts of a work could be an act that violates the right of integrity. As in the pre-VARA case of *Serra v. United States Gen. Servs. Admin.*, 847 F.2d 1045 (2d Cir. 1988), courts seem unable to grasp the concept that removing a site-specific work of conceptual art from its intended "site" destroys the work.

VARA also provides the artist the right to "prevent any destruction of a work of recognized stature." Section 106A(a)(3)(B). The question of what constitutes "a work of recognized stature" is to be determined by the expert testimony of scholars, curators, and, presumably, collectors. See *Carter v. Helmsley-Spear, Inc.*, 861 F. Supp. at 310 (S.D.N.Y. 1994), *aff'd in part, vacated in part, rev'd in part*, 71 F.3d 77 (2d Cir. 1995); *Martin v. City of Indianapolis*, 192 F.3d 608, 611–12 (7th Cir. 1999). The French law has no such recognized stature distinction.

Integrity protection provided to "work[s] of visual art . . . incorporated in or made part of a building in such a way that removing the work from the building will cause the destruction, distortion, mutilation or other modification of the work as described, . . . when the author consented to the installation of the work before [June 1, 1991], or in a written instrument executed on or after [June 1, 1991] that is signed by the owner of the building and the author specifies that installation of the work may subject the work to distortion, mutilation or other modification by reason of its removal" may be limited. 17 U.S.C. §§ 106A(d)(2)(A)–(B); 113. This limitation on protection does not apply when the work can be removed without destroying the work.

Several states have enacted statutes that protect the moral right of integrity. In 1979, California became the first state to enact moral rights legislation. California Art Preservation Act, West's Ann. Cal. Civ. Code § 987. In 1983, New York adopted substantially similar legislation in the Artist's Authorship Rights Act, Art. 12J, N.Y. Arts & Cult. Aff. Law § 14.03. The legislatures of Maine, New Jersey, Louisiana, Nevada, Connecticut, Rhode Island, Utah, Massachusetts, Pennsylvania, and New Mexico have passed similar laws.

The California Act prohibits anyone, except an artist who owns and possesses the work he or she created, from intentionally defacing, mutilating, altering, or destroying a work of fine art. The Act also provides that no person who frames, conserves, or restores a work of art shall deface, mutilate, alter, or destroy the work by any act constituting gross negligence.

A violation of the New York Act occurs if an unauthorized person publicly displays, publishes or reproduces an altered work of fine art as being the work of the artist, or under circumstances in which the work would reasonably be regarded as being the work of the artist, and damage to the artist's reputation is reasonably likely to result. In addition, the artist may bring an action for "just and valid reason" to prevent his or her name from appearing on or in connection with the work of fine art. "Just and valid reason" is defined by the Act as including situations where the work of fine art has been altered, defaced, mutilated, or modified other than by the artist, and damage to the artist's reputation is reasonably likely to result or has resulted therefrom.

Like the California statute, the New York legislation provides an exemption for bona fide conservation unless the conservator is negligent in performing the work. In addition, the New York legislation provides that alterations resulting from the passage of time or from the inherent nature of the materials are not covered unless resulting from gross negligence. Changes that are the ordinary result of a medium of reproduction are not in themselves violations of the Act; nor are changes in works prepared under contract for advertising or trade use unless the contract so provides.

To enforce compliance with the California statute, the work's creator or, in some cases, a representative of the public, may commence an action to obtain injunctive relief or to recover actual and punitive damages. If punitive damages are awarded, the court may select a charitable or educational fine arts organization to receive the award. California Art Preservation Act, West's Ann. Cal. Civ. Code § 989.

Where state legislation and VARA are unavailable, common law theories and federal statutes may provide some protection, but they are by no means as comprehensive as the New York or California laws. There have been cases that found that VARA preempts state art preservation claims to the extent that the state laws provide equivalent rights of integrity and attribution as those provided under VARA. See, e.g., *Board of Managers of Soho International Arts Condominium v. City of New York*, No. 01 Civ. 1226 DAB, 2003 WL 21403333 (S.D.N.Y. June 17, 2003); *Grauer v. Deutsch*, No. 01 CIV.

8672(LAK), 2002 WL 31288937 (S.D.N.Y. Oct. 11, 2002); *Lubner v. City of Los Angeles*, 53 Cal. Rptr. 2d 24 (Ct. App. 2d Dist. 1996). The late Dean William Prosser suggested that there may be a cause of action for invasion of privacy to protect a work from distortion or mutilation. Prosser, *Privacy*, 48 Cal. L. Rev. 383 (1960). Not only is the work of art affected when it is altered, but the public's image of the artist may also be damaged by placing the artist in a "false light." A cause of action has also been suggested under a theory of unfair competition in *Prouty v. National Broadcasting Co.*, 26 F. Supp. 265 (D. Mass. 1939). There, an author's reputation was injured due to the inferior quality of the defendant's radio program, which was based on characters known to the public to have been created by the complaining author.

Section 43(a) of the Lanham Act also has been successfully used, as in *Gilliam v. American Broadcasting Companies*, 538 F.2d 14 (2nd Cir. 1976), where it was held that presentation of a mutilated work accompanied by the author's name violated Section 43(a). In this case, five British writer-actors and one American writer-animator, collectively known as *Monty Python*, had moved to restrain the American Broadcasting Company (ABC) from airing an edited version of several of their BBC television programs. The district court denied the motion but ordered ABC to make the following announcement at the beginning of the program: "The members of Monty Python wish to disassociate themselves from the program which is a compilation of their shows edited by ABC without their approval."

The defendants appealed the district court's order to the court of appeals for the Second Circuit. The circuit court held that the defendants did not have to include the disclaimer, and the show was aired without it. However, after the show was aired and the court heard the plaintiffs' appeal on its damages, the court stated that even if the disclaimer had been included, the disclaimer would not constitute a defense to a violation of Section 43(a). "We are doubtful that a few words could erase the indelible impression that is made by a television broadcast. . . . Furthermore, a disclaimer . . . would go unnoticed by viewers who tuned into the broadcast a few minutes after it had begun."

The *Gilliam* case is also important for its holding on the application of copyright law to cases involving the mutilation of a creative work. The Copyright Revision Act of 1976 does not explicitly deal with the right of integrity, but the right is implicit in Section 106(2), which grants the owner of a copyright the exclusive right to "prepare derivative works based on the copyrighted work." This implies that unless the copyright owner gives away this right through a license, he or she alone has the right to adapt or change the copyrighted work. In *Gilliam*, the court reasoned that since the agreement signed by the Monty Python authors expressly reserved all rights not granted, it followed that in the absence of a grant of a license to make changes, that right was reserved by the authors.

6. EXCESSIVE CRITICISM

A final moral right is the right to be protected from excessive criticism. While the right to freedom of speech demands that critics be allowed to express their opinions, when criticism amounts to an unwarranted, abusive attack on the artist or on his or her work, it may violate the artist's fundamental personal rights. France has resolved this conflict by allowing the artist to publish a reply in such cases. The response of the artist to an unjustified attack must be printed in the next issue of the same publication after receipt of the artist's response.

Unfortunately, there is really no adequate remedy for excessive criticism in the United States. When an unjustifiable attack on the artist constitutes an attack on his or her reputation, there may be an action for libel, but such cases arise infrequently. In addition, given the inherent tension between defamation and the First Amendment, suits against art critics are rarely successful. For example, in *Buckley v. Vidal*, 327 F. Supp. 1051 (S.D.N.Y. 1971), Gore Vidal sued William F. Buckley, Jr., for calling his book *Myra Breckenridge* pornography. The court held that the statement, in context, did not suggest that Gore Vidal was a pornographer. The statement therefore was not defamatory since it did not assail Vidal's character.

B. ECONOMIC RIGHTS

In addition to the *droit moral*, several countries recognize the *droit de suite*, or economic rights. Droit de suite laws (also known as resale royalty laws) give an artist a right to participate in the proceeds realized from the resale of his or her work. While the copyright laws give the creator of a work the right to control reproduction, artists do not benefit as directly as authors do from this aspect of copyright protection. Unlike authors, who derive their primary economic return on a literary work through the sale of multiple copies, artists receive most of their economic returns from the sale of the original works they create. Royalties paid to an artist upon the resale of his or her work put an artist on a more equal footing with an author by giving an artist the right to participate in any exploitive use of his or her creation and by recognizing that increases in the value of art are based on the artist's earlier labors.

The droit de suite, as conceived in France, gives the artist a pecuniary right parallel to that afforded the author through copyright by allowing the artist to collect three percent of the total sales price of his or her work each time it is sold at public auction or through a merchant (including dealers and agents). The French law requires registration of a work by the artist before he or she can claim the right, and a central organization, the Union of Artistic Property, collects and pays the fees to the artist. Many other countries have adopted some form of the droit de suite as well. Although such a pecuniary right can be secured in the United States by contract, there is no federal legislation providing such a right. Early versions of the Visual Artists Rights Act contained a resale royalty provision which would have paid artists seven percent of the appreciated value of a resold work as measured from its preceding purchase price. Congress instead directed the Register of Copyrights, in consultation with the chair of the National Endowment for the Arts, to "study the feasibility of implementing" the proposed or a similar measure.

In 2001, the European Parliament issued a directive requiring a resale right in EU counties. The Commission of the European Parliament investigating this matter noted that its purpose was to resolve disparities in resale rights in the EU. The Commission said that the unequal rights resulted in disproportionate sales in some countries.

The Commission presented the proposal for resale rights in 1996 which was reviewed by the European Parliament in 1997 and revised by the Commission in 1998. The European Council at the urging of the Britain (and its thriving art auction businesses in London) added a ten-year transitional period. However, the Council and the Parliament agreed on a directive on July 3, 2001.

The resale right applies to subsequent sales of original works of graphical or plastic art. The works must be made by the artist himself in limited numbers or under the artist's authority. The right is inalienable and cannot be waived. The right applies to sales involving sellers, buyers, or intermediary art professionals. The resale right does not apply to sales between private persons or entities without an intermediary art professional, or to sales occurring less than three years after the first purchase from the artist when the resale price is less than €10,000. The seller of the art work is responsible for paying the royalty.

The resale royalty is a percentage of the sale price. The percentage is higher for works sold at lower prices. The total amount of resale royalty cannot exceed €12,500. This cap in effect exempts works selling at higher prices from the resale royalty. The directive will also result in a decrease in the set royalty rates in countries such as France, Spain, Belgium, Germany, Denmark, Greece, Finland, and Sweden, which provide higher resale royalties for the works with higher sale prices than the EU directive.

The minimum sale price for resale royalties is €3,000. This price is higher than the minimum prices in France, Germany, Greece, Portugal, Sweden, Finland, Belgium, Denmark, and Spain. Many of those countries do not even have a minimum sale price and the resale royalty applies to all sale prices. The Council arrived at the €3,000 minimum based on the determination that sales under €4,000 are almost always domestic sales.

The beneficiaries of the resale right are the artist or, after the artist's death, the artist's heirs. The member state's laws of succession determine the artist's heirs. The resale right applies only to artists who are citizens of EU countries or citizens of countries which grant the same protection. The resale right endures for the life of the artist plus seventy years.

Member states are responsible for ensuring that royalties are collected and distributed to the artists.

Member states should adopt collective management societies for resale royalties. Although not required by the directive, collective societies can better protect the artists' interests because it is difficult for the individual artist to monitor all the sales of the artist's work and difficult for individual sellers to locate the artist to pay the royalty.

The directive was enacted on October 13, 2001. The directive permitted member states until January 1, 2006, to incorporate the provisions into their national laws. Member states that did not previously have a resale right (Austria, Ireland, Netherlands, United Kingdom) were permitted until January 1, 2010 to add the provisions. The UK did the most foot-dragging and requested a two-year extension. Thus, the directive did not take full effect in the EU until January 1, 2012. See Birgit Brenner, *The Resale Right Directive*, BILD-KUNST (2016), http://www.bildkunst.de/en/copyright/resale-right/resale-right-in-the-european-union.html. See also Wladimir Duchemin, *The Community Directive on the Resale Right*, RIDA Jan 2002 p. 3; Jennifer B. Pfeffer, *The Costs and Legal Impracticalities Facing Implementation of the European Union's Droit de Suite Directive in the United Kingdom*, 24 NW. J. INT'L L. & BUS. 533 (2004).

The United Kingdom finally moved into compliance with the directive with the enactment of the Artist's Resale Rights Regulations 2006, U.K. Artist's Resale Right Regulations 2006 (S.I. 2006/346), which came into force on February 14, 2007. The UK provision allows the right for the same duration as copyright (life plus 70 years), and affords the right to public sales at auction or between dealers where the sale price is over 1,000 pounds. In addition, if the work in question was acquired from the artist within three years of the resale, the sale must exceed 10,000 pounds. The UK regulation mandates a sliding scale of royalty rates applied to the sale based on the sale price with a cap on the maximum royalty payable of 12,500 pounds. It is too early to tell whether the UK's vote to withdraw from the EU on June 23, 2016, will end its participation in the European resale royalty regime.

Of all the states in the United States, only California has adopted a Resale Royalties Act, having done so in 1976. West's Ann.Cal.Civ. Code § 986. Leonard DuBoff, co-author of this book, helped draft the California Resale Royalty Act.

The California Act provided:

> Whenever a work of fine art is sold and the seller resides in California or the sale takes place in California, the seller or the seller's agent shall pay to the artist of such work of fine art; or to such artist's agent; five percent of the amount of such sale.

Fine art is defined as "an original painting, sculpture, or drawing, or an original work of art in glass," but the Act does not apply to the initial sale of a work of fine art where the legal title to the work is vested in the artist, to the resale of a work of fine art for a gross sales price (or fair market value of property, including art taken in trade) of less than $1,000, or to the resale of the work for a gross price less than the purchase price paid by the seller. Also excluded from the Act are sales that occur more than 20 years after the artist's death, resales of works by an art dealer to a purchaser within 10 years of the initial sale of the work by the artist to the dealer, provided all intervening sales are between dealers, and to sales of works of stained glass artistry where the work has been permanently attached to real property and is sold as part of the sale of the real property to which it is attached. For purposes of the statute, an artist is defined as the person who created the art and who is, at the time of resale, either a citizen of the United States or has resided in California for a minimum of two years.

Generally, the responsibility for paying the artist is with the seller, but when a work of fine art is sold at an auction or by a gallery, dealer, broker, museum, or other person acting as the seller's agent, the agent must withhold the five percent, locate the artist, and pay him or her. If the artist cannot be located within 90 days, the royalty must be transferred to the California State Arts Council. The Arts Council then must attempt to locate the artist. If the artist still cannot be located and if the artist does not file a written claim for the money within seven years from the date of the sale, the money becomes the property of the Arts Council for use in acquiring fine art for its Art in Public Places Program.

Unfortunately, a 2016 decision of the federal district court for the Central District of California spells the end of the California Resale Royalty Act.

Estate of Graham v. Sotheby's, Inc., Case Nos. CV–11–08604–MWF–FFM, CV–11–08605–MWF–FFM, CV–11–08622–MWF–PLA, ___ F. Supp. 3d ___, 2016 WL 1464229, 2016 Copr. L. Dec. P 30,914 (C.D. Cal. Apr. 11, 2016). This case reports the decision in a series of consolidated cases which are proposed class actions of artists and their estates and representatives, against Sotheby's, Christie's, and eBay. Earlier in the same litigation, the Ninth Circuit federal court of appeals declared that the CRRA was unconstitutional insofar as it attempted to collect royalties on art transactions occurring outside the State of California. But the Ninth Circuit was willing to sever the out-of-state sales provision and let the rest of the statute continue. See *Sam Francis Foundation v. Christies, Inc.*, 784 F.3d 1320 (9th Cir. May 5, 2015), *cert. denied*, 136 S.Ct. 795 (Jan. 11, 2016). The more recent decision of the Central District of California took up the remaining issues, and declared that the entire CRRA violated the Copyright Act's "first sale doctrine" under 17 U.S.C. § 109(a), and in general, frustrates the purpose and operation of the Copyright Act under theories of direct preemption and indirect preemption, as per 17 U.S.C. § 310(a). As of June 27, 2016, no appeal had been filed in these cases.

CHAPTER 15
FREEDOM OF EXPRESSION

A. CENSORSHIP OF THE ARTS

The atmosphere in which an artist creates should, ideally, be free of external constraints, but art, like any other form of communication, can express ideas in ways that are politically and socially controversial. A fundamental conflict thus arises between the government's legitimate interest in regulating political subversion and obscenity and the guarantee of freedom of speech.

Official attempts to curtail artists' freedom of expression have occurred since early times. During the Middle Ages and the early Renaissance, the Roman Catholic Church was the dominant influence on European society, and naturally enough, the satirical art of the day attacked the organized Church in general and the clergy in particular. Artists such as Hieronymus Bosch and Hans Holbein lashed out at the preoccupation with sin, at the hypocrisy of the priesthood, and even at the papacy. The Church powers were intolerant of such criticism and attempted, through their own laws, to eliminate this anti-Church sentiment. Art produced for Church purposes was placed under the supervision of theologians, and the artists had to adhere strictly to the instructions of their spiritual advisors.

The rise of nationalism during the 16th and 17th centuries placed the power of the state on equal footing with that of the Church. However, as critical artists soon discovered, the state was even less tolerant of criticism than was the Church. In France, Spain, and Germany, artists were harassed or jailed for speaking out through their works against the poverty, oppression, and the injustice of the times. Only in England was some degree of artistic tolerance apparent, and there much of the criticism was directed at the professions. Doctors, the clergy, and especially lawyers were the targets of the vitriolic attacks of social satirists.

The Founding Fathers owed their understanding of the value of freedom of speech and the freedom of the press to the traditions established in the English common law. David Lowenthal, *Censorship is Necessary*, The Weekly Standard, Aug. 23, 1999, reprinted in LAURA K. EGENDORF ED., CENSORSHIP 19 (2001). The freedom of speech and press in Eighteenth Century England was understood to be a freedom from prior restraint and oppressive licensing regimes, not a protection from responsibility and liability for one's words. See 4 William Blackstone, *Commentaries on the Laws of England* 149–53 (1st ed. 1765–69). Words were known to have the potential for harm, stirring up discord and violence in society, and anyone found to have uttered such libels (referred to at the time, and for at least one hundred twenty years after, as "seditious libel") and improper, harmful words would be subject to prosecution after the fact of publication to the full extent of the law. Truth was no defense in a criminal prosecution for seditious libel. It was the very utterance of the libel that mattered in the criminal sense, and true statements had as much potential to stir up the populous into a state of discord and rebellion as false statements.

American lawyers steeped in British law and familiar with British history apparently did not question the need to control subversive voices. Although the experience of the Seventeenth Century "Long Parliament" and the Great Rebellion in England and the restrictions on press freedom before the Rebellion and early in the history of the Commonwealth led to the keen aversion of British law toward prior restraints of speech and the press, little else was counted as "censorship" when British lawyers and jurists referred to the "freedom of speech," if they referred to it at all.

As Europe grew into a continent of nation states, each with divergent interests, the artist-critic turned his or her attention to the inevitable result of nationalism—war. Governments responded by suppressing the protest artist, realizing that the artist's ability to communicate an idea, even to the illiterate, was a dangerous thing. Some governments, however, used the artist to their advantage. Seizing upon this recognized power of the artist to communicate forcefully and effectively, the Germans, for example, cleverly drafted artists during both world wars and employed them successfully in their propaganda machines.

B. THE FIRST AMENDMENT FRAMEWORK

Across the Atlantic, the United States was not immune from social satire expressed in art. The libertarian goals of the founding fathers would appear to make this the most fertile nation for free expression. Yet, not all political criticism has been tolerated, and attempts have been made to suppress objectionable materials.

In 1791, the United States of America amended its Constitution to add the First Amendment: "Congress shall make no law ... abridging the freedom of speech, or of the press ... " Yet, a mere seven years later, Congress passed and President John Adams signed into law the Alien and Sedition Acts of 1798, 1 Stat. 596 (July 14, 1798), which followed the same pattern as Blackstone's prescriptions of laws designed to suppress seditious libel, recounted a century before in England.

Early cases in the life in the nation, such as *Respublica v. Oswald*, 1 U.S. (1 Dall.) 319 (Pa. 1788), followed the British approach to libel (partly in the defamation sense and partly in the seditious libel sense), and even cited Blackstone's *Commentaries* as authority for the law in this area of public and political censorship. The case involved a claim against a newspaper publisher alleged to have published libelous speech against a public figure who was accused of using influence and spreading lies to prejudice the local court against the publisher. The action sought to punish the publisher after the fact of publication; thus, it was not a prior restraint case. The high court upheld the conviction of the publisher.

During the American Civil War, President Lincoln challenged the free press and free speech provisions of the First Amendment by ordering or ratifying the military arrests and detentions of anti-war critics

SEC. B THE FIRST AMENDMENT FRAMEWORK

and political dissenters. Lincoln further suspended the habeas corpus writ, to ensure that the jailed would not receive a hearing and release through this writ procedure. Abraham Lincoln, Proclamation Suspending the Writ of Habeas Corpus (Sept. 24, 1862), in 5 THE COLLECTED WORKS OF ABRAHAM LINCOLN 421, 436, 437 (Roy P. Basler et al. eds., 1953). See also Michael Kent Curtis, *Lincoln, Vallandigham, and Anti-War Speech in the Civil War*, 7 WM. & MARY BILL RTS. J. 105, 191 (1998). At least 14,401 civilians were arrested by the Lincoln administration during the Civil War, see Mark E. Neely, Jr., *The Lincoln Administration and Arbitrary Arrests: A Reconsideration*, 5 JOURNAL OF A. LINCOLN ASSOC. 6, 6–7 (1983), available at http://hdl.handle.net/2027/spo.2629860.0005.103, some of them being newspaper editors and publishers. *Civil War tested Lincoln's tolerance for free speech*, First Amendment Center (Feb. 11, 2009), http://www.firstamendmentcenter.org/. The most publicized of these arrests was in 1863, when President Lincoln ordered the arrest of Clement L. Vallandigham, a prominent Democratic politician and former congressman, for an anti-war political speech he had made a few days before. The outcry in the press over this military arrest and detention, which eventually was commuted by Lincoln to "banishment" of Vallandigham to the confederacy, led the army to temporarily shut down the Chicago Times newspaper. *Id.*; Curtis, *supra*, at 191.

In 2 JOSEPH STORY, COMMENTARIES ON THE CONSTITUTION § 1884, Justice Story stated that "every free man has an undoubted right to lay what sentiments he pleases before the public; to forbid this is to destroy the freedom of the press." But in *Patterson v. Colorado ex rel. Att'y Gen. of Colo.*, 205 U.S. 454, 462 (1907), Justice Holmes declared that the main purpose of the free press provision is "to prevent all such previous 'restraints' upon publications as had been practiced by other governments," but it does "not prevent the subsequent punishment of such as may be deemed contrary to the public welfare."

One case that carried out this formula was *Masses Publishing Co. v. Patten*, 244 F. 535 (S.D.N.Y.), *rev'd*, 246 F. 24 (2d Cir 1917). The case involved a monthly magazine called *The Masses*, which contained cartoons and text of a politically revolutionary nature. In July 1917, the Postmaster General instructed the Postmaster of New York to deny use of the mails for distributing the magazine, alleging that the publication violated the Espionage Act of 1917. The Espionage Act of 1917 mirrored the Sedition Act of 1798 in many ways, although the particular parts at issue in *The Masses* were the prohibitions on speech with an anti-draft and anti-war-effort message. The lower court prohibited the government from withholding from the mail *The Masses* publication, stating that the statute dealt with direct advocacy of resistance to recruiting and enlistment and that the publication fell short of this direct advocacy test. District Judge Learned Hand stated, "It seems to me ... quite plain that none of the language and none of the cartoons in this paper can be thought directly to counsel or advise insubordination or mutiny, without a violation of

SEC. B   THE FIRST AMENDMENT FRAMEWORK

their meaning quite beyond any tolerable understanding." While the cartoons could be said to breed animosity to the draft, there was no intimation that they expressed the idea that one was duty bound to resist conscription.

This decision was overturned by the court of appeals, which held that the decision was within the Postmaster's discretion. The court said that First Amendment rights were not being violated since, notwithstanding the fact that the Masses Publishing Company was prevented from using the mails to distribute its magazine, other means of distribution were still available. Thus, the court stated, publication had not been suppressed.

However, times were about to change. In a series of post-World War I-era cases, *Abrams v. United States*, 250 U.S. 616 (1919); *Schenck v. United States*, 249 U.S. 47 (1919); *Gitlow v. New York*, 268 U.S. 652 (1925), the Supreme Court made its first significant effort at developing a First Amendment doctrine designed to give a measure of protection to unpopular forms of expression. In *Schenck*, Justice Holmes stated that an individual could be prosecuted for speech only upon evidence showing that the "words used are used in such circumstances and are of such a nature as to create a clear and present danger that they will bring about the substantive evils that Congress has a right to prevent." Later, in cases such as *Whitney v. California*, 274 U.S. 357 (1927) (Brandeis, J., concurring), and *New York Times Co. v. Sullivan*, 376 U.S. 254 (1964), the First

Amendment doctrine grew into its modern, robust strength.

In *Brandenburg v. Ohio*, 395 U.S. 444 (1969), the Court put to rest the seditious libel doctrine that in the Twentieth Century had been enacted into criminal syndicalism statutes that forbade advocacy of social change, disruption of industrial production, and insurrection against the wishes of government through such means as union-organizing and public protesting. The Court combined the "clear and present danger" test of *Schenck* with the "direct advocacy" approach of Judge Hand in *Masses Publishing Co.* and Justice Brandeis in *Whitney*, and held,

(1) The advocacy must be "directed to inciting or producing imminent lawless action"; and

(2) The advocacy must be "likely to incite or produce such action."

The *Brandenburg* test thus provides the framework for contemporary free speech analysis. Courts must focus both on the character of the defendant's speech and on the circumstances in which it is made. Regardless of the inciting character of a defendant's speech, he or she cannot be prosecuted unless the speech threatens imminent unlawful conduct and unless there is a probability that lawless action will occur as a result. See, e.g., *R.A.V. v. City of St. Paul, Minnesota*, 505 U.S. 377 (1992). The law has been tweaked to allow prohibitions on "true threats," *Madsen v. Women's Health Center*, 512 U.S. 753 (1994); *Elonis v. United*

States, 135 S. Ct. 2001 (2015), including true threats exhibiting a racially-motivated bias. See *Wisconsin v. Mitchell*, 508 U.S. 476, 489 (1993); *Virginia v. Black*, 538 U.S. 343 (2003); *Elliott v. Virginia*, 593 S.E.2d 263 (Va. 2004).

C. SYMBOLIC SPEECH

As most artists are well aware, there are many forms of expression that go beyond a simple statement of ideas through verbal and written communication. There is a distinction between "pure speech" and "symbolic speech" or "speech plus." Symbolic speech consists of communicative but nonverbal conduct, and speech plus consists of verbal expression within the context of conduct that, in itself, may not be regarded as communicative.

Unfortunately, courts do not necessarily afford nonverbal communication the same deference as so-called pure speech. It has been said that symbolic conduct does not have the same protection as pure speech, and the state may regulate the use of a particular form of nonverbal communication in order to serve a legitimate state interest. The maintenance of the public peace and order is the most frequent argument used against blanket acceptance of visual protest. Yet, this is not to say that the First Amendment offers no protection to symbolic conduct. Conduct may be considered to be protected speech, but the courts have not readily arrived at a basis for determining when conduct will be protected.

As early as 1931, the Supreme Court recognized that nonverbal conduct may be a protected form of speech. Thus, in *Stromberg v. California*, 283 U.S. 359 (1931), the court invalidated a California statute prohibiting the display of a red flag "as a sign, symbol or emblem of opposition to organized government." Chief Justice Hughes' majority opinion stated that a law "so vague and indefinite as to permit the punishment of the fair use" of "the opportunity for free political discussion" was "repugnant to the guaranty of liberty" in the Fourteenth Amendment. In *West Virginia State Board of Education v. Barnette*, 319 U.S. 624 (1943), in a case involving the conduct of Jehovah's Witnesses children who wished to avoid saluting the flag in public schools, the Court spoke eloquently of the power of symbolic speech and expressive conduct as a shortcut from mind to mind, communicating to the illiterate as well as the literate, and held that forced compulsion of the opposite expressive conduct—namely, forcing the children to salute the flag—went against the "fixed star in our Constitutional constellation" that forbids compulsion of adherence and affirmative to any particular belief.

Stromberg and *Barnette* did not, however, create any tests for defining what kinds of expressive conduct and what circumstances fall within the protection of the First Amendment. The court began to set some boundaries in a draft card burning case, *United States v. O'Brien*, 391 U.S. 367 (1968). O'Brien burned his Selective Service Registration card on the steps of the South Boston Courthouse, amidst a crowd of spectators. He was convicted of violating Section 462(b) of the Universal Military Training and Service Act of 1948, as amended in

1965. On appeal, O'Brien argued that the amended statute was unconstitutional because it restricted his freedom of expression. The court rejected this contention, saying, "We cannot accept the view that an apparently limitless variety of conduct can be labeled 'speech' whenever the person engaged in the conduct intends thereby to express an idea." The court also rejected the contention that an action with a clearly noncommunicative aspect is outside any First Amendment protection.

Though O'Brien's action had the requisite communicative element, it does not necessarily follow that it automatically was protected speech. "When speech and nonspeech elements are combined in the same course of conduct, a sufficiently important governmental interest in regulating the nonspeech element—here the destruction of the draft card—can justify incidental limitation on First Amendment freedoms." The important state interest found here was the smooth functioning of the Selective Service System.

The court set forth a four-part test for determining when a governmental interest sufficiently justifies the regulation of expressive conduct:

... (1) [I]f it is within the constitutional power of the Government; (2) if it furthers an important or substantial governmental interest; (3) if the governmental interest is unrelated to the suppression of free expression; and (4) if the incidental restriction on alleged first amendment freedoms is no greater than is essential to the furtherance of that interest.

Finding that the 1965 amendment satisfied each element of the test, the court upheld O'Brien's conviction.

A year later in *Tinker v. Des Moines Independent Community School District*, 393 U.S. 503 (1969), the court reached the opposite result in a case involving elements of symbolic speech. The court held that wearing black armbands in school as an antiwar protest was "closely akin to pure speech" and noted that there was no evidence that the conduct in question had created disorder, in any way interfered with the functioning of the school, or collided with other persons' rights. Yet, even in *Tinker*, the court provided no basis for distinguishing between pure speech and symbolic speech. As Justice Harlan noted, concurring in *Cowgill v. California*, 396 U.S. 371 (1970) (*per curiam*), "The Court has, as yet, not established a test for determining at what point conduct becomes so intertwined with expression that it becomes necessary to weigh the state's interest in proscribing conduct against the constitutionally protected interest in freedom of expression."

This failure to provide for a means of determining when symbolic speech is protected was also apparent in *Schacht v. United States*, 398 U.S. 58 (1970). Schacht had been convicted for performing in an antiwar skit under a federal statute that prohibited the unauthorized wearing of a uniform of any of the Armed Forces of the United States. The statute allowed an exemption for actors portraying members of the Armed Forces "if the portrayal does not tend to discredit that armed force." The Supreme Court overturned the conviction, stating that punishment simply for "speaking out" against the government clearly "would be an unconstitutional abridgement of freedom of speech." The court did not, however, address the symbolic nature of the wearing of an Army uniform.

The modern heir to *Tinker* is the case, *Morse v. Frederick*, 551 U.S. 393 (2007), which held that conduct "interfering with the functioning of the school" might take place outside of the classroom, not during class time, and even off of school property. In *Morse*, students on a "school-sanctioned" event, the viewing of the Olympic torch relay through their Alaska town, "interfered with the functioning of the school" when they unfurled a large banner reading, "Bong Hits 4 Jesus." Thus, the lead student could be suspended in punishment for his speech.

Some resolution of the question of the extent of protection afforded symbolic speech was forthcoming in later cases involving flag desecration. In *Spence v. Washington*, 418 U.S. 405 (1974) (*per curiam*), discussed in Section D, *infra*, the court overturned a conviction under a flag misuse statute, examining both the nature of the activity and the factual context, as well as the environment in which the activity occurred. Like *Tinker*, the *Spence* case evidenced some willingness by the court to view conduct in some circumstances as "closely akin to pure speech," but unlike *Tinker*, the court attempted to develop a working definition that would aid in making the determination of whether the accused had engaged in a protected form of expression.

Applied to cases involving flag desecration, *Spence* thus provided a framework for the First Amendment analysis of expression that is communicative but nonverbal, the keystone of artistic expression.

The Supreme Court continued to apply the *O'Brien* test in *Barnes v. Glen Theatre, Inc.*, 501 U.S. 560 (1991). Here, the court held that an Indiana statute prohibiting public nudity, which operated, in this case, to prohibit nude dancing, did not violate the First Amendment. The court found that the public indecency statute is within the constitutional powers of the state and furthers a substantial government interest in protecting societal order and morality. This interest was found to be unrelated to the suppression of free expression because the perceived evil that Indiana seeks to address is not erotic dancing, but public nudity. Erotic dancing is allowed so long as the performers wear a scant amount of clothing. Because the statute is narrowly tailored, the incidental restriction of First Amendment freedom is no greater than is essential to the furtherance of the government interest. This type of statute was again upheld in *City of Erie v. Pap's A.M.*, 529 U.S. 277 (2000), though in 2002, the Pennsylvania Supreme Court struck down the city ordinance as violative of the state constitution.

D. FLAG DESECRATION AS PROTEST

Some of the most heated debates concerning the freedom of visual expression have centered around the use of the American flag to communicate an idea or sentiment. Flag desecration statutes have been

SEC. D FLAG DESECRATION AS PROTEST

enacted by the federal government and most, if not all, state governments, but whereas the stars and stripes are a symbol of the nation's strength and glory to many, to others the flag is the embodiment of all that is wrong with the government. The American flag has thus been used by artists and many others as a vehicle of public expression and protest.

The central issue in a First Amendment analysis of a flag desecration case is whether the desecration falls within the scope of pure speech or symbolic speech. The use of a flag to express an idea is obviously nonverbal, but in many cases, elements of communication akin to pure speech may be apparent. Yet, as noted in Section B, *supra*, the Supreme Court has not established a framework for distinguishing between protected and nonprotected nonverbal expression.

Prior to 1974, several lower courts held that flag desecration in the context of a visual display was protected by the First Amendment. Thus, in *People v. Von Rosen*, 13 Ill. 2d 68, 147 N.E.2d 327 (1958), the court reversed the conviction of those who had published an illustration which depicted a young woman who was nude except for a large hat, sunglasses, and a piece of cloth that looked exactly like an American flag covering her pubic area. Though the statute itself was held valid, there was no evidence that the publication implicated the statute, preventing breaches of the peace resulting from improper use of the national symbol. Without that showing, the use of the flag in the manner objected to was protected expression.

A similar result was reached in *Korn v. Elkins*, 317 F. Supp. 138 (D. Md. 1970). There, University of Maryland officials refused to permit publication of a student-produced magazine that pictured a burning flag on the cover. The court sustained the students' challenge to the constitutionality of the flag desecration statute upon which the censoring officials had relied. The court indicated that no intertwining of conduct and expression was involved. The case presented only expression in the form of art and, as such, approached pure speech and was protected unless a substantial, countervailing governmental interest was involved.

It was not until *Spence v. Washington* that the Supreme Court provided a context for deciding when expression approaches pure speech. The case involved a student who hung an American flag, with a peace symbol taped on it, upside down from his apartment window as a protest against the Kent State tragedy and the United States' invasion of Cambodia. In finding this conduct to be protected speech, the court considered two factors—the nature of Spence's activity and the factual context and environment in which it was done. *Spence* required that there must be an "intent to convey a particular message" and "a likelihood that the message would be understood by those who observed it." This intent and likelihood of success to communicate could be gleaned from the surrounding circumstances. While the government argued that state action against flag desecration conceivably could still be justified if it could be shown that the state had an interest in (1) preventing a breach of the peace, (2) protecting the sensibilities of passersby, or (3) preserving the flag as an unalloyed symbol of our country, the court held that none of those circumstances had been shown.

The impact of the *Spence* approach to the world of art became apparent in *People v. Radich*, 308 N.Y.S.2d 846, 257 N.E.2d 30 (N.Y.1970), *aff'd sub nom. Radich v. New York*, 401 U.S. 531 (1971), *on writ of habeas corpus, United States ex rel. Radich v. Criminal Court of City of New York*, 385 F. Supp. 165 (S.D.N.Y. 1974). Mr. Radich, a New York gallery owner, was convicted for displaying artworks, one of which employed a United States flag in the form of a phallic symbol, erect and protruding from a cross. The New York Court of Appeals refused to convert what it felt to be a willful act of flag desecration into protected artistic expression and upheld the conviction. An equally divided Supreme Court meant that the lower court's conviction would stand, but Radich was not finished. On a writ of *habeas corpus*, the case was heard again, and this time he was successful. The federal district court, in the *habeas corpus* hearing, applied the *Spence* decision and held that under the circumstances of the context in which the works had been displayed, the display was protected by the First Amendment. Moreover, no imminent unlawful conduct or probability of public disorder had been shown by the state, so regulation on the grounds of a breach of the peace was not warranted. In addition, since the exhibit was on the second floor of a private art gallery, not readily observable by the passing crowds below, the state interest of protecting sensibilities of the public so as to warrant regulation of the activity was not apparent. Finally, since the flag had not been destroyed in the process of communicating the artist's idea, the state had not shown an interest in preserving the flag as an unalloyed symbol.

It is worth noting that the artist, Marc Morrel, was not prosecuted for his act of creating the sculptures involved in the *Radich* case. Could this be because the government was not willing to test how far the courts would go in regulating artistic creation as distinguished from display? It is also interesting to note that Radich's conviction and the courts' conservative views of the facts persisted during the period when hostilities in Vietnam continued. Subsequently, after the United States withdrew from Vietnam, the federal district court appears to have adopted a more liberal attitude. See page 408 for a copy of one of the photographs of the Morrel constructions taken by the New York Police Department and submitted as evidence at trial.

The two-part analysis adopted by the court in *Spence* and employed in *Radich*—first determining whether the conduct is within the protection of the First Amendment, and second, whether, upon the record of the given case, the interests advanced by the state are so substantial as to justify infringement of constitutional rights—differs from the approach in earlier symbolic speech cases. The earlier cases made no initial determination that the individual's conduct actually involved protected First Amendment rights; the court merely assumed this to be so. It is significant that in *Spence* and *Radich*, the courts did not make that assumption, but first considered whether or not the conduct was protected speech. An advantage of this method is that by clarifying the relationship of the competing interests involved, a more exacting balance is possible. Once the court determines that the conduct is protected by the First Amendment, it then decides what degree of protection is appropriate.

In 1989, the Supreme Court in *Texas v. Johnson*, 491 U.S. 397 (1989), determined that desecrating the American flag is political free speech. This case involved a defendant who had burned the flag as part of a protest demonstration during the Republican National Convention. The court held that a state may not foster its own view of the flag by prohibiting expressive conduct relating to it. In effect, the flag desecration statute forbids the expression rather than the conduct, as Texas allows the ceremonious burning of a dirty flag as an expression of respect. Thus, Texas is saying that one may burn the flag to convey one's attitude toward it only if one does not endanger the flag's representation of nationhood and national unity. However, the court concluded, the government may not ensure that a symbol be used to express only one view of a symbol or its referents.

Soon after the *Johnson* decision, the federal government passed the Flag Protection Act of 1989 (18 U.S.C. § 700), which was held unconstitutional in *United States v. Eichman*, 496 U.S. 310 (1990), concluding that "punishing desecration of the flag dilutes the very freedom that makes this emblem so revered, and worth revering."

E. OBSCENITY

1. FROM ROTH TO MILLER

Until the mid-20th century, it was tacitly assumed that obscene materials did not fall within the areas of expression protected by the First Amendment. In a few instances, the Supreme Court hinted as much in *dicta*, but no serious attempt to define obscenity had been made by the court prior to *Roth v. United States*, 354 U.S. 476 (1957). Since then, various attempts to define what is obscene have been made, but none have met with total success. As a result, this area of the law is still the source of much confusion and litigation.

Roth was an obscenity case involving a New York publisher and distributor of books, photographs, and magazines who was convicted of violating a federal obscenity statute by mailing allegedly obscene circulars and advertising an allegedly obscene book. The defendant appealed, claiming that his conduct was protected by the First Amendment, but the Supreme Court rejected this contention.

In its opinion, the court attempted to set out a formula for defining obscenity. It rejected the test used in England, which had been to judge the material according to the effect of an isolated excerpt upon particularly susceptible persons. Instead, the court held that the standard should be "whether to the average person, applying community standards, the dominant theme of the material taken as a whole appeals to prurient interests." To the court, prurient material was that which has "a tendency to excite lustful thoughts," and the applicable community standard was a national standard. Application of this definition became difficult at best.

Sixteen years later, in 1973, the court announced a new obscenity test in a case involving a defendant who was convicted of mailing obscene material. In *Miller v. California*, 413 U.S. 15 (1973), the court carefully noted that "in the area of freedom of speech and press, the courts must always remain sensitive to any infringement on genuinely serious literary, artistic, political or scientific expression." It also reiterated the *Roth* court's emphasis "that sex and obscenity are not synonymous, and a reviewing court must, of necessity, look at the context of the material, as well as its content." With this in mind, the court stated that "[S]tate statutes designed to regulate obscene materials must be carefully limited; we now confine the permissible scope of regulation to works which depict or describe sexual conduct." The court then announced the new test:

(a) Whether the average person applying contemporary community standards would find that the work, taken as a whole, appeals to the prurient interest . . . , (b) whether the works depict or describe, in a patently offensive way, sexual conduct specifically defined by the applicable state law, and (c) whether the work, taken as a whole, lacks serious literary, artistic, political, or scientific value.

In one bold stroke, the court in *Miller* ruled essentially that material of "serious value" could not constitutionally be proscribed as obscenity and delegated to the finders of fact the responsibility for applying the complex *Miller* test. Significantly, the court also held that the First and Fourteenth Amendments do not require that a jury in an obscenity case consider a single, uniform, national standard in determining a particular work's character. Yet, while *Miller* emphasized the necessity of relying on the jury system to define the questions of appeal to the "prurient interest" or of "patent offensiveness," essentially fact questions, it would not be correct to conclude that juries have an unbridled discretion in making these determinations. The appellate courts can conduct an independent review of these factual determinations when necessary. Whereas the court in *Miller* did not clearly face the issue of the application of the local standards formulation to federal prosecutions, the issue was subsequently resolved in *Hamling v. United States*, 418 U.S. 87 (1974), where the concept of local community standards was held equally applicable to federal prosecutions.

In *Pope v. Illinois*, 481 U.S. 497 (1987), the court held that the jury is not to apply community standards when determining "whether the work, taken as a whole, lacks serious literary, artistic, political or scientific value." The proper inquiry is whether a reasonable person would find such value in the material.

Obscenity statutes not incorporating the Miller test have been struck down. In *American Booksellers Ass'n, Inc. v. Hudnut*, 771 F.2d 323 (7th Cir. 1985), the Seventh Circuit struck down an antipornography statute that defined pornography as "the graphic sexually explicit subordination of women, whether in pictures or in words." The ordinance did not refer to prurient interest, offensiveness, standards of the community, or the artistic, literary, political, or scientific value of the work.

Of course, the *Miller* test did not solve all the interpretation problems. Later decisions have had to confront the issues of the size of the community whose standards are to be used and which community standards are to be used when importation or interstate transportation of allegedly obscene materials is involved.

In the customs area, the answer appears to be that it is the community standard of the district where the material was seized that is applicable to the obscenity determination and not the standard of the community of the materials' ultimate destination and use. *United States v. Various Articles of Obscene Merchandise, Schedule #1303*, 562 F.2d 185 (2nd Cir. 1977). This raises a particularly thorny issue in that custom ports are generally in large cities, which would arguably have more relaxed community standards than would smaller communities to which the material may be destined. See page 409 for an example of one of the pieces in the *Kronhausen*

Collection of Erotic Art, which was determined not to be obscene and was, therefore, permitted entry into the United States.

A different rule applies, however, when one uses the United States mail to transmit obscene material. 18 U.S.C. § 1461 makes such transmittal a federal crime. Originally this statute defined the crime as the "deposit" into the mails of obscene matter. Prosecutions thus only occurred in the district where the item was mailed. Congress subsequently defined the crime as a "continuing offense," intending thereby to place it within the purview of 18 U.S.C. § 3237, which permits prosecution in the district of mailing, the district of receipt, or in any intermediate district through which the material passes. This amendment was upheld as constitutional in *Reed Enterprises v. Clark*, 278 F. Supp. 372 (D.D.C 1967), *aff'd*, 390 U.S. 457 (1968). While this permits prosecutions in some districts that have only minimal contacts with the obscene material, in practice, the real benefit has been in permitting prosecution in the district of receipt. Also, though not required to do so, prosecutors generally follow the community standard of the forum district in determining the obscenity question. While this arguably gives rise to some extreme examples of forum shopping, the use of the community standard of the forum district appears to be a desirable result, because the primary purpose of most obscenity laws is to protect the target community from what it feels is obscene material.

If the interstate transportation of obscene materials is carried out not through the mails, but by a common carrier or express company, a similar result is reached. That is, pursuant to 18 U.S.C. § 1462 and 18 U.S.C. § 3237, the activity is again considered a continuing offense for which prosecution may occur in any district from, through, or into which such commerce moves.

The Court is reluctant to expand the reach of nonspeech to new areas of undesirable or potentially harmful speech. In *Brown v. Entertainment Merchants Association*, 564 U.S. 786 (2011), the court struck down a California law regulating and limiting the expression of violent video games.

2. CHILD PORNOGRAPHY

During the late 1970s, there was an increase in child pornography. In response, state legislators enacted strict statutes prohibiting the sale of obscene materials including those portraying sexual activities involving youngsters, as well as materials involving children which may not be characterized as obscene under the *Miller* standard. The court has held that, like fighting words and defamatory statements, portrayals of sexual conduct by children are not constitutionally protected.

In *New York v. Ferber*, 458 U.S. 747 (1982), the Supreme Court had its first opportunity to examine a statute directed at and limited to depictions of sexual activity involving children. In upholding the New York statute, the court held that the test for child pornography is different from that enunciated in *Miller*. Under this test:

> (1) A trier of fact need not find that the material appeals to the prurient interest of the average person; (2) it is not required that the sexual conduct be portrayed in a patently offensive manner; and (3) the material at issue need not be considered as a whole.

Thus, although the *Ferber* court did not enunciate any new standards in this area, it modified the *Miller* guidelines and allowed the states greater leeway in dealing with the problem of child pornography.

The court offered five reasons why the states are entitled to broader regulatory powers in this situation. First, the legislative judgment that the use of children as subjects of sexually explicit materials is harmful to the physiological, emotional, and mental health of the child easily passes muster under the First Amendment. This is because the state's interest in protecting its children is compelling. Second, the *Miller* standards do not reflect the state's particular and more compelling interest in prosecuting those who promote the sexual exploitation of children. The questions under *Miller* of whether a work taken as a whole appeals to the prurient interest of an average person, whether the depiction is "patently offensive," and whether the work taken as a whole contains serious literary, artistic, political, or scientific value bears no connection to the issue of whether a child has been physically or psychologically harmed in the production of the work. Third, the value of permitting live performances and photographic reproductions of children engaged in lewd or sexual conduct is minimal. Finally, recognizing and classifying child pornography as a category of material outside the protection of the First Amendment is not incompatible with earlier decisions where a content-based classification, such as fighting words, has been approved, because the evil to be restricted overwhelmingly outweighs the expressive interests at stake. However, the court was careful to point out that, as with all legislation in this sensitive area, the conduct to be prohibited must be adequately defined by the applicable state law, either as written or as authoritatively construed.

The court also noted that the advertising and selling of child pornography may be prohibited along with its production, since advertising and selling provide an economic motive for the illegal production. However, the court indicated that the distribution of descriptions or other depictions of sexual conduct not otherwise obscene, which do not involve live performance or photographic or other visual reproduction of live performances, retains First Amendment protection. In addition, the court did not close the door on the possibility that in this area, works of serious artistic, scientific, or educational value could receive First Amendment protection; the view that such material would be protected was expressly stated in Justice Brennan's concurring opinion, with which Justice Marshall joined.

In *Osborne v. Ohio*, 495 U.S. 103 (1990), the court held that a state may constitutionally proscribe the private possession of child pornography. The defendant had based his argument on the court's decision in *Stanley v. Georgia*, 394 U.S. 557 (1969), which struck down a Georgia law outlawing the private possession of obscene material. The court concluded that the interests underlying child pornography prohibitions far exceed the interests justifying the law at issue in *Stanley*.

As the use of the World Wide Web has increased, Internet pornography has become a controversial topic. In *Reno v. American Civil Liberties Union*, 521 U.S. 844 (1997), the Supreme Court held that the Communications Decency Act (CDA) of 1996, which made it a crime for any person to post material on the Internet that would be considered indecent or obscene in a manner available to a minor, unconstitutionally "silences some speakers whose messages would be entitled to constitutional protection." The court noted that "as a matter of constitutional tradition in the absence of evidence to the contrary, we presume that governmental regulation of the content of speech is more likely to interfere with the free exchange of ideas than to encourage it. The interest in encouraging freedom of expression in a democratic society outweighs any theoretical but unproven benefit of censorship."

The government responded to *Reno* by passing the Child Online Protection Act (COPA) of 1998 (47 U.S.C. § 223), which also criminalized certain Internet speech. This law was struck down by *Ashcroft v. American Civil Liberties Union*, 542 U.S. 656 (2004). Significant portions of the Child

Pornography Prevention Act of 1996 (CPPA) (18 U.S.C. § 2251 *et seq.*) pertaining to virtual child pornography (that is, sexually explicit images that appear to depict minors but were produced without using any real children) were also struck down in *Ashcroft v. Free Speech Coalition*, 535 U.S. 234 (2002).

Congress enacted the Children's Internet Protection Act (CIPA) in December 2000. CIPA provided that a public library may not receive federal assistance to provide Internet access unless it installs software to block images that constitute obscenity or child pornography and to prevent minors from obtaining access to material that is harmful to them. The Supreme Court held CIPA unconstitutional in *United States v. American Library Association, Inc.*, 539 U.S. 194 (2003).

The Court returned its attention to the problem of the market and distribution chain for child pornography in *United States v. Williams*, 553 U.S. 285 (2008), which upheld the Prosecutorial Remedies and Other Tools to end the Exploitation of Children Today (PROTECT) Act section prohibiting "pandering" and "solicitation" of child pornography. Under the Act, offers to provide and requests to obtain child pornography do not require the actual existence of child pornography backing up these offers. Rather than targeting the underlying material, the Act was construed to ban collateral speech that introduces such material into the child-pornography distribution network. Thus, an internet user who solicits child pornography from an undercover agent violates the statute even if the officer possesses no child pornography, and likewise a person who is selling virtual child pornography but who advertises it as depicting actual children also falls within the reach of the statute.

So called "innocent" or "artistic" nude photographs of young children are swept within the scope of the most aggressively defined prohibitions on child pornography. "Sexting," the practice of underage youths who send pictures of their own or other youth's nude genitalia for fun or flirting or for other purposes, has been prosecuted from time to time as a violation of laws prohibiting the distribution, receipt, or possession of child pornography because there is no mental state required in the law. Simple creation, distribution, receipt, or possession of a picture of a child showing their genitalia meets the definition of the law with no *mens rea* component. The prosecution of these self-created images may be taking the definition of child pornography too far.

3. AN ALTERNATIVE APPROACH TO REGULATION

In recent years, states have begun to use civil rather than criminal sanctions to regulate the dissemination of pornographic material. Typically, a community determines the obscenity of offensive materials in an adjudication to declare the materials or the distributing establishment, or both, a public nuisance. The court then enjoins the distribution of the materials. If the distribution persists, the distributor will be subject to summary contempt proceedings. In this procedure, the community is more likely to prevail and the civil defendant has fewer procedural safeguards. Further, the community need prove obscenity only by a preponderance of the evidence rather than beyond a reasonable doubt. The courts have approved of this regulatory scheme, generally finding that the state's interests in preserving peace, order, and a community's character outweigh the individual's alleged rights.

The government often attempts to regulate art by cutting funding. For instance, the City of San Antonio discontinued funding for a nonprofit art organization that supported gay and lesbian films. The court held that the city had violated the first amendment by defunding the organization based on its viewpoints. *Esperanza Peace and Justice Ctr. v. City of San Antonio*, 316 F. Supp. 2d 433 (W.D. Tex. 2001).

In another instance, the *Sensation: Young British Artists from the Saatchi Collection* exhibit included a work called *The Holy Virgin Mary* by Chris Ofili, which depicted the Virgin Mary with elephant dung on each breast. Shortly before the scheduled opening, the city notified the Brooklyn Museum of Art that it would terminate all funding to the museum unless it canceled the exhibit. The museum brought suit seeking a preliminary injunction to prevent the city from punishing or retaliating against it, as well as for damages, and the city sued to eject the museum from its site. The court granted the museum's motion for preliminary injunction. *Brooklyn Institute of Arts and Sciences v. City of New York*, 64 F. Supp. 2d 184 (E.D.N.Y. 1999). After the ruling, Mayor Rudolph Giuliani and the museum settled their differences and the exhibit ran its course.

Two artworks made on commission for Pasco, Washington's city hall in 1996 were removed due to their alleged sexual nature, resulting in a lawsuit that settled after the Ninth Circuit holding that the removal violated the artists' First Amendment rights. The City of Pasco refused to show Sharon Rupp's sculptures, including one showing a woman mooning her audience, and Janette Hopper's prints, depicting Adam and Eve and including some nudity.

Another way in which states are attacking pornography is through racketeering (RICO) statutes. In *Fort Wayne Books, Inc. v. Indiana*, 489 U.S. 46 (1989), the prosecutor used six counts of distribution of obscene matter as a basis for filing two counts of RICO violations. The court held that because the RICO statute encompassed obscenity laws and because the obscenity law at issue was not unconstitutionally vague, the obscenity charges were not insufficient predicate acts under RICO. The bookstore owner further argued that because the penalties for RICO violations are more severe than the penalties for obscenity offenses, the RICO penalties would have a chilling effect on First Amendment freedoms. The court disagreed, stating that deterrence of the sale of obscene materials is a legitimate goal of state anti-obscenity law. The court did conclude, however, that the pretrial seizure of books and materials was unconstitutional.

Other attempts at censorship do not originate in state action. Artists are frequently victims of an informal brand of censorship that, for whatever reason, is rarely contested in a court of law. Many of these situations involve materials that would not be or have not been held obscene by the courts. Thus, artistic expression may be stifled through public pressure, coercion by civic groups, and behind-the-scene maneuvering by influential university, museum, or community leaders. This informal censorship may, therefore, be more potent than litigation.

For instance, the Seattle Art Museum canceled a show called *Pay for Your Pleasure*, a traveling exhibit that featured a piece of art by someone who murdered people in each community where the exhibit was to be shown. Similarly, Eric Fischl's sculpture *Tumbling Woman*, designed to memorialize those who fell to their deaths from the World Trade Center towers, was removed from Rockefeller Center after numerous complaints from a public still sensitive to such memories.

Acting under the guise of self-appointed guardians of public morality, these censors can be particularly effective in limiting the opportunity of artists to display their works. This strikes at the very heart of the values inherent in the First Amendment, and the artist need not acquiesce, and indeed often has not acquiesced, to these attempts at censorship. This, no doubt, will continue to plague artists, and many battles are yet to be waged since the restraint on free expression of ideas is anathema to the American scheme of justice.

CHAPTER 16
MUSEUMS

A. INTRODUCTION

Museums occupy a unique position in the art world. Like any institution, museums must grapple with the nuts and bolts of managing their investments, personnel and day-to-day activities; yet, due to their sheer size and notoriety, they must do so under scrutiny from donors, their local communities, and the world of art in general. As the largest group of art collectors and the most visible participants in the market, museums influence trends and the behavior of other collectors. As repositories of art and cultural artifacts, they also serve as an important resource for the public. These attributes make museums subject to many legal, ethical, and policy forces that other collectors do not face.

B. THE MUSEUM ORGANIZATION

A museum may be organized as a public or charitable trust, a nonprofit corporation, or a municipal corporation. A public or charitable trust is created by complying with state common law and statutes on trusts. Generally, this requires an owner of property (the settlor) to transfer legal title to trustees who administer the property for the benefit of the public. The document establishing the trust usually sets forth the trustees' names or criteria for their selection, a description of the trust property (referred to as the "*corpus*" of the trust), the trust purpose, and any limitations or conditions imposed by the settlor. See generally Uniform Probate Code (1982); Powell on Real Property (1991); Uniform Commercial Code § 2–201.

A nonprofit corporation is entirely a creature of the laws of the state in which it is formed. It is created by filing articles of incorporation with the state. The articles include the corporation's name, purpose, its duration, names and addresses of the corporate directors, and the names and addresses of the incorporators. State statutes also customarily require the articles of incorporation of a nonprofit corporation to contain a provision that specifies that any corporate funds remaining after dissolution and liquidation will be transferred to a similar organization. At the organizational or first meeting, the bylaws are usually adopted. Bylaws contain the specific rules that govern the internal operation of the organization. Other items traditionally considered at the organizational meeting include naming the officers, authorizing the establishment of bank accounts, and adopting other basic administrative procedures.

Municipal corporations must be created in accordance with the state statutory requirements for the establishment of such organizations.

Both corporations and trusts may become exempt from taxation. In addition to saving the museum money, tax-exempt status is an important criterion for many funding sources. Many private foundations and governmental entities require applicants to be tax exempt before they are eligible to apply for grants and funding. In addition, if a museum has obtained tax-exempt status, then individuals who donate money or property to the institution may be permitted to take charitable deductions for the amounts given the museum. Indeed, for some persons in high income tax brackets, charitable donations may be particularly advantageous for reducing taxable income to more manageable levels. Thus, tax-exempt status acts as a powerful incentive for many people to support the museum.

A museum obtains its tax-exempt status by complying with the formalities required by the Internal Revenue Service, which begins with the filing of IRS Form 1023. If the museum can complete its filing for tax-exempt status within 15 months of its creation, the ruling when issued will apply retroactively. Otherwise, the exemption will apply only to donations received after the ruling. After federal tax-exempt status is obtained, many states and municipalities automatically grant the entity an exemption from state and local taxes. However, as a charitable organization, the museum may be required to file reports with its state's Attorney General before publicly soliciting contributions. Applicable law varies from state to state and should be consulted prior to any charitable fundraising campaign.

In *Georgia O'Keeffe Museum v. County of Santa Fe*, 62 P.3d 754 (N.M. App. 2002), the museum was a private non-profit corporation that was accused by the Santa Fe County tax board of not meeting the requirements for a property tax exemption as a charitable or educational property. The Court of Appeals held that the board should consider the extent of any intrinsic educational value the taxpayer provided to the public and the relationship of taxpayer's off-site programs and activities to the museum, and thus remanded the case. But it also held that the museum's donation of funds to other state museums was insufficient to qualify it for a charitable purposes property tax exemption on its own. The case stands for the proposition that if "educational activities" are the museum's primary claim to tax-exempt status, then the museum's educational activities must be substantial and not just made up of words and window-dressing. The museum must have multiple educational programs that meet regularly, and serve more than a token number of members of the public.

Not all activities of a museum are necessarily exempt from tax once it obtains tax-exempt status. Whereas income derived from donations, deaccessions, admission fees, and membership dues is rarely questioned, income from certain commercial activities may be taxed as unrelated trade or business income. Museums commonly derive additional revenues from selling reproductions of artworks in a gift shop, licensing the copying and sale of items in their collection, operating dining facilities, and engaging in other dealings for profit. Revenues from these activities may become subject to scrutiny by the IRS.

IRC § 511 (codified at 28 U.S.C. § 511) makes all the "unrelated business taxable income" of otherwise exempt corporations and trusts subject to ordinary income tax. An "unrelated trade or business" is defined by Section 513 as:

> ... any trade or business, the conduct of which is not substantially related (aside from the need of such organization for income or funds or the use it makes of the profits derived), to the exercise or performance by such organization of its charitable, educational, or other purpose or function constituting the basis for its exemption.

In order to determine whether an organization's activities are substantially related to the exempt purpose, Treas. Reg. § 1.513–1(d)(2) states that the test is whether the production or distribution of the goods from which the gross income is derived "contributes importantly" to the accomplishment of the exempt purposes of the organization. This test has been applied in several Internal Revenue Service rulings. In Rev. Rul. 73–104, 1973–1 C.B. 263, the sale of greeting cards bearing reproductions of artworks in the museum was held not taxable as unrelated trade or business income. The IRS found that although the activity was unquestionably commercial, it contributed importantly to the museum's educational purpose "by stimulating and enhancing public awareness, interest, and the appreciation of art." The IRS also noted that a broader segment of the public may be encouraged to visit the museum itself to share in its educational functions and programs as a result of seeing the cards.

Present law enables many museums to cover their operating costs by engaging in some profit-making activities, although the museum still must be able to show that such activities contribute substantially to its exempt purpose which ultimately benefits the community. In Rev. Rul. 74–399, 1974–2 C.B. 172, the IRS held that the profitable operation of a cafeteria or dining room, operated for museum staff and the public visiting the museum, was not an unrelated trade or business. However, while the sale of reproductions has been held to further the museum's exempt purpose, the IRS has distinguished the situation of a folk art museum that sold scientific books and city souvenirs along with reproductions of pieces from its collection. According to Rev. Rul. 73–105, 1973–1 C.B. 264, such sales were an unrelated trade or business, even though other items sold in the shop were related to the museum's exempt function. Because the scientific books and souvenirs did not bear a relationship to the museum's artistic endeavor, their sale did not contribute importantly to the organization's exempt purpose. The rule was thus established that sales of a particular line of merchandise could be considered individually to determine their relatedness to the institution's exempt purpose.

The tax court has held that affinity credit card payments by a bank to a charity are royalties and not subject to "unrelated business income tax" (UBIT). *Mississippi State University Alumni, Inc. v.*

Commissioner, T.C. Memo. 1997–397 (U.S. Tax Ct. 1997). Similarly the IRS issued a private letter ruling holding that links from an exempt organization's website to the websites of businesses that provide services to its members do not create UBIT and that such links do not affect the exempt status of royalties or qualified sponsorship payments.

C. TRUSTEE AND DIRECTOR LIABILITY

As a practical matter, there is little difference between the activities of a trustee and those of a corporate director. Both generally are charged with overseeing the museum's policies and assets, although they usually appoint a salaried employee who supervises the museum staff and runs the museum on a day-to-day basis. Yet, the legal responsibilities of trustees and corporate directors may be very different. This is nowhere more apparent and nowhere more confusing than in the area of trustee or director liability for a breach of fiduciary duties. Generally the standards to which trustees will be held are stricter than those applied to corporate directors; yet, the standard applied is not necessarily determined by the individuals' titles in the particular museum. Indeed, it is common for museums to refer to the individuals who serve on the governing board as trustees, even when the institution is created in the form of a nonprofit corporation. However, one trend emerges with increasing clarity: Museum personnel, from trustees to curators, are being held legally accountable for their actions.

Abuses of fiduciary duties in the museum world are more prevalent than one might imagine. This is particularly unfortunate because a museum is an organization with a great deal of visibility. While its primary goal should be education and public service, a museum is also an operating business organization. It buys, sells, pays employees, and performs many of the same functions as its profit-making counterparts. Regrettably, it is not always managed in the same way as a standard business entity, and those who run the museum may treat their museum duties as a hobby rather than as a professional responsibility. For example, the shocking deterioration of some fine Rodin sculptures and the disappearance of many Indian artifacts from the Maryhill Museum led to the intervention of the Washington State Attorney General in *State ex rel. Gorton v. Leppaluoto*, No. 77–11731 (1977). On April 12, 1978, the suit against the board of directors was settled; the self-perpetuating board was almost entirely replaced and converted to an elected body. In addition, the museum, which had been branded by some as a "trading post," was substantially reorganized. Another instance of alleged improper activities by a museum board occurred at Chicago's Harding Museum, where there appeared to have been a mishandling of museum assets, a subsequent sale of museum pieces to pay for the losses which resulted, and extravagant trustee compensation at the time of a serious deficit. See *People ex rel. Scott v. George F. Harding Museum*, 58 Ill. App. 3d 408, 15 Ill. Dec. 973, 374 N.E.2d 756 (1st Dist. 1978). See also *Georgia*

O'Keeffe Foundation (Museum) v. Fisk University, 312 S.W.3d 1, 4 (Tenn. App. 2009).

1. MISMANAGEMENT

The old idea of appointing a figurehead trustee or director for the mere purpose of drawing in more money or tapping his or her private collection—the "give, get, or go" philosophy—is no longer acceptable. Trustees and directors are charged with a fiduciary duty to properly manage the business and assets of the organization. For a trustee, this potential liability for mismanagement arises from his or her responsibility to use the trust property held for the public for a charitable purpose. This is a high standard, requiring complete candor and loyalty. A trustee may be personally liable for negligence or inaction, as well as for fraud and bad faith. A trustee must, at all times, exercise loyalty and due care, preserve the trust property, and avoid questionable transactions. Trustees should be familiar with the nature and purpose of the trust and the contents of all museum documents, including financial statements. They should attend and participate in meetings and know the status of both public and private support.

It is especially important for the trustees to consider the purpose clause included in the creating instrument. The present-day trustee may find him-or herself battling with distant heirs or residuary legatees of the settlor if the museum's current focus and direction differ from the original intent of the creator. A narrow purpose clause may tie the hands of future trustees, rendering the museum sluggish, inflexible, and unable to deal with current needs. Although designed to protect the integrity of the original collection or tract of real property, the purpose clause may prove an administrative and funding nightmare. A more broadly stated purpose allows the trustees greater flexibility in operating the institution in an ever-changing society, though the new course may be inconsistent with the donors' initial intent. Therefore, it is important when creating a public trust to determine whether the trustees should be allowed complete autonomy or whether they should be confined in their activities by some restrictions in the creating instrument.

There is no better case study of the problems raised by a settlor's intent that is extremely detailed and restrictive than that of the Barnes Foundation and its creator, Dr. Albert C. Barnes. The Barnes Foundation was founded in Lower Merion, Pennsylvania in 1922 with the purpose of promoting the advancement of education and appreciation of fine arts. See *In re Barnes Foundation*, No. 58,788, 2004 WL 2903655 (Pa. Com. Pl. Dec. 13, 2004). Barnes was the successful inventor of an antiseptic silver compound, Argyrol. From the fortune generated by Argyrol and other pharmaceutical products, Barnes was able to pursue his interests in psychology, philosophy, education, and art. His art collection grew to be one of the most impressive and extensive collections of Modern art and African art in existence, then and now. Not only was his collecting somewhat eccentric for his times, Dr. Barnes had a profound disdain for the established art intelligentsia, and chose to display his art in unique ways, often displaying "ensembles" of Modern art with African art along with Asian art and ancient Greek, Roman, or Egyptian art, all on the same wall, and often in conjunction with the display of furniture and architectural pieces (door hinges, sconces, and the like).

Dr. Barnes apparently did not want to make the Foundation into a typical museum. He disdained art professionals, experts, and dealers, while he embraced the working class and struggling students. His instructions were that the Foundation galleries were only to be open to visitors by special appointment.

The Barnes Foundation has a large number of valuable assets, particularly Impressionist, Post-Impressionist and early Modern paintings. To put the collection in perspective is a difficult task, but Barnes accumulated 69 Cézannes—more than in all the museums in Paris—as well as 60 Matisses, 44 Picassos, and an astonishing 181 Renoirs. The 2,500 items in the collection include major, career-defining works by (among others) Rousseau, Modigliani, Soutine, Seurat, Degas, and van Gogh. There are also pieces of African sculpture, Asian prints, medieval manuscripts, decorative metalwork, as well as Old Master paintings, including works by El Greco, Peter Paul Rubens, and Titian. James Panero, *Outsmarting Albert Barnes*, PHILANTHROPY (Summer 2011), available at http://www.philanthropyround table.org/topic/donor_intent/outsmarting_albert_ barnes. The value of the collection is conservatively estimated to be in the neighborhood of $25 billion. Nevertheless, in a jaw-dropping irony, the Foundation from the 1990s to the early-2000s had been experiencing serious cash flow problems.

These cash flow problems are due in part to the legacy of Dr. Barnes' original requirements that none of the paintings and sculptures in the collection could be moved, loaned, or sold, and that the Foundation could be opened to visitors by appointment only. More recently, losses were blamed on the zoning limitations of Lower Merion Township that limited the daily attendance to the Foundation to 1,200 visitors. See *In re Barnes Foundation*, No. 58,788, 2004 WL 1960204 (Pa. Com. Pl. Jan. 29, 2004). The inability to raise fees has also resulted in the depletion of the original endowment. In litigation over its operating procedures, the Foundation sought to increase its admission fee to $10 and wanted to increase the number of days the foundation was open. The court approved an increase of the admission fee to $5 and allowed the foundation to be open one more day a week. The Foundation reached an agreement with two large Philadelphia philanthropic groups, the Pew Charitable Trusts and the Lenfest Foundation, to promise to help the foundation raise money on the condition that the gallery is moved into Philadelphia. The two philanthropic groups promised to help raise $150,000,000, of which $100,000,000 would be used to construct a new facility and the other $50,000,000 to replenish the endowment.

This condition requiring relocation resulted in a massive legal dispute. Heinrich Schweizer, *Settlor's*

Intent vs. Trustee's Will: The Barnes Foundation Case, 29 COLUM. J.L. & ARTS 63 (2005); Susan Gary, *The Problems with Donor Intent: Interpretation, Enforcement, and Doing the Right Thing*, 85 CHI.-KENT L. REV. 977, 985–87 (2010). See also John K. Eason, *Motive, Duty, and the Management of Restricted Charitable Gifts*, 45 WAKE FOREST L. REV. 123 (Spring 2010).

Dr. Barnes never intended for his collection to become an art museum, let alone a downtown Philadelphia art museum. Patricia Horn, *A Good Move?*, ARTnews, Feb. 2005, at 49. The relocation to Philadelphia violated the express terms of the Foundation's charter and bylaws, so the Foundation sought to amend those documents. The basis for moving the Foundation's artwork was financial necessity, and the court held that the move was a financial necessity. The court, in 2005, concluded that the Foundation could not sell enough non-gallery assets to achieve financial stability. *In re Barnes Foundation*, 871 A.2d 792 (Pa. 2005). The court also accepted the Foundations' witnesses' testimony that the current system of operation would not generate enough excitement among potential donors to generate increased donations.

The court held that the Foundation could amend its bylaws and indenture because it found that the Foundation showed clearly and convincingly the need to deviate from terms of the indenture, and that there were no viable alternatives. A documentary has been produced presenting a significantly "anti-move" perspective on the entire history of the Barnes

Collection through to the litigation cited here. See *The Art of the Steal* (IFC Films 2009).

In 2006, the Foundation reached its goal of obtaining $150 million dollars to support its move and construction of a new location, and promptly increased its goal by an additional $50 million. See Stephen Salisbury, *Barnes Reaches One Goal, Seeks $50 Million More*, Philadelphia Inquirer, May 17, 2006, at B04. The additional $50 million is said to be for further replenishment of the endowment and for unforeseen costs.

In May 2012, the collection opened to the public at its new location on the Ben Franklin Parkway, the grand boulevard of Philadelphia that ends at the Philadelphia Museum of Art. See http://www.barnesfoundation.org/about/press/coverage/inquirer-091611. Having visited the new location, co-author Michael Murray of this book can say that he appreciates the accessibility of the new location, and the improved opportunity to see one of the most remarkable collections of art that exists in the world. But the case remains as a testament to the courts' willingness to undo and disrespect the intentions of Dr. Barnes.

A trustee is uniformly held to a high standard of care and may be held liable for simple negligence in the management of a trust. A corporate director, on the other hand, is held to a lower standard of care and must be grossly negligent or otherwise be guilty of more than mere mistakes in judgment before liability will be imposed. The majority of jurisdictions thus hold the director to a standard similar to that of the New York statute, which provides for "that degree of diligence, care and skill which ordinarily prudent men would exercise under similar circumstances in like positions." N.Y.-McKinney's Not-for-Profit Corp. Law § 717 (1997). The rationale sometimes given for this "reasonable director" standard is that corporate directors usually have many areas of responsibility, whereas the trustee traditionally is charged only with the management of the trust funds and, therefore, can be expected to devote more time and expertise to that task. See *Stern v. Lucy Webb Hayes Nat. Training School for Deaconesses and Missionaries*, 381 F. Supp. 1003 (D.D.C. 1974).

2. NONMANAGEMENT

In addition to liability for failing to manage the organization properly, directors and trustees also can be held liable for failing to manage it at all. The nonmanagement situation is one in which the trustee or director has improperly delegated duties to others. The trustee may not delegate personal acts, though certain ministerial duties may be delegated. When trustees abdicate responsibility and fail to use the skills for which they were chosen to serve, their duty toward the trust is breached. A trustee has an affirmative duty to maximize the trust income by prudent investment and may not delegate that duty, even to a committee of other trustees. No actual monetary damages need result from a trustee's negligence in order to be held liable for breach of fiduciary duty. While it has been held that a trustee may delegate some ministerial duties and investment responsibilities under extenuating circumstances and with complete, candid disclosure, provided the trustee maintains complete control over the delegate's activities, the degree of permissible delegation is not clear. The prudent trustee, therefore, will avoid delegation of financial responsibilities.

By contrast, a director clearly may delegate some investment responsibilities. The director must maintain some supervisory control, however. Where the directors entrust the management of a corporation entirely to others, relying on their abilities, it has been held in *Heit v. Bixby*, 276 F. Supp. 217 (E.D. Mo. 1967) that they have negligently breached their duty to the corporation. Thus, like trustees, directors cannot function as mere figureheads. Even if the directors are not compensated for their work, they may be held liable for abdicating their duty to run the museum.

3. CONFLICTS OF INTEREST

Another type of breach of a trustee's or a corporate director's fiduciary duty results from transactions that amount to self-dealing. A trustee or director must never be personally enriched at the museum's expense. Whenever a director or trustee buys from or sells to the institution, the transaction is defined as self-dealing, and unless certain precautions are taken, the act will be a breach of fiduciary duty. Even if the trustee or director does not deal with the institution directly but acts through a spouse or agent, a breach of fiduciary duty will occur.

In many publicly owned museums, conflict of interest situations are regulated by statute. The employees of the Smithsonian Institution, for example, are bound by federal regulations that require them to avoid engaging in outside employment or activities that might interfere with the proper discharge of their duties at the Smithsonian. 36 C.F.R. § 504 (1999). These regulations also contain policies regarding acceptance of gifts from those with whom the museum does business, use of museum property and information, and the employees' financial interests as they relate to those of the institution. On the state level, many codes of ethics have been implemented through legislation. These codes vary from state to state.

There is some controversy over inclusion of county and municipal officials in state ethics laws due to the vast number of individuals involved, and the administrative problems posed by such a large, diverse group. California is one of the states that has legislation dealing with the area of conflicts of interest regarding all public officers and employees. Section 1090 of the California Government Code limits the contractual activities of interested state and city officers and employees, prohibiting them from buying from or selling to their own agency. The code also disallows any employment or activity that would conflict with an employee's duties at the agency.

Private, nongovernment supported museums generally are not subject to either state or federal conflict of interest legislation; yet, these institutions are just as vulnerable to having members of their governing boards and employees commit breaches of fiduciary duties. An exception to the lack of statutory sanctions can be found in some state nonprofit corporation codes. See, e.g., California Nonprofit Corporations Code, West's Ann. Cal. Corp. Code § 9243. The California code allows a court to order an interested director to account for any profits made from a self-dealing transaction and pay them to the corporation, to pay the corporation the value of the use of any of its property used in such a transaction, or to return or replace any property lost to the corporation as a result of such a transaction. A self-dealing transaction is defined as any transaction not otherwise properly approved to which the corporation is a party and in which one or more of the directors has a material financial interest. See Principles of the Law of Nonprofit Organizations § 330, illus. R, TD No 1 (2007, and 2016 update).

Common law liability of directors and trustees for their conflicts of interest is based on their duty of complete and unfailing loyalty to the museum and its beneficiaries, its members, and the general public. The consequences of a self-dealing transaction vary between directors and trustees, however. The rules governing trustees are stricter, and any self-dealing transaction is technically a breach of fiduciary duty. The institution need not actually be damaged; injury is presumed.

Precautions can be taken by trustees to avoid liability. Usually it is necessary to obtain approval of the transaction from the Attorney General in the state where the trust is located or from a court. In *Attorney General v. Olson*, 346 Mass. 190, 191 N.E.2d 132 (1963), a trustee proposed selling his house to the trust. To avoid any appearance of impropriety, the trustee had the home independently appraised, and because he was selling the house to the trust for $8,000 under the appraised value, the trustee sought and obtained court approval before completing the transaction.

Corporate directors also may engage in self-dealing transactions without committing an actionable wrong if they take certain precautions. The director must disclose all material facts related to the transaction. The transaction must be fair to the institution and ratified by either a majority of board members who are not involved or a majority of the museum members, if any.

A variation of the self-dealing theme occurs when a board member intercepts opportunities that were to be presented to the museum. Many directors are also private collectors, and this may present difficult choices. A corporate director should not acquire property within the scope of the museum's business, and the director is not released from the obligation to put the museum's interests first simply because the museum is not financially able to purchase the property. Yet, a board member who wishes to acquire an item that might be desired by the museum can disclose all material facts about the property to the institution's board. A majority of impartial directors or members can then decide whether the museum should acquire the item, and if the piece is rejected by the board in good faith, a subsequent acquisition by a director should not be considered a breach of fiduciary duty.

Personal and museum interests may also conflict to the detriment of the museum where the director is the owner of a gallery. If the director owns a competing business, good faith must be exercised at all times, and confidential information obtained through board service must not be abused. Although it is sometimes suggested that dealers should not serve on museum boards, the expertise and connoisseurship might outweigh the danger of harm. The dealer-director may always refrain from participating in a conflicting board decision, leave the room during deliberation, and disclose any interest in the transaction.

If full disclosure and nonparticipation do not prevent a conflict of interest problem, what should a board do to defend an action commenced against it for a breach of fiduciary duty? In some cases, resignation of one or more members of the board may remedy the situation. This may render moot any legal action. However, where money damages are involved, more affirmative board action may be required. The board could set up a special committee to investigate the alleged improprieties, or the board could divide itself into two groups, both to challenge and defend the questionable conduct. The latter course of action, however, may lead to dissension among board members and weaken their effectiveness to deal with other ongoing museum problems. If legal issues arise, the museum board should seek expert legal advice from independent counsel.

Another type of conflict of interest can arise when museums are paid a commission when art they are exhibiting is sold. The fear is that curators will be tempted to show artwork because it would sell rather than because of its artistic merits. While such commissions were fairly common until recently, in the wake of the controversy over the *Sensation* exhibit (see Chapter 15, § E), numerous museums have deleted such clauses from their contracts.

Similar issues surround corporation sponsorships. For instance, the board of the St. Louis Museum of Art declined a $50,000 gift from the Herman Miller Furniture Company intended to help the museum hold an exhibition entitled *The Work of Charles and Ray Eames*. Herman Miller Furniture, which helped finance the show itself, produces and markets *Eames* furniture, causing the board to decline the gift based on the appearance of a conflict of interest.

Businesswoman Catherine Reynolds withdrew most of a promised $38 million donation when the Smithsonian refused to agree to all of her requests regarding the staging of an exhibit honoring American achievers, insisting that the museum must retain ultimate curatorial authority over the exhibition's content, design, and location.

D. MANAGING THE MUSEUM COLLECTION: ACQUISITIONS

In our free enterprise economic system, museums might be thought of as being able to acquire and dispose of any item they desire. Actually, there are many legal and ethical restrictions on museum acquisitions. Acquisition improprieties and outright crimes have written the most spectacular recent history concerning museums, and museums have struggled with public and private challenges to acquisition practices in past and present times. See Jennifer Anglim Kreder, *The Revolution in U.S. Museums Concerning the Ethics of Acquiring Antiquities*, 64 U. MIAMI L. REV. 997 (2010); Jane A. Levin, *The Importance of Provenance Documentation in the Market for Ancient Art and Artifacts: The Future of the Market May Depend on Documenting the Past*, 19 DEPAUL J. ART TECH. & INTELL. PROP. L. 219 (2009). Allegations against major museums concerning their receipt and display of stolen art and cultural property have become front-page news in the early 2000s. Edward Wyatt, *Four California Museums Are Raided*, N.Y. Times (Jan. 25, 2008), http://www.nytimes.com/2008/01/25/us/25raid.html; Stephen K. Urice, *Between Rocks and Hard Places: Unprovenanced Antiquities and the National Stolen Property Act*, 40 N.M. L. REV. 123, 124 (2010). The Metropolitan Museum of Art in New York and the Getty Museum in California have experienced some of the most heated attention in disputes with the government of Italy. Kelly Devine Thomas and Eileen Kinsella, *Looted Antiquities Probe Widens*, ARTnews, Dec. 2005, at 62.

In the early 2000's, the Metropolitan Museum of Art and the government of Italy found themselves in a dispute centered on the 2,500-year-old Greek clay vessel known as the Euphronios Krater. See Lawrence Van Gelder, *The Mysterious Trail of a Treasure, Retraced*, N.Y. Times, Feb. 05, 2006, at 127; Nicole Winfield, *N.Y. Museum will Return Artifacts to Italy: Deal to Correct 'Errors' of the Past*, Boston Globe, Feb. 22, 2006, http://articles.boston.com/2006-02-22/ae/29249552_1_euphronios-krater-morgantina-return-artifacts. The museum had purchased the vessel for $1 million in 1972, and suspicions that it was looted started in 1973. The museum denied the vessel was stolen and would not disclose whom the item was bought from. *Id*. After much pressure, in 2006, the Metropolitan Museum of Art changed its position and agreed to return 21 looted artifacts to Italy, including the Euphronios Krater. See Elisabetta Povoledo, *Italy and U.S. Sign Antiquities Accord*, N.Y. Times, Feb. 22, 2006, at E7. Through shrewd negotiation, the Met turned the situation partially to its own advantage: as part of the agreement, Italy agreed to lend the Met items of equivalent value as those the Met has returned to Italy. *Id*.

Some restrictions on acquisitions originate from practical considerations, based on the museum's decision about how best to utilize its limited resources. Some museums feel they are most effective concentrating on a narrow collection area, while others have very broad collections. Some museums allocate large portions of their budgets to the conservation of ancient works; others prefer to spend their money on modern objects, which generally require less maintenance.

Still other restrictions are based on the responsibilities of the museum within the domestic and international art communities. Museums are the most active buyers in the international art market and have served as major repositories of illicitly acquired art and antiquities. As noted in Chapter 2, *supra*, there are many restrictions based on national treasure laws, criminal statutes, private suits, and import and export regulations; yet, only when there is no market for illicitly obtained objects will the trafficking cease. To this end, many museums have formulated ethical guidelines for the acquisition of art, though in 2003, the collecting policies of several major American museums were criticized at an international conference entitled *Illegal Archeology?* European museum officials and archeologists alleged that U.S. museums continue to buy and show unprovenanced antiques, thereby encouraging the looting of cultural property. See generally Emily A. Graefe, *The Conflicting Obligations of Museums Possessing Nazi-Looted Art*, 51 B.C. L. REV. 473 (2010).

Perhaps the most widely adopted formal statement on ethical acquisitions is the Joint Professional Policy on Museum Acquisitions or The Resolution Concerning the Acquisition of Cultural Properties Originating in Foreign Countries. This statement was formulated by two leading professional societies, the Association of Art Museum Directors (AAMD), composed of 242 art museum directors in the U.S.,

Canada, and Mexico, see https://aamd.org/about/membership, and the International Council of Museums (ICOM), composed of 35,000 members and museum professionals who represent 20,000 museums in 136 countries and territories. See http://icom.museum/the-organisation/icom-in-brief/.

In essence, the Resolution suggests that museums should individually implement the UNESCO Convention on the Means of Prohibiting and Preventing the Illicit Import, Export and Transfer of Ownership of Cultural Property, discussed in Chapter 2, *supra*. The Resolution also suggests that each museum draft a policy on the ethics of acquisition. While policy statements are not legally enforceable against museums, they do serve as effective mechanisms of peer pressure.

The American Association of Museums (AAM) was actively involved in drafting the Native American Graves Protection and Repatriation Act (25 U.S.C. Chapter 32), which, among other things, requires museums to inventory their Native American collections and return human remains and certain classes of Indian artifacts to the lineal descendant or appropriate tribe.

In addition to refusing to acquire works known to be stolen or illegally obtained from their country of origin or in violation of federal statutes intended to protect certain Native American artifacts, museums can protect themselves against embarrassment and potential prosecution by obtaining assurance of good title. This can be done by requiring the seller to warrant that he or she owns or has the power to transfer clear title. This is the surest procedure, but it may be awkward to apply it to donations. Another method is to insist that a responsible museum official make a reasonable inquiry in order to determine whether the museum may acquire valid title. If this is done, the museum should become a bona fide purchaser and hold valid title against all claimants. An important exception to this rule is that if the object has been stolen or wrongfully converted, a bona fide purchaser cannot prevail over the rightful owner. Yet, whereas the bona fide purchaser may have to return the object if the owner demands it, he or she also has a right to restitution of the original purchase price from the person who sold the item pursuant to either an express or implied warranty of title.

Determining validity of title may not be an easy task when a work is acquired by gift, but museum trustees have a duty to the public to exercise "the highest good faith," and that duty should include an obligation to refuse restricted or otherwise questionable gifts. E.g., Elizabeth Dillinger, *Not so Starry Night: The Pension Protection Act's Destruction of Fractional Giving*, 76 UMKC L. REV. 1045 (2007–2008) (Pension Protection Act restricts fractional giving to museums).

For example, in *Redmond v. New Jersey Historical Soc.*, 28 A.2d 189 (N.J. Err. & App. 1942), the decedent's will provided that "if my said son shall die leaving no descendants, . . . the portrait by [Gilbert] Stuart shall go and is hereby bequeathed to the New Jersey Historical Society." The son was 14 years old at the time of his death, and, perhaps for this reason, the executor delivered the painting in 1888 to the society. Its ownership went unchallenged until 1938 when the son's heirs apparently realized the great worth of the painting and the society's questionable title. The court, after examining the will and rejecting the society's claim of adverse possession, awarded the portrait to the heirs.

In addition to ascertaining the validity of a gift, the museum must comply with any conditions attached to it. Failure to do so may result in the loss of the item or monetary damages. Frequently, donations will be made on the condition that they bear the donor's name, remain in the museum's permanent collection in perpetuity or for a fixed period, or always remain on display. These conditions may be legally enforceable or merely precatory or suggestive. In one notable case, the estate of Texas oil heiress Sybil Harrington sued the Metropolitan Opera, alleging that her donation was diverted to nontraditional productions rather than the traditional operas specified by Ms. Harrington.

Another important consideration for some museums is whether they can legally accept gifts under their creating instrument. In *Frick Collection v. Goldstein*, 83 N.Y.S.2d 142 (Sup. Ct. N.Y. Cnty 1948), *aff'd*, 274 A.D. 1053, 86 N.Y.S.2d 464 (1st Dep't 1949), *app. denied*, 275 A.D. 709, 88 N.Y.S.2d 249 (1st Dep't 1949), the institution had been created under the direction of a will which segregated the testator's entire collection, residence, and a $15 million endowment for this purpose. When the trustees sought a declaratory judgment as to the museum's power to accept gifts, it was alleged that the decedent intended the museum to retain the same atmosphere as his private collection. The court rejected this contention and ruled that the Frick Collection could purchase new items and accept donations, but the case does demonstrate the problems that a narrowly drafted will can raise.

Britain's Tate Gallery recently made news when it successfully made a public appeal to artists and private collectors, asking for donations of artwork.

E. LOANS

Museums can also face liability when they acquire objects for display by loan from other museums or from private individuals. Most museums apply the same ethical standards for objects loaned to the museum as are applied to objects to be acquired, which substantially extends the effect of these standards to collectors and other museums. See Allen Wardwell, *The Ethics of Acquisition*, Art in Am., July/Aug. 1973, at 6; Paul Gardner, *Tainted Money*, ARTnews, Apr. 1989 (discussing situations in which several museums found themselves in receipt of stolen art or art previously acquired through fraud); Alexander Stille, *Was This Statue Stolen? Museums Used to Ask Art Historians If a Piece Was Good, Now They Have to Ask Lawyers If It's Legal*, 11 NAT'L L.J. 1 (Nov. 14, 1988); Norman Palmer, *Adrift on a Sea of Troubles: Cross-Border Art Loans and the Specter of Ulterior Title*, 38 VAND. J. TRANSNAT'L L. 947 (2005) (discusses the modern law on unlawfully removed art and its implications on loans).

The museum in a loan situation is a bailee and is subject to the law of bailment. As such, it is responsible for the property in its possession. In general, the standard of care to which a bailee will be held depends on the nature of the bailment. In a gratuitous bailment for the benefit of the bailor, the bailee will be liable only for gross negligence. If the gratuitous bailment is for the bailee's benefit, then the bailee will be liable for even slight negligence. When the bailment is for consideration, ordinary care will govern. However, since the distinction between the degrees of negligence is often difficult to determine, some courts have abolished them and employ only the ordinary care standard. Moreover, the parties may displace these legal doctrines by carefully spelling out their legal duties in a written contract. Many museums do this, fully setting out the obligations of the parties and the precautions, if any, the museum is required to take.

When dealing with loans, a museum should keep careful records. Should the details of the loan be forgotten and the piece be considered part of the permanent collection, an unforeseen legal battle for possession may result. See, e.g., *Lackawanna Chapter of Ry. & Locomotive Historical Soc'y, Inc. v. St. Louis Cnty.*, 606 F.3d 886 (8th Cir. 2010) (documents did not properly lay out a permanent loan or long term loan arrangement for a historic locomotive, and museum-in-possession retained the disputed locomotive).

If the bailee, in whose possession and under whose care and control the goods are held, will not account for the failure or refusal to deliver them on demand, the failure is presumed to be attributed to his or her negligence in caring for the goods, to their wrongful conversion, or to their wrongful retention. If there is injury to, or a loss of, the goods while in the bailee's possession, the burden of proof is on the bailee to show that the loss or destruction did not result from a breach of the bailee's legal duty. Nevertheless, the bailor-lender must pay attention to the communications and accountings of the loaned items sent by the museum, because discrepancies in the lists and descriptions may indicate that the bailee institution has "lost" certain items and the cause of action for recovery or damages from loss might accrue at the time of loss or at the time of a communication indicating a possible loss. In *Airis v. Metro. Zoological Park & Museum Dist.*, 332 S.W.3d 279 (Mo. App. 2011), the claimant's cause of action to recover items loaned to a museum several decades earlier accrued and eventually became time-barred when the claimant or his father received communications from the museum in the 1970s and 1980s that did not list, describe, or itemize the claimed items, and the claim was held to have run from the dates of these communications that suggested that the items had in fact gone missing and had been "lost" by the museum.

In similar fashion, the museum may feel that it has gained legal title to the piece through adverse possession. Adverse possession occurs when there is an actual, open, notorious, and exclusive retention of the property for a statutorily specified period. While possession is strong evidence of ownership, possession alone is not sufficient to establish title; the technical legal requirements must be fulfilled before a museum gains actual and legal ownership through adverse possession. If these requirements are not fulfilled, the museum could be sued by the rightful owner, or his or her successors, for recovery of the piece.

To be safe, the museum should attempt to notify the owners, or their heirs, of items which remain in the institution's possession for a long period of time; then the exact status of the lender's relationship to those items can be determined. If the heirs cannot be located, the museum should attempt to give constructive notice by publication of the museum's intention to retain the piece as its own. This should have the effect of beginning the running of the statute of limitations for adverse possession. Some states have enacted special legislation to aid museums in clarifying their relationship to pieces in their possession with unclear titles. See, e.g., O.R.S. 358 *et seq.*; West's RCWA 27.40.034, providing a procedure for vesting clear title in the institutions.

F. MANAGING THE MUSEUM COLLECTION: DEACCESSIONS

The term "deaccession" when applied to a museum's collection means the removal of an item either by moving the item to another collection, i.e., from the display collection to a study collection within the museum, or by disposing of the item outside of the institution.

There are numerous reasons why a museum might desire to deaccession part of its collection. It might wish to reduce storage, insurance, or restoration costs. There may not be storage space available. The collection may have duplicates (repetition of similar themes in a similar medium). The museum may have made a policy decision to specialize in certain types of art, thus restricting the scope of the collection and making retention of a piece undesirable. The sale may be necessary in order to finance the acquisition of an expensive masterpiece believed to have great public appeal. Finally, there may be a need to correct an imbalance between the collection itself and other museum activities. With operating costs rising, museums may be forced to reduce their present holdings and curtail acquisitions. Some deaccessioning decisions are more questionable than others. See D.K. Row, *Salem Museum Voids Exhibit Sales Policy: "Matter Of Perception"—Hallie Ford Museum's Director Cancels the Sale of Artists' Works*, The Oregonian, Jan. 27, 2009, available at http://www.oregonlive.com/entertainment/oregonian/index.ssf?/base/entertainment/1233015907195670.xml&coll=7 (Hallie Ford Museum of Art cancelled its lucrative but controversial policy of selling artworks by exhibiting artists which created the perception that the museum was making curatorial decisions based on salability, not merit); Robin Pogrebin, *Museum Sells Pieces of its Past, Reviving a Debate*, N.Y. Times, Dec. 5, 2010, available at http://www.nytimes.com/2010/12/06/arts/design/06sales.html

(over several years, the Philadelphia History Museum has sold more than 2,000 items in an effort to cull its collection of 100,000 artifacts and raise money for a $5.8 million renovation of its 1826 building).

Deaccessioning pieces out of the institution has been criticized by several authorities, who believe that sale of part of a collection should occur only under special circumstances after much careful consideration and with close supervision. See generally Stephen E. Weil, *Deaccession Practices in American Museums*, Museum News 44–50 (Feb. 1987); Edward Manisty & Julian Smith, *Proposed Scheme For Reforming Museum Deaccessioning*, The Art Newspaper, available at http://theartnewspaper.com/comment/articles/authors/162920 (Nov. 2010); Laura R. Katzman & Karol A. Lawson, *The (Im)permanent Collection: Lessons From a Deaccession*, American Association of Museums, available at http://www.aam-us.org/pubs/mn/deaccession.cfm; Christopher Knight, *Museum Deaccessioning Done Right*, L.A. Times, Mar. 15, 2009, available at http://articles.latimes.com/2009/mar/15/entertainment/ca-deaccession15. Some feel that any trade or sale should be outlawed, unless it is to another museum. The rationale for this exception is that when an object is sold or transferred to another institution, it still is available to the public. This argument ignores the likelihood of a future purchaser lending the creation back to the museum for display. It is also possible to sell merely a limited interest and retain a reversion. The institution could thus obtain necessary present capital and still have the piece when the term has expired. In addition, a conveyance could be used that specifies that the buyer will allow the art to be displayed periodically after the sale.

There are many logical reasons for exercising great caution when considering whether to deaccession an object. Fashions do change. For example, during the 1930s, impressionist paintings were relatively new and not sought after. Later, they were among the most popular and highest priced works available in the art market. A museum could lose irreplaceable pieces or be placed in the embarrassing position of having to pay a premium to reacquire an object it had previously deaccessioned. There is a rumor that the curator of the Louvre once rejected a donation because the paintings were too modern at the time. Years later, when the Louvre purchased these same paintings, they were quite expensive.

While deaccessioning fakes and forgeries might at first seem desirable, care still is necessary in this area. Many fakes become valuable in their own right. If Michelangelo's copy of Guiraldo were still extant, it would be far more precious than the original. Moreover, a conclusion that a work is not authentic is not always correct. The notorious situation involving the Metropolitan Museum's *Etruscan Horse* is a prime example. The piece, which was once considered one of the finest examples of ancient bronze, was subsequently pronounced a fake. This was because a seam was discovered on the work, and the method of casting bronze that would have produced such a seam was unknown to Etruscan artisans. Fortunately, a museum official removed the wax coating that had been put on the bronze to protect it. The controversial seam disappeared with the wax. Subsequently, scientific tests verified the authenticity of the piece. It is fortunate that the museum did not deaccession the bronze during its unpopular period. A photograph of the Etruscan Horse appears at page 410.

Another problem arises when the sale offends the public, contributors, their heirs, or other museums. When the Metropolitan Museum acquired Valazquez's *Portrait of Juan de Pareja*, its price exceeded the funds available, and the museum found it necessary to deaccession some items to cover the cost. An immediate furor arose, partly because some of the works sold were from the Adelaide Milton de Groot Collection. Ms. de Groot had been courted by many museums in the hope that her collection would be donated to them. In bequeathing her collection to the Metropolitan, Ms. de Groot indicated that it was her desire to have the pieces remain together and made available to the public. When the Metropolitan decided to deaccession the works, it sought the advice of counsel and was advised that the language in the will was merely precatory and not legally binding. Yet, the other museums who had courted Ms. de Groot were understandably incensed. To Ms. de Groot's relatives and friends, the apparent disregard of her wishes was insulting.

The ensuing scandal brought official intervention. While the New York Attorney General agreed that the language in Ms. de Groot's will was merely precatory and that the museum's action was technically legal, he suggested that there might be a need for state regulation of all deaccessioning. Yet, at a public hearing, with very few exceptions, the museum directors stated that the de Groot situation was unique and that none of them would be guilty of this type of alleged breach of ethics.

Unfortunately, the de Groot situation is not unique. A similar debate followed the St. Louis Mercantile Library's deaccessioning of some George Bingham drawings. Critics alleged that the sale violated the spirit of the 1898 gift of the drawings to the library by the then-mayor John How. Again, legislation was discussed but not enacted.

Yet another divisive issue is whether funds obtained through deaccessioning can be used for purposes other than art acquisition. The Guggenheim sold nearly $15 million worth of artwork in 1999 and 2000, depositing most of the proceeds in a restricted art fund in its endowment. The AAMD investigated the museum to determine whether this violated the AAMD's code of ethics. At issue was whether the fund was created to serve as collateral for a $54 million bond issue and whether the art collection was placed at risk. The Guggenheim eventually approved an amendment to its written collection management policy to prohibit using proceeds from deaccessioned art for any purpose other than art acquisitions (the Guggenheim's previous policy had reflected the less stringent standards of the AAM, which allows such monies to also be used for costs relating to direct care of the collection).

Case law in the area of deaccessioning is sparse. Aside from overt violations of the conditions of a trust, deaccessioning will be actionable only if it amounts to a breach of the trustee's or director's fiduciary duty to manage the assets of the museum. See Megan Loving, *An Arm and a Van Gogh: Selling Art Collections From Charitable Contributions for Capital Gain is a High Price to Pay*, 1 EST. PLANNING & CMTY. PROP. L. J. 455 (Summer 2009); Jorja Ackers Ciriliana, *Let Them Sell Art: Why a Broader Deaccession Policy Today Could Save Museums Tomorrow*, 20 S. CAL. INTERDISC. L.J. 365 (Winter 2011); Scott Andrews, *The Struggle to Save the Museo Alameda Hinges on a Big Bottle*, San Antonio Current, Sept. 21, 2011, available at http://sacurrent.com/arts/visualart/the-struggle-to-save-the-museo-alameda-hinges-on-a-big-bottle-1.1206560; Robin Pogrebin, *Bill to Halt Certain Sales of Artwork May be Dead*, N.Y. Times, Aug. 10, 2010, http://www.nytimes.com/2010/08/11/arts/design/11selloff.html; Patty Gerstenblith, *Acquisition and Deacquisition of Museum Collections and the Fiduciary Obligations of Museums to the Public*, 11 CARDOZO J. INT'L & COMP. L. 409 (2003).

In 2009, Brandeis University drew criticism for planning to close its Rose Art Museum and dispose of its entire collection of 6,000 works, including famous works of American Art from the 1960s and 70s by Warhol, Lichtenstein, and Paik. Geoff Edgers and Peter Schworm, *Brandeis to Sell School's Art*

Collection, Boston Globe, Jan. 26, 2009, http://www.boston.com/ae/theater_arts/articles/2009/01/26/brandeis_to_sell_schools_art_collection/. The plans were scaled back considerably, and then scrapped. *Brandeis, plaintiffs settle Rose Art Museum lawsuit*, http://www.brandeis.edu/now/2011/june/rose.html (June 30, 2011). See also Linda Sugin, *Tax-Exempt Organizations and the State: New Conditions on Exempt Status: Lifting the Museum's Burden From the Backs of the University: Should the Art Collection Be Treated as Part of the Endowment?*, 44 NEW ENG. L. REV. 541 (2010).

The Buffalo Fine Arts Academy (operating the Albright-Knox Art Gallery) was sued over a deaccession plan for breach of fiduciary duties and other alleged corporate misbehavior. The court denied the plaintiffs' request for a preliminary injunction of the sale, finding a lack of likelihood of success on the merits, but the case stands as a warning that decisions concerning deaccession are not just a matter of good public relations but carry legal consequences, too. See *Dennis v. Buffalo Fine Arts Academy*, 15 Misc. 3d 1106(A), 836 N.Y.S.2d 498 (Erie Cty. 2007).

Yet, few unpopular deaccessions go that far, and so most of the responsibility falls within the scope of self-regulation. Procedures set up by the Metropolitan Museum shortly after the de Groot scandal in 1973 are a good model for self-regulation for many museums. They require disclosure, outside appraisals of the work to be removed from the collection, a vote by the acquisitions committee, and notice to the public before sale or exchange of the piece. These procedures, like many self-regulating museum procedures in the area of museum management, are perhaps the best means available for protecting the interests of the public and the art community in protecting the museum's resources and assets.

Proposed deaccessioning guidelines have also been promulgated by the AAMD, the AAM, and the American Association of State and Local History (AASLH).

G. LOCATION OF THE COLLECTION

A surprisingly common issue in collection management is where, geographically speaking, the collection will be housed. Recently, two major museums have been plagued with disputes over location.

In 2000, two members of the board of the Terra Museum of American Art accused fellow members of plotting to relocate the museum to Washington, D.C. In 2001, the parties agreed to a mediated settlement stipulating that the museum would stay in the Chicago area, but the founder's widow appealed the settlement, contending that two board members were intimidated into approving the settlement by the office of the Illinois Attorney General. After years of low attendance, however, the board announced that the museum would close, with many works placed at the Art Institute of Chicago on long-term loan.

As discussed in section C.1 above, the Barnes Foundation sought to move its collection from suburban Philadelphia to a downtown area despite its founder's restrictions, filing a petition in court in 2002 to change the foundation's governing rules. The financially-strapped Barnes Foundation had been founded not as a museum, but as a school for teaching art appreciation. In 2005, the court ruled to allow the relocation of the collection.

A relatively new issue is whether a museum should display some of its collection on the Internet. Many museums, including the Guggenheim, the Metropolitan Museum of Art, and the Whitney, have chosen to display artwork on their websites.

H. LABOR RELATIONS

Even small museums encounter labor problems, and may find their employees organizing themselves into bargaining units. Museum employees are frequently underpaid, and many work more for the satisfaction and prestige of participating in the museum's activities than they do for pecuniary rewards. Yet, when employees feel that museum policies are wrong or that the board is not responsive to their concerns, their frustration can erupt into painful and costly labor disputes.

Some notorious examples of strife between museum management and employees demonstrate the importance of a clearly stated personnel policy and salary and benefit guidelines. At the Queens Museum in New York, for example, an exdirector and several dissident trustees accused the board of failing to establish standards of professional practice and of neglecting to set up salary and benefit schedules. They then staged a two-day job action. In another incident, picketers at the Brooklyn Museum demonstrated during employee efforts to choose a collective bargaining agent for about 80 of the museum's clerks and professionals. These seem to be extreme examples, but even more subtle and damaging effects are possible if a museum fails to provide adequate labor policies and grievance practices from the beginning. At the Museum of Modern Art, as at many other institutions, the museum staff attached great importance to their inability to participate in policy decisions, which was exacerbated by the high turnover of museum directors and the inaccessibility of the board of trustees. The employees' seven-week strike in the early 1970s resulted in more than just a new union contract. In the period following the strike, many observers felt that the employees' bitterness resulted in a loss of the spontaneity and intimacy that had previously characterized the museum. In the spring of 2000, staff again walked out. The strike was precipitated by a collapse in negotiations between the museum's management and the Professional and Administration Staff Association, a union of archivists, curators, and conservators.

In order to protect their interests, many museum employees have elected to organize formally under the National Labor Relations Act, 29 U.S.C. § 151 *et seq*. The question of whether the museum and the employees' grievances are subject to regulation by the National Labor Relations Board (NLRB) depends on whether the museum is considered a governmental entity. If so, the NLRB will not exercise jurisdiction. Yet, where a museum is a private entity engaged in commercial and educational activities, the NLRB may exercise jurisdiction, even if the museum is a nonprofit entity.

Four basic criteria determine whether the NLRB will have jurisdiction. The institution must have operating revenues that exceed $1 million annually; it must have interstate transactions valued at more than $50,000; it must have substantial private sources of operating revenue; and the operating control must be in the hands of trustees who are not subject to government control. A smaller institution may be excluded simply because its operating budget is considerably less than the $1 million specified in this rather mechanically applied formula. Section 7 of the National Labor Relations Act (NLRA) gives employees the right to "engage in other concerted activities for the purpose of collective bargaining or other mutual aid or protection." The NLRB has held that certain types of conversations, such as those about work conditions, are considered "inherently concerted," even when the employees aren't unionized and aren't thinking of taking any group action. *MikLin Enterprises, Inc. v. N.L.R.B.*, 818 F.3d 397, 405 (8th Cir. 2016) (employees do not lose protection under the National Labor Relations Act for their concerted activity simply by appealing to the public); National Labor Relations Act, § 7, 29 U.S.C.A. § 157.

Unfortunately, the NLRB has refused to issue general rules and guidelines relating to the organization of employees of museums. Therefore, each case is separately considered. The legally determinative issue is not what the museum's intent has been in a particular dispute with an employee but the actual conduct and its effect. Thus, an unfair practices claim may be sustained even if the museum has made good faith efforts to cooperate and deal fairly with employees. The museum will be liable in damages to the wronged employee based on the actual, though unintended, results of the institution's employment practices.

Thus, great care should be taken to avoid potential labor disputes by providing fair personnel policies, responsible grievance procedures, and opportunities for employees to express their opinions in major policy decisions. A museum's employees are as important an asset as its collection.

I. CODES OF ETHICS

In addition to the Joint Professional Policy on Museum Acquisitions promulgated by the AAMD, ICOM, and the deaccessioning policies discussed in this chapter, *supra*, many museums have adopted broad codes of ethics covering most of the museum's functions. In May 1991, the AAM adopted The AAM Code of Ethics for Museums, which requires its members to have an institutional code of ethics that, among other things, generally embraces and reflects its code, and now has guidelines, position papers, and policies on many aspects of museum operation, from deaccessioning to proper collection of art and antiquities. See https://aamd.org/standards-and-practices (latest update, June 2, 2016).

The AAM code does not cover individual responsibilities but, rather, addresses the institution as a whole. The code was based on fundamental precepts developed by its membership and focuses on three areas: (1) loyalty to the institution, (2) stewardship, and (3) public programs.

In 2000, the AAM adopted new guidelines on how museums should oversee displays of art borrowed from private collections, and in 2001, it adopted guidelines to help direct museums on soliciting and accepting corporate sponsorships.

J. CONCLUSION

Proper care by a museum in managing its collections, personnel, and business practices is essential. It not only benefits the individuals who work in the museum but also the public and members of the art community.

CHAPTER 17
RIGHT OF PUBLICITY

A. INTRODUCTION

Publication of the name, image, or likeness of a celebrity is a serious business. The exploitation of celebrity entertainers, sports figures, and just plain famous people is a huge, high-dollar industry in the United States. At his peak as a golfer, Tiger Woods made approximately 10–15 million dollars a year playing golf and winning tournaments, but simultaneously made ten times that amount licensing his name, image, and goodwill for the endorsement of a number of companies—including Nike, Buick, Gillette, EA Sports, Titleist, and his own company, ETW Corporation. Even now, in 2015–2016, with his golf career on a downward swing, Woods still is earning $50 million in sponsorships, which is 83 times his golf earnings of $600,000 in 2015. Jesse Oxfeld, Tiger Woods Earns 83 Times More Money Endorsing Things Than Playing Golf Plus other athletes' income stats, Adweek (Jun. 30, 2015, 1:55pm EDT), http://www.adweek.com/news/advertising-branding/tiger-woods-earns-83-times-more-money-endorsing-things-playing-golf-165649. The sprinter Usain Bolt's disparity of earnings is even greater: his $21 million in endorsements in 2015 is 1,400 times greater than the $15,000 he earned winning foot races. *Id.* With that much money tied up in just two sports figures, one can understand the motivation to recognize and protect rights in the use and exploitation of a celebrity's name and image. The law has responded by defining and protecting the rights of celebrities to control and protect their valuable personae and a wide-range of their personal attributes from unconsented exploitation.

Artists and people working in the arts field are as likely as anyone to become entangled in a dispute over the use of another person's name, likeness, or persona. Artists often communicate through symbolic speech (images or names and the meanings connoted by the images or names), and celebrities have an instrumental purpose of "standing for something." If symbols are a shortcut from mind to mind, *West Virginia Board of Education v. Barnette*, 319 U.S. 624, 632 (1943), celebrities and sports figures can be a shorthand expression for bravery, hubris, debauchery, sophistication, or many other aspects of the human condition. A few artists achieve celebrity-status of their own and will seek to protect it, but most artists and those working with them or in partnership with them, will face the law from the perspective of an alleged infringer of personality rights.

B. WHAT THE RIGHT OF PUBLICITY PROTECTS

The right of publicity protects a person's name, image, likeness, persona, and often their voice or other distinctive characteristics, from unauthorized commercial exploitation by others. The right has been construed very broadly—basically anything that is exploited by the celebrity herself, or calls to mind, or even is associated with the celebrity, can be protected by the right of publicity. Consider the following examples:

Celebrity	What was protected
Johnny Carson (former host of the Tonight Show)	The phrase, "Here's Johnny," spoken by Ed McMahon at the start of the Tonight Show. – *Carson v. Here's Johnny Portable Toilets*, 698 F.2d 831 (6th Cir. 1983)
Bette Midler (singer, performer)	The sound of her singing voice. – *Midler v. Ford Motor Co.*, 849 F.2d 460 (9th Cir. 1988)
John Facenda (longtime voiceover announcer for NFL films)	The sound of his announcer voice. – *Facenda v. N.F.L. Films, Inc.*, 543 F.3d 1007 (3d Cir. 2008)
Dustin Hoffman (film star)	His appearance as a character he portrayed in Tootsie. – *Hoffman v. Capital Cities/ABC, Inc.*, 255 F.3d 1180 (9th Cir. 2001)

Celebrity	What was protected
Muhammad Ali (boxer)	His silhouette and moniker of "The Greatest." – *Ali v. Playgirl, Inc.*, 447 F. Supp. 723 (S.D.N.Y. 1978)
Don Newcombe (pitcher for MLB Dodgers)	His "slouch" on the pitcher's mound and his jersey number. – *Newcombe v. Adolf Coors Co.*, 157 F.3d 686 (9th Cir. 1998)
Don Henley (singer for the Eagles)	His name. – *Henley v. Dillard Dep't Stores*, 46 F. Supp. 2d 587 (N.D. Tex. 1999)
Kareem Abdul-Jabbar (college and professional basketball player)	His appearance playing college basketball (under the name Lew Alcindor). – *Abdul-Jabbar v. General Motors Corp.*, 85 F.3d 407 (9th Cir. 1996)
John Dillinger (Depression-era bank robber, FBI's Public Enemy No. 1)	His name and reputation as a machine-gun wielding criminal. – *Dillinger, LLC v. Electronic Arts Inc.*, 795 F. Supp. 2d 829 (S.D. Ind. 2011)

Celebrity	What was protected
Ginger Rogers (film star, dancer)	Her first name, "Ginger," and reputation as a ballroom dancer – *Rogers v. Grimaldi*, 875 F.2d 994 (2d Cir. 1989)
Tony Twist (hockey player)	His name and reputation as an "enforcer" – *Doe v. TCI Cablevision*, 110 S.W.3d 363 (Mo. 2003)

The general idea is that persons have the right to control the exploitation of their names and other features of their personalities, and a wrong is done when someone usurps that right without permission.

C. REQUIREMENTS OF A RIGHT OF PUBLICITY CLAIM

The basic requirements (elements) of a right of publicity claim are:

(a) defendant's appropriation of plaintiff's name, image, or likeness or other aspects of plaintiff's identity;

(b) use of these elements of personality to the defendant's advantage, commercially or otherwise;

(c) with lack of consent; and

(d) causing injury to the plaintiff.

E.g., Restatement (Third) of Unfair Competition §§ 46–49 (1995); Restatement (Second) of Torts § 652 (1977); *Hart v. Elec. Arts, Inc.*, 717 F.3d 141, 151 & n.13 (3d Cir. 2013); *Comedy III Prods., Inc. v. Gary Saderup, Inc.*, 21 P.3d 797, 801 (Cal. 2001).

The injury must be connected to and caused by the actions of the defendant. The right of publicity allows a person to recover damages only for pecuniary gain from misappropriation of their name, image, or likeness. In contrast to the right of privacy, the right of publicity is not intended to protect the person's feelings, but provides a cause of action where a defendant has been unjustly enriched by misappropriation of the person's valuable public persona or image. If plaintiff has other injuries caused by the defendant, such as severe emotional distress, the plaintiff can allege and attempt to prove other claims against the defendant, such as a traditional privacy claim, or a claim for intentional infliction of emotional distress. But a publicity claim is for publicity-type damages.

The right of publicity protects a person from losing the benefit of her work in creating a publicly recognizable persona. In some jurisdictions, it may also be necessary to have a recognizable publicity to protect. In these jurisdictions, establishing the fame or value of one's image or likeness is a necessary element for the cause of action. See, e.g., *Ji v. Bose Corp.*, 538 F. Supp. 2d 349, 351 (D. Mass. 2008), *aff'd*, 626 F.3d 116 (1st Cir. 2010) (plaintiff model did not establish that she had a recognizable and valuable image and likeness to protect).

D. COMMERCIAL SPEECH AND ADVERTISING

The paradigmatic claim for violation of a right of publicity comes from the unauthorized and unconsented use of a celebrity's image or likeness in advertising. Advertising is referred to in the law as commercial speech, and commercial speech is the lowest form of protected speech in the first amendment cosmos. (Anything lower is unprotected speech that is highly regulated or outright banned—obscenity, fighting words, true threats, and child pornography. *See* Chapter 15, *supra*).

A use of an image in advertising also brings to the forefront the most dishonorable motives for using a celebrity image: to get a viewer to stop and look, or to assume some kind of support or endorsement by the celebrity of the product or service being advertised. Commercial speech rarely edifies or educates the audience, it rarely enriches the listeners. It may be entertaining for a few seconds, but always in the context of a crass pitch for sales. Therefore, the use of a celebrity image in a purely commercial communication will almost always result in a victory for the celebrity in a right of publicity claim.

Many of the cases already discussed above—*Midler, Abdul-Jabbar, Newcombe, Henley,* and *Doe*—presented this type of claim, and in each of these cases the celebrity prevailed. These cases show the risk of using any celebrity's name, image, or likeness in a commercial venture in an advertising or promotional sense without getting authorization and without paying for the value of the image.

Carson v. Here's Johnny Portable Toilets, 698 F.2d 831 (6th Cir. 1983), is another typical case of the commercial speech genre. Johnny Carson, the former late night comedian and host of "The Tonight Show," sued an outdoor toilet supply company that helpfully went by the name that caused the lawsuit in the first place: "Here's Johnny Portable Toilets," with the byline: "World's Foremost Commodian" used in its advertising and promotions. The basis for the assertion of publicity rights was that Carson was intimately connected to the phrase "Here's Johnny" because in the opening of every Tonight Show broadcast, Carson's sidekick, Ed McMahon, announced Carson with the phrase, "Heea-eeeeeers Johnny." As noted earlier, that reflects a rather broad interpretation of publicity rights. Nevertheless, Carson prevailed.

Not every commercial speech use of a celebrity's image fails the test. Even though uses of celebrity images in commercial advertising is the paradigmatic right of publicity claim that celebrities win, the tables are turned when the advertising is of a previous protected use, such as a use in a bona fide news or public interest reporting context. For example, in *Booth v. Curtis Publishing Company*, 15 App. Div. 2d. 343, 223 N.Y.S.2d 737 (1st Dep't), *aff'd mem.*, 11 N.Y.2d 907, 182 N.E.2d. 812, 228 N.Y.S.2d 468 (1962), Shirley Booth, a well-known actress (at the time), brought an action against Curtis Publishing Company for the unauthorized use of her image in a magazine and subsequently in another medium as an advertisement for the first publication. The pictures were taken by a photographer of a travel magazine while the actress was on vacation in Jamaica. The photos were later published in the travel magazine and then used as a part of an advertisement for the magazine. The New York court held that the use of the actress's image in this instance was protected by the First Amendment of the U.S. Constitution. Addressing the original photograph, published by a travel magazine, the court held that the reproduction was for news purposes; therefore, it was not a violation of privacy. Furthermore, the court held that the republication of the photograph as an advertisement of the magazine was also permissible. The court held that the reproduction of the photos was allowable as long as it was incidental advertising of the news medium. The court explained that a publication can best prove its worth through an extraction from past editions.

In *Namath v. Sports Illustrated*, 371 N.Y.S.2d 10, 11 (N.Y. App. Div. 1st Dept. 1975), *aff'd*, 352 N.E.2d 584 (N.Y. 1976), Sports Illustrated used a picture of Joe Namath, with his consent, in an issue of the magazine. Namath sued when, later, Sports Illustrated republished the picture as an advertisement of the magazine. The court held, where the use of a professional athlete's photograph was merely incidental to the advertising of the publisher's magazine, in which the athlete had earlier been properly and fairly depicted, and the language of the advertisement did not indicate the athlete's endorsement of the magazine, then there was no invasion of athlete's right to privacy in violation of N.Y. Civil Rights Law.

The defendant in *Montana v. San Jose Mercury News, Inc.*, 34 Cal. App. 4th 790, 40 Cal. Rptr. 2d 639, 640 (6th Dist. 1995), reported the San Francisco 49er's Super Bowl victories in 1989 and 1990 with cover photos of the star quarterback, Joe Montana. It further commemorated the victories with a bonus, "Souvenir Section," with large blow-ups of the celebratory Montana. Then the newspaper created posters of several of the images from the souvenir section, some of which were sold for $5, but the rest were given away. Montana sued, believing that the newspaper had strayed from its protected status as an outlet of news. The court stood by the newspaper, stating that the "First Amendment protects [defendant's 49er Super Bowl victory] posters . . . because the posters themselves report newsworthy items of public interest." The newspaper had previously printed a front page story on the San Francisco 49er's multiple Super Bowl victories and in conjunction with that news story, printed a picture featuring the 49er's quarterback Joe Montana. Both the news story itself and Mr. Montana's involvement in it were considered to be newsworthy. The posters merely reprinted the front page of the newspaper's reporting of this newsworthy story. The newspaper did not create a poster solely to exploit the image of Joe Montana.

E. BALANCING PUBLICITY RIGHTS WITH FREE SPEECH RIGHTS

Publicity rights, like other intellectual property rights, are protected by imposing limits on other people's speech. In copyright or trademark, the protection of the copyright or trademark owner's rights stops other people from printing and publishing the copyrighted or trademarked words and images. With the right of publicity, the protection of the right limits how people can express the image, likeness, name, and other essential characteristics of the celebrity in media. Because of this fact, publicity rights constantly must be balanced against the free speech and free press rights of other speakers.

An example of the balance is seen in *Zacchini v. Scripps-Howard Broadcasting Co.*, 433 U.S. 562 (1977). *Zacchini* is the only case on the right of publicity issued by the United States Supreme Court. The case also has very unusual facts, because it involves the "human cannonball" act of Hugo Zacchini. Zacchini spent his formative years learning and perfecting a craft that culminates in public performances that last all of 15 seconds. He climbs up to the mouth of the barrel of the cannon, waives a gallant greeting to the crowd, climbs down into the barrel, and is fired through the air to a waiting net. The whole act easily can be captured for airing in the "human interest" segment of the last two minutes of a nightly news broadcast. And that is exactly what happened. *Id.* at 564.

Scripps Howard, the respondent, was the owner of a television station who sent a reporter to the county fair where Mr. Zacchini was performing. The reporter was told by Zacchini not to film the act for the news, but the reporter surreptitiously filmed it anyway—all 15 seconds of it—and the station then aired it in the "human interest" segment at the end of the late evening news broadcast. Zacchini sued the station, and the case made it through the federal court system and all the way to the U.S. Supreme Court, where the Court, *id.* at 576–77, explained and justified the right of publicity on three public policy grounds:

(1) **Don't take for free what everyone else pays for.** This is a classic equitable policy against what is called ***unjust enrichment***. Everyone was supposed to pay to see Zacchini, not just turn on the nightly news and see him perform his entire act for free.

(2) **The need to reward the sweat of the brow of entertainers and celebrities who spend years perfecting their craft.** This is pretty close to the British justification for protecting intellectual property rights—because someone labored to create something original, they should therefore be rewarded for the labor. This theory does not always work in right of publicity scenarios. For every Zacchini and Tiger Woods who spend years perfecting their craft, there are Paris Hiltons and Kim Kardashians who do little or nothing to earn their celebrity status.

(3) **The need to encourage people to invest effort in creative endeavors that lead to celebrity because that will enrich society as a whole.** This is the exact American public policy supporting the

American recognition of intellectual property rights. The United States protects the works of artists, authors, and inventors not because it wants them to be directly rewarded for their labor and good works, but because it wants the general public to benefit from new, creative, original works and inventions. The author or inventor is rewarded as a secondary consequence of this public policy. With *Zacchini*, this theory is stretched a bit (which probably explains why it is listed third, and after the "British" theory for rewarding effort) because the general public gets little more than a gasp from the spectacle of Zacchini's achievements. Yet, entertainment is a recognized public good, and Zacchini delivers entertainment.

The outcome of the case may come as a bit of a surprise to those who understand the strength of the free press rights in America (*see* Chapter 15, *supra*), because Zacchini won, and he won against the First Amendment freedom of press broadcast rights of a news station. A bona fide member of the press ultimately was punished (in the civil law sense—paying damages) for reporting the news so that Mr. Zacchini could enjoy his publicity rights.

News reporting has other limits. The press has a privilege to report matters of legitimate public interest even though such reports might intrude on matters otherwise private. Images of private citizens who are involved in news stories must be used in a manner directly related to the reporting of the newsworthy event, but not exploited for other commercial purposes. In *Shulman v. Group W Prods., Inc.*, 18 Cal. 4th 200, 74 Cal. Rptr. 2d 843, 955 P.2d 469 (1998), a car accident victim was filmed in the hands of an EMT crew. The court held, "The contents of the publication or broadcast are protected only if they have 'some substantial relevance to a matter of legitimate public interest.' Thus, recent decisions have generally tested newsworthiness with regard to such individuals by assessing the logical relationship or nexus, or the lack thereof, between the events or activities that brought the person into the public eye and the particular facts disclosed."

F. FAIR USE

The need to balance free speech rights with publicity rights has led to the creation of a doctrine of fair use in right of publicity law. However, unlike in other areas of intellectual property law, the courts do not agree on the standards for evaluating what is fair in right of publicity cases. There are no fewer than *five* separate and distinct fair use tests that have been applied by courts in right of publicity cases. All of them speak to the same issue: the proper balance of first amendment expression and other public policy benefits weighed against the protection of publicity rights.

Cardtoons—Balancing test	10th Circuit court balanced the value of the expression of the use under the First Amendment against the value of the celebrity name-image-likeness that was used. *Cardtoons, L.C. v. Major League Baseball Players Ass'n*, 95 F.3d 959, 968–76 (10th Cir. 1996)
Rogers—Relatedness test	2nd Circuit court considered whether the use of the celebrity name-image-likeness is directly related to the content of the expression (fair use), or if instead it is a disguised advertisement and exploitation (not fair use). *Rogers v. Grimaldi*, 875 F.2d 994, 999–1005 (2d Cir. 1989)
Comedy III—Transformative test	California court evaluated whether the artist adds value to the depiction of a celebrity beyond the value of the celebrity image either through artistic additions or because of the status of the artist (e.g., a famous artist, such as Warhol). The test

	asks if people would sooner buy the work for the art/artist or for the celebrity image. *Comedy III Prods., Inc. v. Gary Saderup, Inc.*, 21 P.3d 797, 804–08 (Cal. 2001)
Simeonov—NY Artistic Expression test	New York court ruled that any artist can make a representation of a celebrity if done in "limited numbers." *Simeonov v. Tiegs*, 602 N.Y.S.2d 1014, 1018 (Civ. Ct. N.Y. Cty. 1993)
CBC, Doe—Predominant Purpose test	8th Circuit and Missouri courts determined whether the predominant purpose of the activity is for expressive, artistic, news purposes (fair use), or is it predominantly to unfairly exploit the celebrity name-image-likeness (not fair use). *C.B.C. Distribution & Mktg., Inc. v. Major League Baseball Advanced Media, L.P.*, 505 F.3d 818, 820 (8th Cir. 2007); *Doe v. TCI Cablevision*, 110 S.W.3d 363 (Mo. 2003)

ETW Corp. v. Jireh Pub., 332 F.3d 915 (6th Cir. 2003), presents a fairly typical fair use scenario of a celebrity who wants to control his rights and those who want to tell his tale to the world. When Tiger Woods (ETW) won the 1997 Masters Golf Tournament, his first major tournament victory as a professional golfer, he was the youngest golfer ever to win the Masters (age 21), he won it with the largest margin of victory ever in the Masters (12 strokes under his closest opponent), he was the first person of African American ancestry to win the tournament, and the first of Asian American ancestry (owing to his father being African American and his mother being Asian American). In short, a lot of history was made at that golf tournament. Tiger also became established as a public figure around whom a great deal of public interest is focused. This made him newsworthy and a subject of public affairs attention and commentary.

Rick Rush, a sports artist, and his publisher, Jireh (the first-named defendant in the case), wanted to celebrate and commemorate the history that Tiger Woods made in Augusta during that tournament (and make a little money in the process). Rush created a painting that was serialized into a "limited" edition of 5,000 serigraphs. ETW and Woods sued Rush and Jireh, and the court considered whether the artist and his publisher enjoyed a fair use right to use the images of Tiger.

The court applied many of the fair use tests listed above to determine fair use. The court was pleased with the expression evident in Rick Rush's art work.

The court found that Rush had provided worthwhile commentary on the sports and historical interest value of the Tiger Woods Masters tournament victory, thus giving him strong weights to throw into the scale on *Cardtoons'* balancing test. Rush prevailed on the balancing test. The court found that his entire effort to depict and describe the historical events revolved around the name, image, and likeness of Tiger, so the relatedness test of *Rogers* was satisfied in Rush's favor. And the court applied the *Comedy III* transformative test, and found that Rush's artistic treatment, additions, and embellishments (the multiple images, the backdrop, the addition of Butler Cabin, the addition of ghostly images of past champions, the addition of the famous leader board) all combined to sufficiently transform the image of Tiger in a manner that allowed Rush to prevail on that test, too. The result: fair use victory for Rick Rush.

More recently, collegiate athletes have sued video game manufacturers for publicity rights allegedly exploited in digital football simulation games. In a pair of cases, *Hart v. Electronic Arts*, 717 F.3d 141, 165–70 (3d Cir. 2013), and *In re NCAA Student-Athlete Name & Likeness Licensing Litig.*, 724 F.3d 1268 (9th Cir. 2013), *aff'g*, *Keller v. Elecs. Arts, Inc.*, No. C 09–1967 CW, 2010 WL 530108, at *1 (N.D. Cal. Feb. 8, 2010), the courts considered the rights of student athletes to control their images and likenesses when the students' sports league, the NCAA, had licensed all of the other intellectual property associated with college football—the names of the teams, the uniforms, the team logos, the fight songs, the appearance of the stadiums, and much more—to EA Sports, the manufacturer of the football simulation games.

In *Hart*, the District Court for the District of New Jersey noted that NCAA student athletes were not permitted to license and profit from their actual identities as players under strictly enforced NCAA rules. The student athletes could not sell their own jerseys or sell autographs or engage in other commercial activities relating to their athletic endeavors. This undercut the logic of the suit severely; it seemed that even if the rest of their complaint stated a cause of action for violations of publicity rights, there were no functional damages. The game maker also successfully alleged fair uses in defense of the suit, the most important of which was that the game was transformative. Hart's suit was dismissed, and the *Hart* case went up on appeal.

On appeal, the United States Court of Appeals for the Third Circuit carefully examined whether defendant EA Sports was entitled to the first amendment defense recognized by the District Court. The Third Circuit reviewed three of the prevailing fair use tests: the Predominant Purpose Test (*Doe, CBC* test), the Relatedness Test (*Rogers* test), and the Transformative Test (*Comedy III* test), and determined that the transformative test from California state law was the most apt for the situation of Hart's case.

The Third Circuit painstakingly broke down the issue of the strong first amendment protection for expressive media such as video games, and the meaning and application of the transformative test. In spite of the completely different meaning, purpose, context, and message, and the transformation from a real life player in actual football games to a completely fanciful, visual recreation in a digital virtual reality of a computerized football simulation game, the Court made the remarkable observation that there was no real difference between a depiction of Hart the actual football player in actual football games, and the avatar appearance of Quarterback No. 13 for Rutgers in the football simulation computer game. EA Sports has not made sufficient change in "context, meaning, and expression" from the actual Hart's appearance to the avatar in the video game to justify the label of transformation and the fair use protection that goes with the label.

The issue in *NCAA Athletes Name & Likeness Licensing Litigation* was framed differently, because the court had to respond to a motion by EA Sports that the entire lawsuit was a "Strategic lawsuit against public participation" (SLAPP) under California's anti-SLAPP statute—meaning that the only reason for the suit was to put pressure on EA Sports to cease exercising its free expression rights, which it typically exercised by making and selling video games. The District Court denied the motion for the somewhat unusual reasoning that the motion was improper because EA Sports did not have first amendment rights and protections in the video game that would need to be protected in the anti-SLAPP motion. This signaled that the lawsuit of the athletes had merit, and was not just a bullying technique to "quiet" the video game maker's speech. And the reason the suit had merit was that EA Sports did not enjoy a transformative fair use (*Comedy III* test) over the images of the athletes. The Ninth Circuit agreed, and affirmed the case on appeal.

In essence, the Ninth Circuit opinion followed *Hart*: it agreed that the transformative test was the superior test (it considered the Relatedness test of *Rogers*, too), and it found that the treatments of the athletes' images was not transformative. The lawsuit only represents a disposition on the anti-SLAPP motion to dismiss, but the ruling indicates that the athletes' claims have merit and are likely to succeed, so it telegraphs to the parties that EA Sports is not going to sail through the case on the strength of its first amendment defenses.

Rogers' Relatedness test and *Comedy III*'s Transformative test have grown to be the most popular tests affording protection to both publicity interests and first amendment artistic expression concerns. *Cardtoons* continues to be cited and discussed, but it has not been followed in making the ultimate determination of whether a use is fair or not in many years. *ETW Corp.*, 332 F.3d at 915, worked through the analysis under the *Cardtoons'* test, but also applied the *Rogers'* Relatedness Test and *Comedy III*'s Transformative Test. *C.B.C.*, 505 F.3d at 822–24, also cited and discussed the *Cardtoons'* test, but ultimately applied the Predominant Purpose Test from *Doe*, 110 S.W.3d at 374. *Simeonov* gets mentioned in cases that involve fine arts, but it rarely has been used out of New York State, and never as the sole test of fair use. *Doe* and *CBC* are used less often than the tests from *Rogers* and *Comedy III*, but they are cited from time to time. *Hart*, 717 F.3d at 151, cited and discussed the Predominant Purpose Test from *Doe*, 110 S.W.3d at 374, but ultimately settled on the Transformative Test. The important take-away from this discussion is that courts, no matter where they are located, rarely pick one test and run with it. Instead, courts treat the tests as a buffet where they can have a little of this test, run a little analysis through a different test, and ultimately finish up with a run through of a third test. See *Hart*, 717 F.3d at 151–54. The state of the law is disjointed, and things are not likely to get much better in a "predictability of outcome" sense until one test becomes the norm in right of publicity situations.

In June 2016, Kanye West created one of the most interesting and potentially complicated right of publicity fair use problems by his creation and airing of a music video for his song, *Famous*. The video presented what appeared to be computer-generated imagery (CGI)-enhanced or CGI-created depictions of twelve nude, sleeping celebrities, partially covered by a loose sheet, all lying in the same hyper-extended bed. The celebrities were West, his wife Kim Kardashian, family-relation Caitlyn (the former Bruce) Jenner, and mega-pop star Taylor Swift; singers/celebrities Rihanna, Chris Brown, Ray J, and Amber Rose; Vogue editor Anna Wintour; presumptive Republican presidential nominee Donald Trump, and former president George W. Bush; and the famous but recently disgraced Bill Cosby. Some of the sleeping celebrities have had clashes or disagreements with West in the past, most notably Taylor Swift, who was upstaged by West at the 2009 MTV Video Music Award Ceremony. But others, like Trump, Bush, Wintour, and Cosby, were chosen for reasons known only to West. See Colin Stutz, *Kanye West Nuzzles Naked Taylor Swift, Donald Trump & Bill Cosby in 'Famous' Video*, Billboard.com (June 25, 2016), available at http://www.billboard.com/articles/columns/hip-hop/7416556/kanye-west-naked-taylor-swift-donald-trump-famous-video-premiere.

The work was an audio-visual recreation of a well-known Vincent Desiderio painting entitled, *Sleep*. This fact does not suggest the placement of this event as a problem or case study in the copyright chapter (Chapter 12) of this book because Vincent Desiderio apparently is honored by Kanye West's reimagining of his painting, and approves of the homage, and says so in writing in a piece featured on Wmagazine.com. Vincent Desiderio, *On Kanye West's "Famous" Video, From the Artist Who Inspired It,* Wmagazine.com (June 27, 2016 at 5:02 PM), available at http://www.wmagazine.com/culture/2016/06/kanye-west-famous-video-artist-vincent-desiderio-reaction/. See also Joe Coscarelli, *Artist Who Inspired Kanye West's 'Famous' Video: 'I Was Really Speechless'*, NY Times, June 29, 2016, at C3, available at http://www.nytimes.com/2016/06/29/arts/music/kanye-west-vincent-desiderio-famous-sleep.html?_r=0.

Kanye West, Vincent Desiderio, and other commentators have described the video as a provocative, voyeuristic commentary on celebrity itself, showing the vulnerability of stars (naked, sleeping) under the scrutiny of fans and gawkers, ironically placing all viewers in the role of gawker and voyeur for looking at the video. Desiderio calls it "art," and affirms West as a modern Warhol, an artist who expresses and mirrors the times he lives in through a continuous process of life as performance art. See Coscarelli, *supra.*

In the days immediately after the premiere of the video, West actually appeared to be courting a lawsuit, and tweeted an invitation or warning, "Can somebody sue me already #I'll wait." As of the date of this update, June 29, 2016, no one has stepped forward to sue West over the video. See Daniel Kreps, *Kanye West Talks 'Famous' Visual, Invites Lawsuits,* Rollingstone.com (June 25, 2016), available at http://www.rollingstone.com/music/news/kanye-west-talks-famous-visual-invites-lawsuits-20160625#ixzz4D4O W1bFZ.

The issues raised by the video are many—federal Lanham Act "false endorsement" issues, state law right of publicity issues, fair use issues under federal or state law, not to mention choice of law and choice of forum issues—and it may be that the video is so grand and sensationalized that no one will feel bold enough to step up to challenge West. See Eriq Gardner, *Kanye West's 'Famous' Video Is Infamous, But Will Any Celebrity Dare Sue?,* Billboard.com (June 28, 2016), available at http://www.billboard.com/articles/news/7423175/kanye-west-famous-legal-analysis.

PHOTOGRAPHS OF ARTWORK

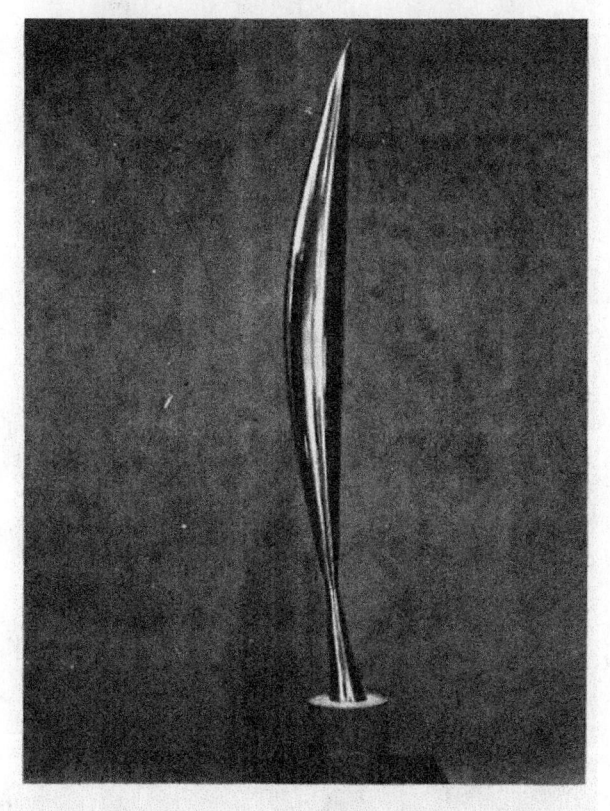

Brancusi, *Bird in Space*, Collection, The Museum of Modern Art, New York. Given anonymously.

Elgin Marbles in the Duveen Gallery of the British Museum. Reproduced with the permission of the copyright holders, the Trustees of the British Museum.

PHOTOGRAPHS OF ARTWORK 397

Machaquila, Stela II., photographed by Ian Graham of the Peabody Museum of Archeology and Enthenology. This photo was taken in the jungles of Guatemala before the piece was illegally removed by Clyde Hollingshead. Doctor Graham's photos and sketches were used as evidence in the *U.S. v. Hollingshead* case.

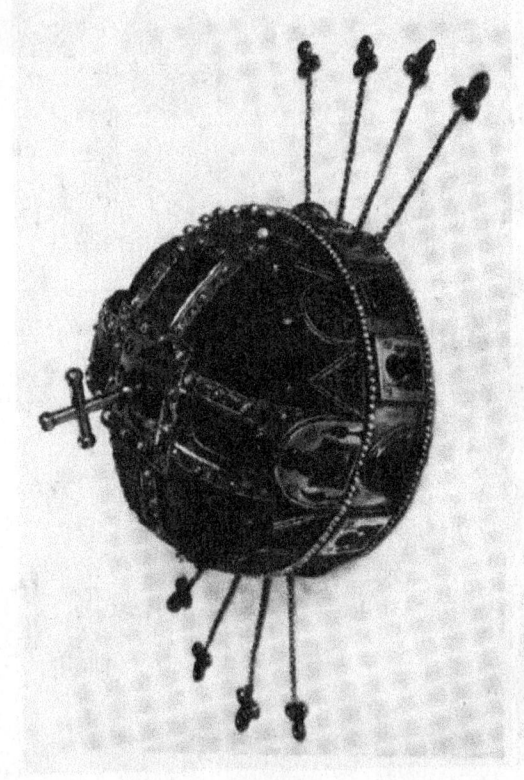

Crown of St. Stephans. Courtesy of the National Gallery of Art. Photograph by William J. Sumits.

Sun Yat-Sen, stainless steel & rose-red granite W.P.A. St. Mary's Plaza, San Francisco. Copyright © C. Boddy, 1983.

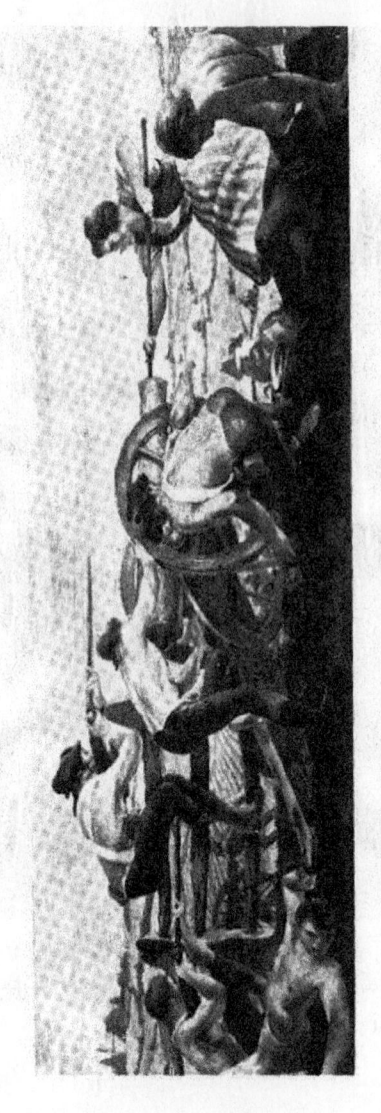

Foster, Sketch for Mural for Freehold, New Jersey, Post Office, "Molly Pitcher". Photograph by courtesy of the National Gallery of Art, Washington, D.C.

PHOTOGRAPHS OF ARTWORK

Deutsch, *Sketch for Mural in Readley, California, Post Office, "Grape Picking"*. Photograph by courtesy of the National Gallery of Art, Washington, D.C.

402   PHOTOGRAPHS OF ARTWORK

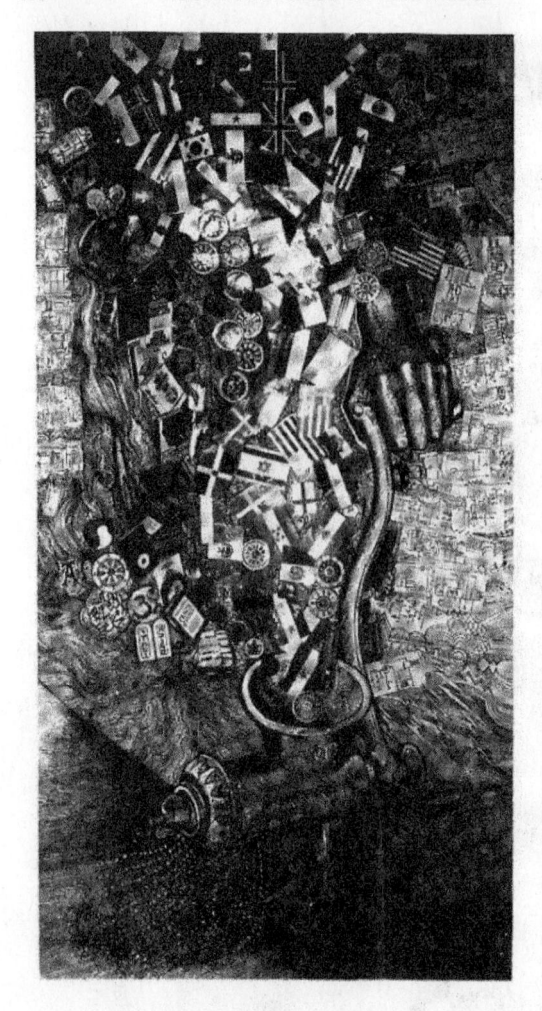

Asmar, *The Mills of the Gods Grind Slowly, But They Grind Exceedingly Small*, West '79, The Law, "Hurled into a universal grinder, scattered symbols of man's creation pulverize into gold, sparkling particles—Stars?", Asmar.

PHOTOGRAPHS OF ARTWORK 403

Grand Central Terminal exterior photograph, 1914 by Irving Underhill. Reprinted with permission of the Photo Library Department of the Museum of the City of New York.

Chicago Picasso, photo by Kee Chang, CACI.

Photograph of the lamp which was the subject of the *Esquire v. Ringer* case, courtesy of Professor Alan Latman, New York University School of Law.

Original **Rogers** photograph and the **Koons** sculpture which was found to be an infringement.

Winged Wolves, by Moses Sanchez, Denver, Colorado. Reproduced with permission of the artist.

408   PHOTOGRAPHS OF ARTWORK

Photo by New York City Police Department Photographic Unit, Color Section, introduced into evidence in *People v. Radich.*

Shunchosai, woodblock print, 1770s. Reproduced by permission of Doctors Phyllis and Eberhard Kronhausen for the National Sex Forum.

Statuette of a Horse, Bronze. Courtesy of the Metropolitan Museum of Art, Fletcher Fund, 1923.

INDEX

References are to Pages

ACQUISITIONS
Museums, 348–354

ACT OF STATE DOCTRINE
War, art as victim, 38

ADVERTISEMENTS AND ADVERTISING
Insurance, advertising injury, 123–125

AFGHAN ART
Victim of war, 34

AID TO THE ARTS
    Generally, 167–182
Applications, National Endowment for the Arts, 170
Block grants, 170–171
Bufano sculpture, 169
Charitable contribution, tax deductible, 174
Decency clause, National Endowment for the Arts, 172–173
Deductions, tax deductible charitable contribution, 174
Funding, National Endowment for the Arts, 170–174
Historical development, 167–188
Indirect aid, National Endowment for the Arts, 176–181
Investments, National Endowment for the Arts, 174
Landmark preservation, indirect aid, 177–181
National Endowment for the Arts, 170–174
    Applications, 170
    Block grants, 170–171
    Charitable contribution, tax deductible, 174
    Decency clause, 172–173
    Deductions, tax deductible charitable contribution, 174
    Funding, 173
    Indirect aid, 176–181
    Investments, 174

411

Landmark preservation, indirect aid, 177–181
Percentage allocation for art, indirect aid, 176–177
Tax deductible charitable contribution, 174
West's Art and Law Program, 174
Percentage allocation for art, indirect aid, 176–177
Tax deductible charitable contribution, 174
West's Art and Law Program, National Endowment for the Arts, 174
Works Progress Administration (WPA), 168

ALARM SYSTEMS
Insurance, 111

AMERICAN JOBS CREATION ACT OF 2004
Intellectual property donations, 162

ANGKOR WAT
Victim of war, 33

ANTICYBERSQUATTING CONSUMER PROTECTION ACT
Trademark infringement, 259

ANTIWAR PROTEST
Freedom of expression, wearing of black armbands, 303–304

APPLICATIONS
Aid to the arts, National Endowment for the Arts, 170

APPRAISERS AND APPRAISALS
Insurance, appraisal requirement, 121
Taxation, charitable contributions, 137

APPROPRIATION ART
Copyright infringement, 237

ARCHAEOLOGICAL RESOURCES PROTECTION ACT OF 1979
International movement, 28

ART DEFINED
Customs definition, 1–8

ART EXPERTS
See Authentication

ART WARRANTY STATUTES
Forgeries, fakes and frauds, 100–103

ARTIST-DEALER RELATIONSHIP
Working artists, 188–194

ARTISTS
Taxation, 151–166

AUCTIONS
  Generally, 61–74
  Bidding, 62–74
    Brancusi sculpture, 72
    Copyright, blind bidding, 202
    Disclosed and undisclosed bidding, 62–63
    Fraudulent auctioning techniques, 65–71
    Phantom bids, 64
    Problems, 65–74
    Puffing, 64
    "Ring" formation, 65
    Sealed bids, 63
    Shilling, 64
    Tactics, 64–65
    Uniform Commercial Code, 64, 66
    Withdrawing goods or bids, 66–67
  Brancusi sculpture, 71
  Christie's auction house, 73, 78
  Cyberauctions, 62
  Disclosed and undisclosed bidding, 62–63
  Forgeries, fakes and frauds
    Raoul Duffy paintings forged, 92
    Techniques, fraudulent auctioning techniques, 65–71
  Houses
    Christie's auction house, 73, 78
    Investing in art, auction houses, 57–58
    Phillips auction house, 78
    Sotheby Park Bernet, 56–57, 68, 73, 78, 82–83
  Internet, cyberauctions, 62
  Investing in art
    Auction houses, 57–58
    Methods of acquisition, 57–60

Methods of acquisition, 57–60
Phantom bids, 64
Phillips auction house, 78
Price fixing, 73
Problems, bidding, 65–74
Puffing, bidding, 64
"Ring" formation, bidding, 65
Sealed bids, 63
Shilling, bidding, 64
Sotheby Park Bernet, 56–57, 68, 73, 78, 82–83
Tactics, bidding, 64–65
Telecast sales, 62
Uniform Commercial Code, bidding, 64, 66
Withdrawing goods or bids, 66–67

AUTHENTICATION
Generally, 75–109
See also Forgeries, Fakes and Frauds
Art experts, 79–86
    Chemical analysis, 86
    Da Vinci, Leonardo, paintings by, 81
    "Fair comment" defense, 81–86
    Fission tracks analysis, 86
    Louvre, painting by Leonardo da Vinci, 81
    Obsidian hydration analysis, 86
    Potassium-argon analysis, 86
    Reynolds, Sir Joshua, painting by, 83–84
    Scientific category, 79–80
    Stylistic category, 79–80
    Thermoluminescent analysis, 86
Chemical analysis, 86
Common law remedies against seller, 87–92
Da Vinci, Leonardo, paintings by, 81
Establishing authenticity, 75–79
"Fair comment" defense, 81–86
Fission tracks analysis, 86
Investment, art as, 75
Lanham Act, 87
Louvre, painting by Leonardo da Vinci, 81
Obsidian hydration analysis, 86

Potassium-argon analysis, 86
Professional negligence, 82
Reynolds, Sir Joshua, painting by, 83–84
Scientific category, art experts, 79–80
Slander of title, 83
Stylistic category, art experts, 79–80
Thermoluminescent analysis, 86

BACON, FRANCIS
Gallery dispute, 192

BAILMENT
Museums, loans, 354–355
Working artist, galleries and commissions, 189

BANKRUPTCY
Trademark infringement, 257

BARNES FOUNDATION
Dispute over location, 366

BERNE CONVENTION
Copyright, Revision Act of 1976, 223–224, 229
General Agreement on Tariffs and Trade (GATT), 229
Moral rights, 267, 268

BIDDING
See Auctions

BILATERAL TREATIES
International movement, 21–22

BIRD IN FLIGHT
Brancusi, 2–3

BLACK ARMBANDS
Freedom of expression, antiwar protest, 303–304

BLIND BIDDING
Copyright, 202

BLOCK GRANTS
Aid to the arts, National Endowment for the Arts, 170–171

BOSCH, HIERONYMUS
Freedom of expression, 293

BRANCUSI
Auctions, Brancusi sculpture, 72
Bird in Flight, 2–3, 395 (photograph)

BRANDENBURG TEST
Freedom of expression, 301

BRAQUE
Forgery of works of, 78

BROOKLYN MUSEUM OF ART
Funding, 324

BUFANO
Aid to the arts, Bufano sculpture, 169
Photograph, 399

BUSINESS EXPENSES
Taxation, business expense deductions, 156–158

C CORPORATION
Taxation, 153–155

CAPITAL ASSET
Defined, 128–129

CAPITAL EXPENSES
Taxation, 133

CAPITAL GAIN
Taxation, 129, 135

CARTOONS
Copyright, Revision Act of 1976, 218–219

CELLINI
Generally, 7

CENSORSHIP OF THE ARTS
Freedom of expression, 293–294

CENTRAL AMERICA
Pre-Columbian antiquities, 10, 29

CERTIFICATE OF COPY REGISTRATION
Copyright, Revision Act of 1976, 218

CHAGALL, MARC
Forgery of works of, 78
War, art as victim, 36

CHARACTERIZING INCOME
Taxation, 151–155

CHARITIES
Aid to the arts, tax deductible charitable contributions, 174
Museums, organization as charitable trust, 327–333
Taxation of charitable contributions, 135–140, 141, 147, 174
Working artists, charitable purposes, 186

CHILD ONLINE PROTECTION ACT OF 1998
Freedom of expression, 320

CHILD PORNOGRAPHY
Freedom of expression, 317–322

CHILD PORNOGRAPHY PREVENTION ACT OF 1996
Freedom of expression, 320

CHILDREN'S INTERNET PROTECTION ACT
Freedom of expression, 320

CHRISTIE'S AUCTION HOUSE
   Generally, 56–57, 78
Price Fixing, 73

CITY OF PASCO
Removal of murals, 324

CLEAR AND PRESENT DANGER TEST
Freedom of expression, 301–302

COLLECTION
Museums, management of collection, 357–365

COLLECTORS AND DEALERS
Taxation, 127–150

COMMISSIONS
Working artists, 188–194

COMMUNICATIONS DECENCY ACT OF 1996
Freedom of expression, 320

COMPREHENSIVE OR ALL-RISK POLICIES
Insurance, 118

COMPUTERS
See Internet

CONFLICTS OF INTEREST
Museums, 342–347

CONSIGNMENT
Working artists, 187–188

CONSTITUTIONAL LAW
Copyright, constitutional basis, 199
First Amendment. See Freedom of Expression

CONSTRUCTION OR INTERPRETATION
Insurance contract, 116–118

CONTRACTS OR POLICIES
See Insurance

COOPERATIVE GALLERY
Working artists, 184

COPYRIGHT
    Generally, 199–244
  See also Trademark
Berne Convention, Revision Act of 1976, 223–224, 229
Bids and bidding, blind bidding, 202
Blind bidding, 202
Cartoons, Revision Act of 1976, 218–219
Certificate of copy registration, Revision Act of 1976, 220
Constitutional basis, 199
Copyright Act of 1909, 200

INDEX

Criminal action for infringement, 236
Damages for infringement, 234–235
Deposit requirements, Revision Act of 1976, 226–228
Duration, Revision Act of 1976, 228–233
Elements of infringement, 233–234
Fair use, 236–239
Fixation requirement, Revision Act of 1976, 212–214
Formalities, Revision Act of 1976, 219–228
General Agreement on Tariffs and Trade (GATT), 228–229
Infringement
    Generally, 233–244
  Criminal action, 236
  Damages, 234–235
  Elements of infringement, 233–234
  Fair use, 236–239
  Insurance, 125
  Parody, 239–244
  Remedies, 234–236
Insurance, infringement, 125
Original work of authorship, Revision Act of 1976, 209–212
Parody, infringement, 239–244
Publication, Revision Act of 1976, 221–223
Remedies for infringement, 234–236
Renewal, Revision Act of 1976, 228
Revision Act of 1976
  Berne Convention, 229
  Berne Convention Implementation Act, 224
  Cartoons, 204, 218–219
  Certificate of copy registration, 220
  Deposit requirements, 226–228
  Duration, 228–233
  Fixation requirement, 212–214
  Formalities, 219–228
  General Agreement on Tariffs and Trade (GATT), 228–229
  Original work of authorship, 209–212
  Publication, 221–223
  Renewal, 228
  Scope of protection, 203–209
  Sole intrinsic function language, 215–218
  Source country, 229–230

Statutory subject matter, 209–219
Universal Copyright Convention, 222
Work made for hire doctrine, 205–206
Scope of protection, Revision Act of 1976, 203–209
Sole intrinsic function language, Revision Act of 1976, 215–218
Source country, Revision Act of 1976, 229–230
Statutory subject matter, Revision Act of 1976, 209–219
Universal Copyright Convention, 223
Work made for hire doctrine, Revision Act of 1976, 205–206

COPYRIGHT ACT OF 1909
Generally, 200

COTTAGE INDUSTRIES
Working artists, federal laws inhibiting cottage industries, 196

CRIMINAL MATTERS
Copyright, criminal action for infringement, 236

CRITICISM
Moral rights, 284

CROSS BURNINGS
Freedom of expression, cross burnings as bias-motivated crime, 306–307

CROWN OF ST. STEPHAN'S
Generally, 43–44, 398 (photograph)

CUSTOMS
Customs definition of art, 7–8
Definition of art, 1–8
Harmonized Schedule, 3–58
Imports, customs definition of art, 1

CYBERAUCTIONS
Generally, 62

DA VINCI, LEONARDO, PAINTINGS BY
Authentication, 81

DALI, SALVADOR
Investing in art, 54
Moral rights, integrity, 277

Trademark, trade dress, 266

DAMAGES
Copyright infringement, 234–235
Trademark infringement, 256–257

DEACCESSIONS
Museums, 357–365

DEALERS AND COLLECTORS
Taxation, 127–150

DECENCY CLAUSE
Aid to the arts, National Endowment for the Arts, 172–173

DEDUCTIONS
Aid to the arts, tax deductible charitable contribution, 174
Taxation, 130–135, 148–149, 194
Working artists, tax deductions for working conditions, 194

DEFENSES
Insurance, 125

DEFINITION OF ART
Customs, 1–8
Fine arts, 1, 2

DEPOSITS
Copyright deposit requirements, Revision Act of 1976, 226–228

DESTRUCTION
International movement, 9

DIEBENKORN, RICHARD
Bidding tactics, 64

DILUTION
Trademark, 259–261

DISCLAIMERS
Forgeries, fakes and frauds, 100

DISCLOSED AND UNDISCLOSED BIDDING
Auctions, 62–63

DRAFT CARD BURNING
Freedom of expression, 302–303

DUBUFFET
Forgery of works of, 78

DÜERER, ALBRECHT
Stolen paintings, 39

DUMBARTON OAKS MUSEUM
Sixth-century Byzantine silver, 16

DURATION
Copyright, Revision Act of 1976, 228–233

EBAY
Cancellation of sale for fraud, 65

ECONOMIC RIGHTS
  Generally, 285–291
Resale Royalties Act, 289–291

EDUCATIONAL PURPOSES
Working artists, 186, 187

ELEMENTS OF INFRINGEMENT
Copyright, 233–234

ELGIN MARBLES
International movement, 11–12
Photograph, 396

ESTATE PLANNING
Taxation, 140–144, 162–166

ETHNOLOGICAL MATERIALS
International movement, 24

ETRUSCAN HORSE
Museums, 361
Photograph, 410

EXCESSIVE CRITICISM
Moral rights, 284

INDEX

EXEMPTIONS
Working artists, working conditions, 186, 194

EXPENSES
Tax deductions, 130–135

EXPORT RESTRICTIONS
International movement, 17–19
Matisse, 19

EXPRESS WARRANTIES
Forgeries, fakes and frauds, 95–98, 100–101

FABERGE
Generally, 7

FAIR COMMENT DEFENSE
Authentication, 81–86

FAIR USE
Copyright, 235, 236–239, 240–244
Freedom of expression, symbolic speech, 302
Trademark, 257–259, 261

FAIRS OR CRAFT EXHIBITS
Working artists, 184

FAKES
See Forgeries, Fakes and Frauds

FAMILY PARTNERSHIP
Taxation, creation of family partnership, 153

FEDERAL COMMON LAW
Trademark, 247–252

FEDERAL REGISTRATION
Trademark, 252–256

FIGHTING WORDS
Freedom of expression, 306–307

FINE ARTS
Definition of art, 1, 2

FINE PRINT AND MULTIPLES LEGISLATION
Forgeries, fakes and frauds, 103–104

FIRE
Selective Service Card, freedom of expression in burning of, 302–303

FIRE POLICIES
Insurance, 111–112, 119

FIRST AMENDMENT
See also Freedom of Expression
Authentication, art experts, 81
Aid to the Arts, indirect aid, 181

FISCHL, ERIC
Freedom of expression, 325

FIXATION REQUIREMENT
Copyright, Revision Act of 1976, 212–214

FLAG DESECRATION
Freedom of expression, 304, 307–312
Photograph, 408

FORGERIES, FAKES AND FRAUDS
Art warranty statutes, 100–103
Auctions. See Auctions
Authentication
    Braque, forgery of works of, 78
    Chagall, forgery of works by, 78
    Dubuffet, forgery of works of, 78
    Forgery, 75–76
    Forgery, generally, 87
    Fraud, generally, 88
    Giacometti, forgery of works of, 78
    Vermeers, forgery of, 76
Braque, forgery of works of, 78
Chagall, forgery of works by, 78
Disclaimers, 100
Dubuffet, forgery of works of, 78
Express warranties, 95–98, 100–101
Fine print and multiples legislation, 103–105

Giacometti, forgery of works of, 78
Implied warranties, 98–100
Indian Arts and Crafts Board, 107
Insurance contracts or policies, 123
Museums, deaccession of forgeries or fakes, 361
Mutual mistake, contract doctrine of, 91
Native Americans, Indian Arts and Crafts Board, 107
Negligent misstatement, purchasers remedies, 88–91
Picasso, signature forgery, 94
Preventive measures, 107–109
Puffing, express warranties, 95
Purchasers remedies
    Generally, 87–92
  Auction, forged Raoul Duffy paintings, 92
  Mutual mistake, contract doctrine of, 91
  Negligent misstatement, 88–91
  Warranties, 92–103
Rembrandt painting, express warranties, 96
Remington sculpture, 103–104
Sculpture, 103–104
Signature on Picasso print, forgery of, 94
Tax deductions, 133
The Misses Werthheimer painting, 98
Uniform Commercial Code, 93–94, 99–100
Vermeers, forgery of, 76
Warranties, purchasers remedies, 92–103

FORMALITIES
Copyright, Revision Act of 1976, 219–228

FRAUDS
See Forgeries, Fakes and Frauds

FREEDOM OF EXPRESSION
    Generally, 293–325
  See also Museums
Alternative approach to pornography, 322–325
Antiwar protest, wearing of black armbands, 303–304
Black armbands, antiwar protest, 303–304
Bosch, Hieronymus, 293
Brandenburg test, 300

Censorship of the arts, 293–294
Child pornography, 317–322
Clear and present danger test, 301–302
Cross burnings as bias-motivated crime, 306–307
Draft card burning, 302–303
Fighting words, 306–307
First Amendment framework, generally, 294–301
Flag desecration, 304, 307–312
Internet pornography, 319–322
Nude dancing, 306
Obscenity, 312–325, 409 (photograph)
Political criticism, 293–302
Pornography
   Alternative approach to pornography, 322–325
   Child pornography, 317–322
   Internet pornography, 319–322
Public nudity, 306
Selective Service card, burning of, 302–303
Symbolic speech, 301–307

FUNDING
National Endowment for the Arts, aid to the arts, 170–174

GALLERIES
Investing in art, 57–58
Working artists, 188–194

GENERAL AGREEMENT ON TARIFFS AND TRADE (GATT)
Copyright, 228–229

GIACOMETTI
Forgery of works of, 77

GIFTS
Taxation, 127–128, 147

GROSS INCOME
Taxation, gross income defined, 127

GUGGENHEIM
Deaccession, 362
Internet, 366

HAGUE CONVENTIONS
War, art as victim, 35, 39

HARMONIZED SCHEDULE
Customs, 4–5

HEALTH HAZARDS
Working artists, 197

HEIROGLYPHS
International movement, 10

HIRSCHFELD, AL
Dispute with dealer, 191

HISTORICAL DEVELOPMENT
Aid to the arts, 167–188

HOUSES
See Auctions

IMPLIED WARRANTIES
Forgeries, fakes and frauds, 98–100

IMPORTS
Customs definition of art, 1
Restrictions, international movement, 20–21

INCOME
Taxation, property characterizing income, 127–129

INCORPORATION
Taxation, 165

INDIAN ARTIFACTS
International movement, 15–16

INDIAN ARTS AND CRAFTS BOARD
Forgeries, fakes and frauds, 108

INDIRECT AID
National Endowment for the Arts, 176–181

INFRINGEMENT
See Copyright, Trademark

Damages. See Damages
Insurance, 125
Trademark, 125, 256–259

INSTALLMENT METHOD OF ACCOUNTING
Taxation, 152

INSURABLE INTEREST
Generally, 116

INSURANCE
    Generally, 111–126
Advertising injury, 125
Alarm systems, 111
Appraisal requirement, 121
Comprehensive or all-risk policies, 118
Construction or interpretation of contract, 116–118
Contracts or policies
        Generally, 114–120
    Advertising injury, 125
    Appraisal requirement, 121
    Comprehensive or all-risk policies, 118
    Construction or interpretation of contract, 116–118
    Copyright infringements, 125
    Defenses, 125
    Fire policies, 119
    Forgery, 124
    Fraud, 123
    Insurable interest, 116
    Open or unvalued policy, 120
    Patent infringements, 125
    Personal household policy, 117–118
    Recovery, 120–126
    Reformation of contract, 123
    Remedies, 120–126
    Riders, 114
    Self-insurance, 126
    Theft, 120
    Trademark infringement cases, 125
    Unscheduled personal property, 124
    Valued policy, 120–123

Vasarely painting, 115
Copyright infringements, 125
Defenses, 125
Fire and fire policies, 111–112, 119
Forgery, contracts or policies, 124
Fraud, contracts or policies, 123
Infringement cases, 125
Insurable interest, 116
National Endowment for the Arts' Arts and Artifacts Indemnity program, 112
Nuclear risks covered under National Endowment for the Arts' Arts and Artifacts Indemnity program, 113
Open or unvalued policy, 120
Patent infringements, 125
Personal household policy, 117–118
Premiums, 111
Recovery, 120–126
Reformation of contract, 123
Remedies, 120–126
Riders, 114
Self-insurance, 126
Theft, 111–112, 119
Trademark infringement cases, 125
Traveling exhibits, 112
Unscheduled personal property, 124
Valued policy, 120, 123
Vasarely painting, 116
War risks covered under National Endowment for the Arts' Arts and Artifacts Indemnity program, 112

INTEGRITY
Moral rights, 277–284

INTER VIVOS TRANSFERS
Taxation, estate planning, 141–142

INTERNATIONAL MOVEMENT
  Generally, 9–31
Destruction, 9
Egyptian antiquities, 31
Elgin marbles, 11–12

Export restrictions, 17–19
Extradition, Treaty of, 21–22
Hieroglyphs, 10
Import restrictions, 19–21
Indian artifacts, 14
Kennewick Man, 15
Looting, 9
Mayan language, 10
Mexican antiquities laws, 22
Parthenon, 11, 12
Paul Getty Museum, 15
Sanctions for vandalism and theft, 26–32
Self-regulation by nongovernmental organizations, 26
Tellico Dam and Reservoir Project, Indian archaeological sites, 11
Tennessee Valley Authority, 11
Theft, 9, 26–32
Treaties, 21–25
UNIDROIT, 25
Uniform Commercial Code, 19
Zuni war gods, 13

INTERNET

Anticybersquatting Consumer Protection Act, 259
Auctions, cyberauctions, 62
Cyberauctions, 62
Display of museum collections, 366
Freedom of expression, internet pornography, 317–322
Online galleries, 57
Trademark infringement, Anticybersquatting Consumer Protection Act, 259

INVESTING IN ART

Generally, 49–60
See also Auctions
Authentication, art as investment, 75
Dali, Salvador, 54
Factors and considerations, 54–57
Galleries, 58
Methods of acquisition, 57–60
National Endowment for the Arts, aid to the arts, 174

Racketeer Influenced and Corrupt Organizations Act (RICO), 53–54
Securities Act of 1933, 52–53
Taxation
    Generally, 56
  Tax shelters, investment tax credit, 149

IRAQ'S NATIONAL MUSEUM OF ANTIQUITIES
Victim of war, 35

JERUSALEM
International movement, 11

JUDICIAL SOLUTIONS
War, art as victim, 36–42

KENNEWICK MAN
Ownership of skeleton, 15

KLIMT, GUSTAV
Paintings as victim of war, 40

KOSOVO
Victim of war, 34

KUWAITI NATIONAL MUSEUM
Victim of war, 35

LABELING OF HAZARDOUS ART MATERIALS ACT (LHAMA)
Working artists, 197

LABOR RELATIONS
Museums, 366–369

LANDMARK PRESERVATION
Indirect aid to the arts, 177–181
Photograph, 403

LANHAM ACT
Authentication, 87–88
Moral rights, 275–277, 281–284
Trademark, 246, 251–252, 261

LIEBER CODE
War, art as victim, 35

LIMITED LIABILITY COMPANIES
Taxation, 153–155

LIQUIDATION
Taxation, 165–166

LOANS
Museums, 354–357

LOOTING
International movement, 9

LOUVRE
Authentication of painting by Leonardo da Vinci, 81
Museums, deaccessions, 360

MADRID PROTOCOL
Generally, 262

MANAGEMENT
See Museums

MARITAL DEDUCTION
Taxation, estate planning, 141

MATISSE
Export restrictions, 19

MEI/MOSES FINE ART INDEX
Generally, 50

METROPOLITAN OPERA
Conditions of donation, 354

MEXICAN ANTIQUITIES LAWS
International movement, 22

MISMANAGEMENT
Museums, 335–341

MORAL RIGHTS
   Generally, 267–284

Criticism, 284
Excessive criticism, 284
Integrity, 277–284
Lanham Act, 275–277, 281–284
Name attribution, 273–277
Revision Act of 1976, 272–273
Withdrawal right, 273

MUNCH, EDVARD
Uninsured, 112

MUSEUMS
Generally, 327–370
Acquisitions, 16–17, 348–354
Bailment, loans, 354–355
Charitable trust, organization of museum as, 327–333
Collection, management of, 348–354, 357–365
Commissions, 347
Conflicts of interest, 342–347
Corporate sponsorships, 347, 369–370
Deaccessions, 357–365
Etruscan Horse, 361
Forgeries or fakes, deaccession of, 361
Labor relations, 366–369
Loans, 354–357
Location of collection, 365–366
Management
    Generally, 348–354
  Collection, management of, 348–354, 357–365
Mismanagement, 335–341
National Labor Relations Act, 367
National Labor Relations Board, 367
Nonmanagement, 341–342
Nonprofit corporation, 327–333, 343
Organization, 327–333
Public trust, organization of museum as, 327–333
Rodin sculptures, deterioration of, 335
Self-dealing, 343–345
Trust, organization of museum as, generally, 327–333
UNESCO, 351
Unrelated business income tax, 333

MUTUAL MISTAKE
Forgeries, fakes and frauds, contract doctrine of mutual mistake, 91

NAME ATTRIBUTION
Moral rights, 273–277
Photograph, 407

NATIONAL ENDOWMENT FOR THE ARTS
See Aid to the Arts
Insurance, National Endowment for the Arts' Arts and Artifacts Indemnity program, 112

NATIONAL LABOR RELATIONS ACT
Museums, 367

NATIONAL LABOR RELATIONS BOARD
Museums, 367

NATIVE AMERICAN GRAVES PROTECTION AND REPATRIATION ACT
International movement, 28

NATIVE AMERICANS
Forgeries, fakes and frauds, Indian Arts and Crafts Board, 108

NEGLIGENT MISSTATEMENT
Forgeries, fakes and frauds, purchasers remedies, 88–91

NET CAPITAL GAIN DEFINED
Taxation, 128

NONMANAGEMENT
Museums, 341–342

NONPROFIT CORPORATION
Museums, 327–333, 343

NUCLEAR RISKS
Insurance, nuclear risks covered under National Endowment for the Arts' Arts and Artifacts Indemnity program, 112

NUDE DANCING
Freedom of expression, 306

OBSCENITY
See Freedom of Expression

OFILI, CHRIS
Freedom of expression, 322

OPEN OR UNVALUED POLICY
Insurance, 120

ORDINARY INCOME
Taxation, 128–129, 134

ORGANIZATION OF MUSEUMS
Generally, 327–333

ORIGINAL WORK OF AUTHORSHIP
Copyright, Revision Act of 1976, 209–212

PARODY
Copyright infringement, 239–244
Photograph, 406

PARTHENON
International movement, 11, 12

PARTNERSHIP
Taxation, creation of family partnership, 153

PATENT INFRINGEMENTS
Insurance, 125

PAUL GETTY MUSEUM
International movement, 16

PAY FOR YOUR PLEASURE
Freedom of expression, 325

PERCENTAGES
Indirect aid, percentage allocation for art, 176–177

PERSONAL HOUSEHOLD POLICY
Insurance, 117–118

PHANTOM BIDS
Auctions, 64

PHILLIPS AUCTION HOUSE
Generally, 78

PICASSO
Art as an investment, 50
Copyright, formalities, 219–221
Photograph, 404
Record price, 50
Signature forgery, 94
Trademark, 251–252

PLACES TO WORK AND SELL
Working artists, 183–188

POLITICAL CRITICISM
Freedom of expression, 293–302

PORNOGRAPHY
See Freedom of Expression

PREMIUMS
Insurance, 111

PREVENTIVE MEASURES
Forgeries, fakes and frauds, 107–109

PRINCIPAL REGISTER
Trademark, 254–255

PROFESSIONAL NEGLIGENCE
Authentication, 82

PUBLIC NUDITY
Freedom of expression, 306

PUBLIC TRUST
Museums, organization of as public trust, 327–333

PUBLICATION
Copyright, Revision Act of 1976, 221–223

PUFFING
Auctions, bidding, 64
Express warranties, forgeries, fakes and frauds, 95

PURCHASERS REMEDIES
See Forgeries, Fakes and Frauds

RACKETEER INFLUENCED AND CORRUPT ORGANIZATIONS ACT (RICO)
Freedom of expression, pornography, 324–325
Investing in art, 53–54

RECOVERY
Insurance, 120–126

REFORMATION OF CONTRACT
Insurance, 123

REMBRANDT
Forgeries, fakes and frauds, Rembrandt painting, 96

REMEDIES
Copyright infringement, 234–236
Insurance, 120–126
Purchasers remedies. See Forgeries, Fakes and Frauds

REMINGTON SCULPTURE
Forgeries, fakes and frauds, 103–104

RENEWAL
Copyright, Revision Act of 1976, 228

RENTAL OF ARTWORK
Generally, 57

RESALE ROYALTIES ACT
Copyright, common law rights, 201
Economic rights, 289–291

REVISION ACT OF 1976
See Copyright
Moral rights, 272–273

REYNOLDS, SIR JOSHUA
Authentication of painting by, 83–84

RIDERS
Insurance, 114

RING FORMATION
Auctions, bidding, 65

RODIN
Museums, deterioration of Rodin sculptures, 335

SALES TAXES
Fraud, 150

SAN SALVADOR CONVENTION
International movement, 22

SANCTIONS
International movement, sanctions for vandalism and theft, 26–32

SATISFACTION GUARANTEE
Working artists, 192

SCHIELE, EGON
Paintings as victim of war, 42

SCIENTIFIC MATTERS
Authentication, scientific category, 79–80
Working artists, scientific purposes, 186

SCREAM, THE
Uninsured, 112

SCULPTURE
Customs definition of art, 2–3, 4–5
Forgeries, fakes and frauds, 103–104

SEALED BIDS
Auctions, 63

SEATTLE ART MUSEUM
Freedom of expression, 325

SECURITIES ACT OF 1933
Investing in art, 51–52

SELECTIVE SERVICE CARD
Freedom of expression, burning of Selective Service card, 302–303

SELF-DEALING
Museums, 343–345

SELF-INSURANCE
Generally, 126

SELF-REGULATION
International movement, self-regulation by nongovernmental organizations, 26

SELTZER, STEVE
Art expert, 86

SENSATION: YOUNG BRITISH ARTISTS FROM THE SOATCHI COLLECTION
Deletion of commission clauses as result of controversy, 347
Freedom of expression, 322

SHILLING
   See also Puffing
Auctions, bidding, 64

SIGNATURES
Forgery of signature on Picasso print, 94

SIR JOSHUA REYNOLDS
Authentication of painting by, 83–84

SIXTH-CENTURY BYZANTINE SILVER
Dumbarton Oaks Museum, 16

SLANDER OF TITLE
Authentication, 83

SOLE INTRINSIC FUNCTION LANGUAGE
Copyright, Revision Act of 1976, 215–218
Photograph, 405

SONNY BONO COPYRIGHT TERM EXTENSION ACT OF 1998
Generally, 230

SOTHEBY PARK BERNET
   Generally, 56–57, 68, 78, 82–83
Price Fixing, 73

SOURCE COUNTRY
Copyright, Revision Act of 1976, 229–230

STATE TRADEMARK LAWS
Generally, 261–262

STATUTORY SUBJECT MATTER
Copyright, Revision Act of 1976, 209–219

STELAE
International movement, 10
Photograph of Machaquila, 397

STYLISTIC EXPERTS
Authentication, art experts, 79–80

SUPPLEMENTAL REGISTER
Trademark, 255–256

SYMBOLIC SPEECH
Freedom of expression, 301–307

TACTICS
Auctions, bidding, 64–65

TARIFF ACT OF 1930
Generally, 3

TATE GALLERY
Public appeal for donations of artwork, 354

TAX SHELTERS
Generally, 144–150

TAXATION
Aid to the arts, tax deductible charitable contribution, 174
Appraisals, charitable contributions, 138
Artists, 151–166
Business expense deductions, 156–158
C corporation, 153–155
Capital asset defined, 128–129
Capital expenses, 133
Capital gain, 129, 135
Characterizing income, 151–155

INDEX

Charitable contributions, 135–140, 141, 147, 160–162, 174
Collectors and dealers, 127–150
Dealers and collectors, 127–150
Deductions, 130–135, 149, 156–160, 174, 194
Donations, 163–164
Estate planning, 140–144, 162–166
Expenses, deductions, 130–135
Family partnership, creation of, 153
Forgery, deductions, 133
Gifts, 124–125, 147
Gross income defined, 127
Income, property characterizing, 127–129
Incorporation, 165
Installment method of accounting, 152
Inter vivos transfers, estate planning, 141–142
Investing in art. See Investing in Art
Limited liability companies, 153–155
Liquidation, 165–166
Marital deduction, estate planning, 141
Net capital gain defined, 129
Ordinary income, 128–129, 134
Tax shelters, 144–150
Theft, deductions, 134
Trade or business deduction, 129–131
Trusts, estate planning, 144
Working artists, 186, 194
Working conditions, tax deductions, 194

TELECAST SALES
Auctions, 62

TELLICO DAM AND RESERVOIR PROJECT
International movement, Indian archaeological sites, 11

TENNESSEE VALLEY AUTHORITY
International movement, Indian archaeological sites, 11

TERRA MUSEUM OF AMERICAN ART
Dispute over location, 366

THE MISSES WERTHHEIMER PAINTING
Forgeries, fakes and frauds, 97

THEFT
Insurance, 111–112
International movement, 9, 25–32
Tax deductions, 134

THERMOLUMINESCENT ANALYSIS
Authentication, 86

TRADE DRESS
Trademark, 264–266

TRADEMARK
    Generally, 246–266
    See also Copyright
Anticybersquatting Consumer Protection Act, infringement, 259
Background, 246–247
Bankruptcy, infringement, 257
Damages, infringement, 256–257
Dilution, 259–261
Federal common law, 247–252
Federal registration, 252–256
Image as, 259
Infringement, 125, 256–259
Insurance, trademark infringement cases, 125
Internet, Anticybersquatting Consumer Protection Act, 259
Lanham Act, 246, 251–252, 261
Picasso, 251–252
Principal Register, 254–255
State trademark laws, 261–262
Supplemental Register, 255–256
Trade dress, 264–266
Trademark Law Revision Act (TLRA), 246, 252–256

TRADEMARK LAW REVISION ACT (TLRA)
Generally, 246, 252–256

TREASURES FROM WAWAL CASTLE IN KRAKOW
War, art as victim, 43

TREATIES
Extradition, Treaty of, 21–22
International movement, 20–26

TRUSTS
See Museums
Taxation, estate planning, 144

UNESCO
International movement, 23, 25–26
Museums, 351
War, art as victim, 46

UNIDROIT
International movement, 26

UNIFORM COMMERCIAL CODE
Auctions, bidding, 64, 66
Forgeries, fakes and frauds, 93–94, 98–99
International movement, 19
Working artists, 189–190

UNIVERSAL COPYRIGHT CONVENTION
Generally, 222

UNRELATED BUSINESS INCOME TAX
Museums, 333

UNSCHEDULED PERSONAL PROPERTY
Insurance, 124

VALUED POLICY
Insurance, 120–123

VAN GOGH
Art as investment, 50

VANDALISM
International movement, sanctions for vandalism and theft, 26–32

VASARELY PAINTING
Insurance, 116

VERMEER
Forgery of, 76

VERSAILLES, TREATY OF
War, art as victim, 36

WAR, ART AS VICTIM
Generally, 33–47
Act of State Doctrine, 38
Altmann, Maria, 42
Chagall, Marc, 36
Hague Conventions, 35, 39
Iraq's National Museum of Antiquities, 35
Judicial solutions, 36–42
Kosovo, 35
Kuwaiti National Museum, 35
Lieber Code, 35
Nonjudicial solutions, 42–47
Treasures from Wawal Castle in Krakow, 43
UNESCO, 46
Versailles, Treaty of, 36
Wawal Castle in Krakow, treasures from, 43
Weimar Art Collection, 39–40

WAR RISKS
Insurance, war risks covered under National Endowment for the Arts' Arts and Artifacts Indemnity program, 112

WARRANTIES
Forgeries, fakes and frauds, purchasers remedies, 92–103

WAWAL CASTLE IN KRAKOW
War, art as victim, 43

WEIMAR ART COLLECTION
War, art as victim, 39–40

WEST'S ART AND LAW PROGRAM
National Endowment for the Arts, aid to the arts, 174
Photograph, 402

WITHDRAWAL
Auctions, withdrawing goods or bids, 66–67
Moral rights, withdrawal right, 273

WOODS, TIGER
Image as trademark, 259

WORK MADE FOR HIRE DOCTRINE
Copyright, Revision Act of 1976, 205–206

WORKING ARTISTS
Generally, 183–198
Artist-dealer relationship, 188–194
Charitable purposes, 186
Commissions, 188–194
Consignment, 187–188
Cooperative gallery, 184
Cottage industries, federal laws inhibiting, 196
Deductions, tax deductions for working conditions, 194
Educational purposes, 186, 187
Exemptions, 186, 194
Fairs or craft exhibits, 184
Galleries, 188–194
Health hazards, 197
Labeling of Hazardous Art Materials Act (LHAMA), 197
Places to work and sell, 183–188
Satisfaction guarantee, 192
Scientific purposes, 186
Taxation, 186, 194
Uniform Commercial Code, 189–190
Working conditions, 194–198

WORKING CONDITIONS
Working artists, 194–198

WORKS PROGRESS ADMINISTRATION (WPA)
Aid to the arts, 168
Photographs, 399, 400, 401

WORLD INTELLECTUAL PROPERTY ASSOCIATION
Trademarks, 263

WORLD TRADE CENTER
Freedom of expression, 325

ZUNI WAR GODS
International movement, 13

1-18-5c

Wayne
KF4288 .D83 2017
DuBoff, Leonard D., author
Art law in a nutshell

WEST ACADEMIC PUBLISHING'S LAW SCHOOL ADVISORY BOARD

JESSE H. CHOPER
Professor of Law and Dean Emeritus,
University of California, Berkeley

JOSHUA DRESSLER
Distinguished University Professor, Frank R. Strong Chair in Law
Michael E. Moritz College of Law, The Ohio State University

YALE KAMISAR
Professor of Law Emeritus, University of San Diego
Professor of Law Emeritus, University of Michigan

MARY KAY KANE
Professor of Law, Chancellor and Dean Emeritus,
University of California, Hastings College of the Law

LARRY D. KRAMER
President, William and Flora Hewlett Foundation

JONATHAN R. MACEY
Professor of Law, Yale Law School

ARTHUR R. MILLER
University Professor, New York University
Formerly Bruce Bromley Professor of Law, Harvard University

GRANT S. NELSON
Professor of Law, Pepperdine University
Professor of Law Emeritus, University of California, Los Angeles

A. BENJAMIN SPENCER
Earle K. Shawe Professor of Law,
University of Virginia School of Law

JAMES J. WHITE
Robert A. Sullivan Professor of Law Emeritus,
University of Michigan